New Proclamation
Year C 2013

P9-CCK-416

Easter through Christ the King
March 30, 2013—November 24, 2013

Mary Donovan Turner

Eric D. Barreto

Walter C. Bouzard

Lance Pape

David B. Lott, Editor

Fortress Press

Minneapolis

NEW PROCLAMATION
Year C 2013
Easter through Christ the King
March 30, 2013—November 24, 2013

Copyright © 2012 Fortress Press, an imprint of Augsburg Fortress. All rights reserved. Except for brief quotations in critical articles or reviews, no part of this book may be reproduced in any manner without prior written permission from the publisher. Visit http://www.augsburgfortress.org/copyrights/contact.asp or write to Permissions, Augsburg Fortress, Box 1209, Minneapolis, MN 55440.

Unless otherwise noted, scripture quotations are the author's own translation or from the New Revised Standard Version Bible, copyright © 1989 by the Division of Christian Education of the National Council of Churches of Christ in the USA, and are used with permission.

Scriptures marked RSV are from the Revised Standard Version of the Bible, copyright © 1952 [2nd edition, 1971] by the Division of Christian Education of the National Council of the Churches of Christ in the United States of America. Used with permission. All rights reserved.

Scriptures marked NAB are taken from the *New American Bible*, copyright © 1970 by the Confraternity of Christian Doctrine, Washington, DC, and are used by permission of the copyright owner. All rights reserved.

Cover design: Laurie Ingram
Cover illustration: Nicholas Wilton
Book design: Sharon Martin
Illustrations: Joel Nickel, Margaret Adams Parker, Robyn Sand Anderson, Margaret Bartenstein Bussey, and M.P. (Paula) Wiggins, © 2010 Augsburg Fortress.

Library of Congress Cataloging-in-Publication Data
The Library of Congress has catalogued this series as follows.
New Proclamation: Year C 2013 Easter through Christ the King
p. cm.
Includes bibliographical references.
ISBN 978-0-8066-9631-7
1. Church year. I. Moloney, Francis J.
BV30 .N48 2001
2511.6dc21 2001023746

Library of Congress Cataloging-in-Publication Data
ISBN 978-1-4514-0260-5

The paper used in this publication meets the minimum requirements of American National Standard for Information Sciences—Permanence of Paper for Printed Library Materials, ANSI Z329.48-1984.

Manufactured in the U.S.A.

15 14 13 12 1 2 3 4 5 6 7 8

Contents

Preface
David B. Lott vii

Easter
Mary Donovan Turner

Introduction 1

March 30–31, 2013
Resurrection of Our Lord / Easter Vigil 3

March 31, 2013
Resurrection of Our Lord / Easter Day 7

March 31, 2013
Resurrection of Our Lord / Easter Evening 14

April 7, 2013
Second Sunday of Easter 18

April 14, 2013
Third Sunday of Easter 24

April 21, 2013
Fourth Sunday of Easter 29

April 28, 2013
Fifth Sunday of Easter 34

May 5, 2013
Sixth Sunday of Easter 40

May 9, 2013 / May 12, 2013
Ascension of Our Lord / Ascension Sunday 47

May 12, 2013
Seventh Sunday of Easter 52

May 19, 2013
Day of Pentecost 59

Time after Pentecost / Ordinary Time
Trinity Sunday through Lectionary 16 / Proper 11
Eric D. Barreto

Introduction 65

May 26, 2013
Holy Trinity Sunday / First Sunday after Pentecost 66

June 2, 2013
Lectionary 9 / Ninth Sunday in Ordinary Time / Proper 4 (RCL)
Solemnity of Corpus Christi (Body and Blood of Christ) (LFM)
Second Sunday after Pentecost 72

June 9, 2013
Lectionary 10 / Tenth Sunday in Ordinary Time / Proper 5
Third Sunday after Pentecost 80

June 16, 2013
Lectionary 11 / Eleventh Sunday in Ordinary Time / Proper 6
Fourth Sunday after Pentecost 86

June 23, 2013
Lectionary 12 / Twelfth Sunday in Ordinary Time / Proper 7
Fifth Sunday after Pentecost 92

June 30, 2013
Lectionary 13 / Thirteenth Sunday in Ordinary Time / Proper 8
Sixth Sunday after Pentecost 98

July 7, 2013
Lectionary 14 / Fourteenth Sunday in Ordinary Time / Proper 9
Seventh Sunday after Pentecost 104

July 14, 2013
Lectionary 15 / Fifteenth Sunday in Ordinary Time / Proper 10
Eighth Sunday after Pentecost 110

July 21, 2013
Lectionary 16 / Sixteenth Sunday in Ordinary Time / Proper 11
Ninth Sunday after Pentecost 116

Time after Pentecost / Ordinary Time
Lectionary 17 / Proper 12 through
Lectionary 26 / Proper 21
Walter C. Bouzard

Introduction 123

July 28, 2013
Lectionary 17 / Seventeenth Sunday in Ordinary Time / Proper 12
Tenth Sunday after Pentecost 125

August 4, 2013
Lectionary 18 / Eighteenth Sunday in Ordinary Time / Proper 13
Eleventh Sunday after Pentecost 132

August 11, 2013
Lectionary 19 / Nineteenth Sunday in Ordinary Time / Proper 14
Twelfth Sunday after Pentecost 138

August 18, 2013
Lectionary 20 / Twentieth Sunday in Ordinary Time / Proper 15
Thirteenth Sunday after Pentecost 146

August 25, 2013
Lectionary 21 / Twenty-First Sunday in Ordinary Time / Proper 16
Fourteenth Sunday after Pentecost 153

September 1, 2013
Lectionary 22 / Twenty-Second Sunday in Ordinary Time / Proper 17
Fifteenth Sunday after Pentecost 161

September 8, 2013
Lectionary 23 / Twenty-Third Sunday in Ordinary Time / Proper 18
Sixteenth Sunday after Pentecost 167

September 15, 2013
Lectionary 24 / Twenty-Fourth Sunday in Ordinary Time / Proper 19
Seventeenth Sunday after Pentecost 173

September 22, 2013
Lectionary 25 / Twenty-Fifth Sunday in Ordinary Time / Proper 20
Eighteenth Sunday after Pentecost 179

September 29, 2013
Lectionary 26 / Twenty-Sixth Sunday in Ordinary Time / Proper 21
Nineteenth Sunday after Pentecost 185

Time after Pentecost / Ordinary Time
Lectionary 27 / Proper 22 through Christ the King / Reign of Christ
Lance Pape

Introduction 191

October 6, 2013
Lectionary 27 / Twenty-Seventh Sunday in Ordinary Time / Proper 22
Twentieth Sunday after Pentecost 193

October 13, 2013
Lectionary 28 / Twenty-Eighth Sunday in Ordinary Time / Proper 23
Twenty-First Sunday after Pentecost 199

October 20, 2013
Lectionary 29 / Twenty-Ninth Sunday in Ordinary Time / Proper 24
Twenty-Second Sunday after Pentecost 205

October 27, 2013
Lectionary 30 / Thirtieth Sunday in Ordinary Time / Proper 25
Twenty-Third Sunday after Pentecost 210

November 1, 2013 / November 3, 2013
All Saints Day / Sunday 215

November 3, 2013
Lectionary 31 / Thirty-First Sunday in Ordinary Time / Proper 26
Twenty-Fourth Sunday after Pentecost 221

November 10, 2013
Lectionary 32 / Thirty-Second Sunday in Ordinary Time / Proper 27
Twenty-Fifth Sunday after Pentecost 226

November 17, 2013
Lectionary 33 / Thirty-Third Sunday in Ordinary Time / Proper 28
Twenty-Sixth Sunday after Pentecost 232

November 24, 2013
Christ the King or Reign of Christ Sunday
Lectionary 34 / Last Sunday in Ordinary Time / Proper 29
Twenty-Seventh Sunday after Pentecost 238

November 28, 2013 (USA) / October 14, 2013 (Canada)
Thanksgiving Day 243

Preface

For nearly four decades Fortress Press has offered an ecumenical preaching resource built around the three-year lectionary cycle, a tradition that this latest edition of *New Proclamation* continues. *New Proclamation* is grounded in the belief that a deeper understanding of the biblical pericopes in both their historical and liturgical contexts is the best means to inform and inspire preachers to deliver engaging and effective sermons. For this reason, the most capable North American biblical scholars and homileticians are invited to contribute to *New Proclamation*.

New Proclamation has always distinguished itself from most other lectionary resources by offering brand-new editions each year, each dated according to the church year in which it will first be used, and featuring a fresh set of authors. Yet each edition is planned as a timeless resource that preachers will want to keep on their bookshelves for future reference for years to come. In addition, *New Proclamation*, true to its ecumenical scope, has traditionally offered commentary on all of the major lectionary traditions. Now, reflecting changes in practices among the mainline Protestant denominations, those number just two: the *Revised Common Lectionary* (RCL) and the Roman Catholic *Lectionary for Mass* (LFM).

New Proclamation is published in two volumes per year. The first volume, published earlier this year, covered all the Sunday lections and major festivals from Advent through Easter Vigil. This second volume begins with new commentary on the Easter Vigil and covers the remaining Sunday lections and major festivals through Christ the King Sunday as well as Thanksgiving Day. For those churches that celebrate minor feast days and solemnities, including saints' days and the Feast of the Transfiguration (August 6), denominational days such as Body and Blood of Christ (Corpus Christi) (June 10) or Reformation (October 31), and national days and topical celebrations, a separate volume covering the texts for those days is available: *New Proclamation Commentary on Feasts, Holy Days, and Other Celebrations* (ed. David B. Lott; Fortress Press, 2007).

We invite you to visit this volume's companion Web site, www.NewProclamation.com, which offers access not only to this book's contents, but also to commentary from earlier editions, up-to-the-minute thoughts on the connection between texts and current events, user forums, and other resources to help you develop your sermons and enhance your preaching.

This edition continues the high quality of the content that *New Proclamation* provides to preachers and those interested in studying the lectionary texts. Each writer offers an introduction to her or his commentary that provides insights into the background and spiritual significance of that season (or portion thereof), as well as ideas for planning one's preaching during that time. In addition, the application of biblical texts to contemporary situations is an important concern of each contributor. Exegetical work is concise, and thoughts on how the texts address today's world, congregational issues, and personal situations have a prominent role.

This volume, as with others in the *New Proclamation* series, brings together both veteran writers and newer voices. Readers will note how each author uniquely brings a perspective of social justice to the weekly readings. Mary Donovan Turner and Walter Bouzard are both Hebrew Bible scholars who draw especially on that particular background in their offerings. Turner, who as a homiletics professor helps women to find their voice in preaching, provides practical guidance for forming sermons in the Easter season. As a student of the Psalms, Bouzard shows how these responsive readings can also be fruitful preaching texts. Eric Barreto, a professor of New Testament, is the first person of Hispanic background to contribute to *New Proclamation*; his lively contributions help preachers to understand how context—both the text's and our own—affects how we hear and proclaim the text. And Lance Pape closes out the volume with his bracing and direct commentary, which draws on both his nearly two decades of ordained ministry as well as his more recent work as a professor of homiletics. We are grateful to each of these contributors for their insights and their commitment to effective Christian preaching, and are confident that you will find in this volume ideas, stimulation, and encouragement for your ministry of proclamation.

David B. Lott

Easter

Mary Donovan Turner

The progression of the lectionary readings through the season of Easter takes us both "back" and into the "future." Throughout the seven weeks in the first readings, we make our way through pivotal events in the life of the early church as recorded in Acts. We encounter Peter and Paul and the varied ways they are on the front edge of carrying the movement forward. Empowered by God's Spirit, they heal and teach and argue with officials; they are both imprisoned but still the church grows and is empowered to do its work. This is an interesting progression because when the Easter season is over on Pentecost Sunday, we go back in time to the birth of the church in Jerusalem.

During the Easter season we also have the opportunity to explore parts of the book of Revelation; we often believe that only the bravest of preachers should go there. But there is much to learn about faithfulness, complacency, hope, and resilience from the lections that are assigned.

Note several strong threads that run throughout the season. The first has to do with inclusion. In hymnic fashion many of the psalms and the readings in Revelation speak of the day when all nations and all peoples will know God. And, episode by episode in the book of Acts, the church is encouraged to make a larger circle, accept those previously labeled unclean, and make the boundaries about who can be baptized more permeable. It is a call to expand our peripheral vision and to see who is now not included. How do we overturn or revolutionize an us-versus-them kind of world? That is the question that faces us during Easter, Year C!

Another strong thread throughout the season has to do with calls to live faithfully. The calls to love one another and to live righteously are woven throughout the Easter-season tapestry. This is a season of joy but also of challenge. Global social issues like poverty and violence will not escape our notice.

I am taken by the fact that many of the stories in Acts and the visions in Revelation tell of times, both present and future, when the church, or the group gathered around the Lamb, is growing by great numbers. The great gathered multitudes are seen as part of the hope. What does that mean to us today as churches diminish in size and number?

The lections for the Easter season in Year C are a challenge—and a joy. You will notice on many occasions that I invite you to look at the lections holistically. That is, you will be invited to explore either the text's historical context or its literary context—the verses or units that come before or after. Sometimes it is the context that gives us the clue for this week's sermon. And when the assigned lection invites you to read only selected verses of the psalm, I invite you to read it in its entirety so that important repetitions of words and phrases, theological complexities, and sometimes the drama's plot will not escape your attention.

Some of the lections will probably be very familiar to you and some will take you into unfamiliar territory. Both journeys—into the familiar and unfamiliar—are important paths toward personal and communal discovery. Enjoy.

March 30–31, 2013
Resurrection of Our Lord / Easter Vigil

Revised Common Lectionary (RCL)

Genesis 1:1—2:4a
Psalm 136:1-9, 23-36

Genesis 7:1-5, 11-18; 8:6-18; 9:8-13
Psalm 46
Genesis 22:1-18

Psalm 16
Exodus 14:10-31; 15:20-21
Exodus 15:1b-13, 17-18
Isaiah 55:1-11
Isaiah 12:2-6
Proverbs 8:1-8, 19-21; 9:4b-6 or
Baruch 3:9-15, 32—4:4
Psalm 19
Ezekiel 36:24-28
Psalm 42 and Psalm 43
Ezekiel 37:1-14
Psalm 143
Zephaniah 3:14-20
Psalm 98

Evangelical Lutheran Worship adds:

Jonah 1:1—2:1
Jonah 2:2-3 (4-6) 7-9
Isaiah 61:1-4, 9-11
Deuteronomy 32:1-4, 7, 36a, 43a
Daniel 3:1-29
Song of the Three 35–65
Romans 6:3-11
Psalm 114
John 20:1-8 or Luke 24:1-12 (ELW)

Lectionary for Mass (LFM)

Genesis 1:1—2:2 or 1:1, 26-31a
Psalm 104:1-2, 5-6, 10-12, 13-14, 24-35; or Psalm 33:4-5, 6-7, 12-13, 20-22

Genesis 22:1-18 or 22:1-2, 9a, 10-13, 15-18
Psalm 16:5 + 8, 9-10, 11
Exodus 14:15—15:1
Exodus 15:1-2, 3-4, 5-6, 17-18
Isaiah 54:5-14
Psalm 30:2 + 4, 5-6, 11-12a + 13b
Isaiah 55:1-11
Isaiah 12:2-3, 4bcd, 5-6
Baruch 3:9-15, 32—4:4
Psalm 19:8, 9, 10, 11
Ezekiel 36:16-17a, 18-28
Psalm 42:3, 5; 43:3, 4; or Isaiah 51:12-13, 14-15, 18-19

Romans 6:3-11
Psalm 118:1-2, 16-17, 22-23
Luke 24:1-12

The Easter Vigil is the first celebration of the resurrection of Jesus. In different places, times, and traditions, the service has taken on differing liturgical rituals and functions. Often the service has been the time when adult catechumens are baptized, received into full communion with the church. Baptismal vows are renewed. The service is held during the hours of darkness on the evening of Holy Saturday and into Easter morning. It can include a "Service of Light." The service ends with Eucharist.

Many traditions would consider this the most important service of the church year; during worship the Alleluias that have been absent during Lent are sung with joy and celebration. The service ushers in the Easter season, which will last fifty days and until Pentecost. In its long history, the texts chosen for the vigil have been changed, and in contemporary settings different texts are read in different traditions. In them, however, there is a ritual recounting of the story of God and humanity beginning with the creation story and continuing through the Torah, Writings, and Prophets. The ritual drama is seen as a recounting of God's deliverance of God's people time and again throughout the course of history, culminating in the raising of Jesus on the day of resurrection.

It is also a story about God's people—a recounting of the times they were faithful, times they turned away from covenant in both memory and practice, times they suffered because of confused priorities, times they were void of spirit or oppressed. And yet, through the centuries in waves of despair and ultimate hope, God remained with them. That is the story recounted here. This is a dance between God and people, and though the metaphor of dance may seem frivolous, and while no metaphor is perfect, the dance does illustrate the people's on-again/off-again relationship to the covenant. Sometimes they are on the dance floor, in perfect rhythm. Sometimes the people leave the floor; sometimes they choose other dance partners. But God remains there, perhaps at first angry or jealous that the people have walked away, but committed to the dance nonetheless. We find God patiently waiting there, steadfast and vulnerable, for the people to hear the music and return.

In the Old Testament it is God's *hesed* that is foundational for this kind of loyalty. *Hesed* is often translated "steadfast love"—and that is what it is. This is God's unconditional, "I will never let you go" kind of love that is manifest over and over again through the Old Testament story. When God is disappointed, angry, lonely, troubled, God waits on the people and loves them back. Always. That is how the story ends, because, as God says through the prophet Hosea, "I am God and not person." This is a promise of presence.

It is best, then, to see the varied lessons for the Easter Vigil as the stories of the people's goings and comings. The psalms between the lections sing the celebration of the God who kept *hesed* and who kept bringing salvation and redemption when the people were in dire need of it.

The liturgies for both RCL and LFM begin with the recounting of God creating the world and everything in it and calling it good. Psalm 136 (RCL) and the alternative psalm for LFM, Psalm 33, which follow the telling of the creation story, set the stage for the recounting of the story of *hesed* that stands the test of time. Psalm 136, twenty-six times, and in every verse, calls the community to give thanks because God's *hesed* has endured forever. And in Psalm 33 (vv. 5, 18, 22) the community is reminded that their hope lies in God's steadfast love. The psalm ends with a prayer that this kind of love remain with them forever.

These psalms set the stage, then, for what will unfold in the telling of the stories of the flood, the deliverance from Egypt, and the exile. Through the words of the prophets we will experience the plight of a people who need to be called back into righteousness and into relationship with the God who waits for them. Through the writings we will be called back to wisdom.

Surely this is a long story of redemption! It brings gratitude and hopefulness and joy as we celebrate the life of Jesus the Christ who was sent into the world to show us how this undying love of God was made manifest in his own death. That is the irony and the wonder of the Easter season. Hallelujah!

This interesting context for the Easter Vigil creates a wealth of preaching challenges! The RCL lists as readings for the Vigil nine Old Testament lessons with corresponding psalms and songs. *Evangelical Lutheran Worship* adds three additional Old Testament readings, a reading from an epistle, four psalms, and a Gospel lesson with an alternative. The LFM lists seven Old Testament readings, eight psalms or songs, an epistle, and a Gospel reading from Luke. The challenge, then, becomes immediately clear. Generally the homily/sermon at the Easter Vigil is shorter than on other worship occasions. Is it possible to allow the stories to speak for themselves? How does the preacher "get out of the way" so that the lessons can speak in their own voice? How does the preacher engage the Old Testament lessons in traditions and contexts where preaching is generally from the New Testament? What needs to be said about the lessons in congregations and communities that are virtually illiterate when it comes to Scripture? Will listeners have a framework in which to put the stories of Abraham, Moses, Jonah, and the prophets? How can we help them make sense of this?

The preacher has many choices, some of which will be outlined here.

1. The preacher can read through the lections and choose a theme or word or theological concept that can serve as a lens through which the lections can be seen. One overarching theme is relationship; the lections show God's ongoing relationship with humanity, how God came and intervened in the life of the people, bringing what they needed to carry on—forgiveness, renewed spirit, challenge, wisdom, transformation.

2. The lections introduce us to our spiritual ancestors on whose shoulders we stand. To bring their names and briefly what we know about them helps the community "fill in" parts of the family tree. We can identify our noble and faithful and obedient ancestors and also the "skeletons in the closet." All of them know of God's grace.

3. If there will be baptisms at the Easter Vigil, themes that reflect the tradition's understanding of baptism could be highlighted—new life, community, and so forth. The one New Testament reading listed as a Vigil lection that does *not* appear later

during the Easter season is Romans 6:3-11. Paul's understanding of baptism is clear. We who are baptized were baptized into Jesus' death. This is not a physical death, but it is death to a way of life that is formed and molded by the world around us. We can walk in a new way. Our old life is resurrected because we have been forgiven of our sins. How is this understanding of baptism embraced or not embraced by your own tradition? What does your baptism liturgy say about what happens when the infant or the adult has water sprinkled or poured on him or her? When they are immersed in the pool of water? This conversation about baptism is linked to the theology and the celebration of the resurrection. We have choices about the ways we live our lives. We can wrest ourselves free from self-indulgent and individualistic thinking. We can engage in Christopraxis; we can pattern ourselves after the life of Jesus as it is described in the Gospels and not be bound to less satisfying, less sacred living.

4. The preacher could choose one of the Vigil lections that also appears as a reading on Easter or Easter evening. For the RCL and LFM these readings are John 20:1-8; Luke 24:1-12 (ELW alt.); Psalm 114; and Psalm 118. See the commentaries for these texts under Easter Day and Easter Evening, below.

Whatever the preacher decides in relation to the content and form of the sermon (this is a particularly good occasion for a narrative sermon), it will be good and helpful to start by reading the texts. Read them slowly. What do you see and hear as you read? What words are repeated or what themes are prevalent? How will each individual text contribute to the drama of worship; what part does each play in the Easter "plot"? How do these readings build anticipation for the story and the energy and the blessing of resurrection?

While there is no single identified theme that incorporates all the Vigil lections, there are some strong threads that run between them. Recently reading through the texts, I was struck by the prevalence of water imagery throughout. God creates the waters, floods the earth with the waters, parts the waters so that the Israelites can pass over into the wilderness. The prophet Isaiah says to his listeners, "Everyone who thirsts come to the water," and he talks about the rain and the snow coming down to replenish the earth. Ezekiel talks about the water that cleanses us and also brings to us a vision of a valley of dry bones, a valley where there is no water. Jonah is thrown into the sea. And Paul talks about the waters of baptism that symbolize the new life that we can have through the resurrected Jesus.

What do you see and hear and taste and feel as you read through this incredible story of salvation and redemption brought to every generation by a faithful and loving and gracious God?

Note

1. See also explicit references to *hesed* in these Easter Vigil readings: Exodus 15; Psalms 33, 42, 51, 98, 118, 136, 143; Isaiah 54, 55; Jonah 2.

March 31, 2013
Resurrection of Our Lord / Easter Day

Revised Common Lectionary (RCL)

Acts 10:34-43 or Isaiah 65:17-25
Psalm 118:1-2, 14-24
1 Corinthians 15:19-26 or Acts 10:34-43
Luke 24:1-12 or John 20:1-18

Lectionary for Mass (LFM)

Acts 10:34a, 37-43
Psalm 118:1-2, 16-17, 22-23
Colossians 3:1-4 or 1 Corinthians 5:6b-8
John 20:1-9

First Reading
Acts 10:34-43 (RCL)
Acts 10:34a, 37-43 (LFM)

When the reader arrives at the tenth chapter of Acts, the church that was born on the day of Pentecost has experienced its first growing pains. In fits and starts those who gathered in prayer and who had the Holy Spirit fall down upon them began prophesying and testifying to the risen Jesus. This is a story about the Holy Spirit. In the beginning chapters of Acts, the Holy Spirit comes and almost inevitably moves those who have received the Spirit to bold speech. The early chapters of Acts are also dotted with challenges to preaching the gospel boldly. Government authorities who were threatened by the power and the appeal of the resurrection message, and individuals like Saul of Tarsus, worked mightily to silence Jesus' disciples. But as the story is told, the courage brought by God's Spirit is mightier than the fear and the many challenges they encounter—imprisonment and, in Stephen's case, even death. Still they heal. Still they teach. Still they preach, prophesy, and give testimony. Count how many times these three words appear in Acts' first chapters!

In today's reading from Acts the themes of prophesying and testifying continue. Cornelius, a centurion in Caesarea, is prompted by God to call for Peter, asking him to come for a visit. In the meantime, Peter receives a vision about those things he considers profane or unclean. God says to him, "What God has made clean, you must not call profane" (10:10). Peter goes to Cornelius and explains to him the vision he has received. It is in this context, then, that we read 10:34-43. This is Peter's last sermon in

Acts, perhaps a synthesis of the most important things he has learned. Peter begins to speak to Cornelius, his servants, and all those gathered by saying, "I truly understand that God shows no partiality." He testifies to the baptism of Jesus where Jesus was anointed with power, the life of Jesus filled with good deeds and healing, the death and crucifixion of Jesus, the resurrection and the postresurrection sightings of Jesus. And he says that everyone who believes in Jesus receives forgiveness in his name.

It is as this story continues, and after the end of the reading designated by the lectionaries, that we realize the significance of the testimony. The Holy Spirit that has consistently and constantly empowered the disciples falls once again on Peter. He speaks and those who hear realize that God's Spirit is poured out on Jew and Gentile alike! Those who once were separate come together and all are baptized in the name of Jesus Christ. The extended narrative (Acts 10:1—11:18), of which today's lection is part, bears witness to the inclusiveness of the gospel; the resurrection story knows no boundaries! It builds bridges over what once was a great divide.

It is interesting that on this Easter Day the lections not only recount the resurrection story, but begin to spin out the implications of it, its meanings and its significance for those who lived in a world where the landscape knew walls and barriers that could not be crossed. The tension in Scripture between the chosen and the universal is in some sense heightened and also resolved. God is impartial, but we know we are very partial.

Isaiah 65:17-25 (RCL alt.)

The reading from Isaiah provides a very different experience from the reading in Acts. It is not a narrative but a poetic rendering of a word from God; this is a word about transformation and healing. This is a word of hope.

Isaiah 65 is the penultimate chapter in these writings by an anonymous prophet, usually identified as Third Isaiah. This prophet is writing to a people who have been carried away into the Babylonian exile, then freed by Cyrus of Persia who overcame the Babylonians, and who are now finding themselves back home. Their struggles and challenges are not over, even if they are now restored to the lands of their ancestors. There are theological questions about God and the devastation they have endured. There are questions about worship and about how they are to live life as a restored people.

In the first half of Isaiah 65, God recounts the past experiences with the Israelite people. In the past, they did not seek God; they did not ask God to help them. Isaiah paints a compelling picture of God calling out to the people, "Here I am, here I am" (65:1). But the nation turned the other way. The waywardness and the unfaithfulness of the people are graphically recounted. And then, abruptly in verse 17, the tone and tenor of God's message change. No longer is the story of the unfaithful people being told. God is creating new heavens and a new earth. The former things, their apostasy and their wanderings, will not even be remembered! The God who once created the heavens and the earth is creating still, and out of the ruins of Jerusalem, pulled forth from her troubled and devastated history, there comes something new. "Behold, I am about to create new heavens and a new earth!" (v. 17).

Many times in verses 17-25 we encounter the words *joy*, *delight*, and *blessing*. For the tired and worn nation, here is the good news. Jerusalem will be a safe place, a place where the community can live and grow old. They can build houses and live in them. They can establish themselves and have a home. They will grow their food and be able to eat it. They will not be at war; they will not be taken away into exile. There will be no hurt or destruction; and the vision seen by First Isaiah about the wolf and the lamb? It will come to pass because the Creator God is creating still—we see evidence of this new creation in our own world, don't we? That is what we celebrate on Easter Sunday. We are joyful, and Third Isaiah depicts a God who is joyful. What does that mean that we serve a joyful God?

The people exhale. Something better is coming. It is held out as a hope by a God who can bring joy out of their despair and who is forever faithful—even to a wandering people. But that is not all. We are called to use our faithful imaginations to see and co-create the world Isaiah could envision. A resurrection people is a commissioned people! On Easter Sunday there are people in the world who will wake up and, for another day, be surrounded by violence. In their own backyards, they will witness nations fighting against nations. People will wake up hungry, and perhaps displaced from their homes because of drought or a search for safety. The vision of Third Isaiah is that someday these things will no longer be. Children will be born and live long lives, not lives destined for calamity. People will plant vineyards and have good shelter that is stable and permanent and safe (vv. 20-23). The wolf and the lamb will dwell together. This will come to pass if we allow God's Spirit to stir our imaginations and our passions to make it so.

Psalmody

Psalm 118:1-2, 14-24 (RCL)
Psalm 118:1-2, 16-17, 22-23 (LFM)

Psalm 118 is part of a group of psalms (113–118) sung at festival gatherings—Passover, Tabernacles, and the Feast of Weeks. These are songs of great celebration, of family and community gatherings.

The lectionary frequently "cuts" the psalm into small units; both the RCL and LFM renderings for Psalm 118 bear witness to this tendency. And while only the verses indicated above might be read in worship, the preacher would be wise to read the psalm as a full unit. Only in this way can the exquisite repetitions of words and phrases be found, repetitions that lead us to understand more comprehensively the psalmist's theological affirmations. Only in reading the psalm in its entirety can we see how the drama of worship is played out as the leader speaks and worshipers repeat his affirmations, as the worshipers enter the temple and as testimonies are made to the everlasting and steadfast nature of God who is faithfully present during all that life brings to us.

Notice, for instance, the repetitions in verses 1-4. The lectionary doesn't allow us to see the fullness of the affirmation in verse l, repeated then in verses 2, 3, and 4 by Israel, the house of Aaron, and finally all who fear the Lord. The gathered community is giving thanks because of God's steadfast love, God's *hesed.* A look at the meaning of *hesed* in the Hebrew Bible will yield a wealth of ideas and portraits of the Old Testament God who will not let the people go.

These liturgical affirmations, perhaps uttered outside the temple, are followed by personal testimony in verses 5-18. While it is not clear if this is one voice or several, the extensive use of metaphor and imagery can be embraced by anyone who has suffered challenges or persecution. Note the repetitions of the Lord "on my side" in verses 6 and 7, the Lord as refuge in verses 8 and 9. Is it the king who is worshiping? He testifies that the Lord cut off the nations who were surrounding him. They surrounded him like bees and blazed like a fire. He was pushed so that he was falling. But then the Lord helped him. The drama continues as the worshipers enter the temple (vv. 19ff.) and give praise for their salvation.

An individual worshiper gives thanks to God that he has been saved (v. 21). This is followed by a communal affirmation that this is God's doing and it is marvelous in "our" eyes. The community hears the testimony of the individual and gives thanks for the story of deliverance. How does that happen in your own church community? How are stories spoken and heard and affirmed by the community?

The worshiper says, "The stone that the builders rejected has become the chief cornerstone . . ." (v. 22). This is a reminder that the joy of Easter is at its most profound and wondrous only when we have traveled with Jesus to the cross and crucifixion. The vision of the restored earth is profoundly moving only when we allow ourselves to witness and touch the devastation and suffering of life as people are now experiencing it.

Second Reading
1 Corinthians 15:19-26 (RCL)

It is not difficult to see why the text from 1 Corinthians 15 was chosen for Easter Day. Beginning in 15:1 is a rather long, rambling, circuitous exposition, wherein Paul outlines for the community in Corinth the importance of the resurrection, specifically the bodily resurrection of Jesus. If Christ has not been raised from the dead, our faith has been in vain. More, if Christ has not been raised, we are the people most to be pitied (v. 19). Thinking through this passage will provide a good opportunity for the preacher to reflect on her own theology of resurrection. Does the preacher affirm a physical and bodily resurrection of Jesus? Or an understanding that is metaphorical and that speaks of grace and new beginnings? Is the resurrection of Jesus an important or mandatory element in one's understanding of salvation? Does salvation come after death or is one's salvation in this life also? Is it the death of Jesus or the life of Jesus that is ultimately important? How do these understandings inform the kind of sermon we preach in our communities on Easter Sunday? While all of these questions will not make it into an Easter Sunday sermon, these questions are vital to our faith, and in teaching and preaching the careful pastor will be sure to address them. Rest assured, these are questions on the minds and in the hearts of those in the listening community.

Most interesting in the Corinthians text is the understanding of Jesus as destroyer—the one who destroys every ruler and every authority and power. Who are the enemies of Jesus? How are the disciples of Jesus also called to destroy authorities and powers that seek to dominate and subjugate and oppress? (vv. 24ff.). What kinds of ideas and attitudes need to be destroyed in the world in which we live?

Colossians 3:1-4 or 1 Corinthians 5:6b-8 (LFM)

Both readings for the LFM are abbreviated, intended no doubt to help communities understand how the new life in Christ is made manifest in us. The one who believes in the resurrected life of Jesus does not go about living in a business-as-usual way. New energy, new perspectives, new priorities, and new ways of living in relationship are given birth in those who believe. This is a part of the good news. Though the writers of Colossians and Corinthians use different language and metaphors, the essence of their message shows great similarity.

In Colossians 2, the crucifixion and resurrection of Jesus are signs of forgiveness; our trespasses are set aside, nailed to the cross (v. 14). But in chapter 3 there is a change in focus. The author moves from what has been forgiven to the ways we ourselves need to "put to death" some of our ways of behaving in the world so that we might put on something more Christlike. In the verses immediately following today's lection, what are "put to death" are fornication, impurity, passion, evil desire, greed, and the like. We now clothe ourselves with love, which binds us in harmony, kindness, humility, and so forth. A new way of living is resurrected when we believe in the risen Christ. One important thing that happens as we embrace and clothe ourselves in this new way of living: there is no longer Geek and Jew, circumcised and uncircumcised, barbarian, Scythian, slave, and free; but Christ is all and is in all. For the writer of Colossians, the resurrection is our call to inclusivity.

Paul in 1 Corinthians lays out for us also the ways that the sacrifice of Christ on the cross affects our living. Using the metaphors of yeast and leavened and unleavened bread, he calls the people in Corinth as they celebrate the festival of the resurrection not to use bread leavened with the yeast of malice and evil. Rather, they are to use new yeast of sincerity and truth. New life comes not automatically or instantaneously because Jesus has been resurrected. Because Jesus has died for us, we work to put on the spirit of Christ.

Acts 10:34-43 (RCL alt.)

For commentary on this lesson, please see the first reading, above.

Gospel

Luke 24:1-12 (ELW, RCL alt.)

The resurrection narrative in Luke is like the Johannine narrative in that it is the women who go to the tomb. Here, however, it is Mary Magdalene, Joanna, Mary the mother of James, and other women who come with their prepared spices to anoint the body. They also see two men who remind them that Jesus had foretold what had now happened—he was crucified and rose again on the third day. The women remember the words Jesus had spoken, and they go to tell the disciples what they have seen and heard. Significantly, the disciples do not believe them and go to the tomb to substantiate what the women have said. The disciples on the road to Emmaus remember that the male disciples went to the tomb and found it "just as the women had said" (24:24).

It is significant that the women are the first at the tomb to hear the news of the resurrection. But equally significant, the women were also present at the crucifixion (23:49) and at the burial (23:55). There is something about this kind of "staying power" that is significant—the ability to be present to the suffering and harsh realities of the world as well as present to the joy when those are overthrown. We need one to understand the profound nature of the other.

The women did not expect resurrection and an empty tomb! But the gardener reminds them that Jesus himself had told them that this would happen. They then remember what had been said. The implications of the resurrection were not immediately evident to the women or the disciples or even to the early church, and we are still processing them today. What does this mean—for what we believe and how we live? What does it mean for the preacher's community?

John 20:1-18 (RCL, ELW alt.)
John 20:1-9 (LFM)

The RCL and LFM both begin with John's story of Mary going to the tomb on the first day, while it was still dark. As the reader of John would expect, one of the important elements in the story is that the disciple who followed Peter into the tomb came to believe. From the beginning of the Gospel of John, the author has told us that this is a story about believing. In the prologue, John tells us that in the beginning was the Word, the Word was with God, and the Word was God. What came into being with the Word was life, and the life was the light of all people. John was sent by God to testify to this light, so that all might *believe* through him. This is the purpose of telling the story.

Throughout the Gospel story, then, the word *belief* (in its several forms) appears nearly one hundred times in the Gospel's twenty chapters! And the word appears in every chapter of the Gospel except for two. The writer depicts Jesus as one who teaches about himself and his relationship with God. This is not a Gospel with parables that teach disciples how to live their lives as followers of Jesus. This is a Gospel that tells us who Jesus is.

This story in John shares with the Synoptics memories of the importance of women on resurrection morning. In all of them, Mary Magdalene (or Mary Magdalene with other women) comes and discovers the empty tomb. Here, Mary is alone when she makes her way in the dark to find that the stone had been rolled away. She runs to tell Simon Peter and the disciple whom Jesus loved; immediately they make their way to the tomb and go inside to find the linen wrappings lying there. The disciples leave. But Mary stays.

Mary's grief is understandable here. She had lost Jesus once; she was there at the crucifixion. Now she has lost him again. She looks into the tomb and sees the two angels sitting there. She turns and sees Jesus, but like the disciples on the road to Emmaus, she does not recognize him.

In their exchange, Mary recognizes Jesus when he says her name. He tells her to go away because he is ascending to "my Father and your Father, to my God and your God" (20:17). Mary is the first to have a postresurrection experience with Jesus; she is the first to proclaim the good news when she goes to the disciples and says, "I have seen the Lord" (v. 18).

One wonders if this was really good news to Mary. Yes, she was assured that the spirit of Jesus was alive in the world. But her human grief would linger. Jesus was not available to her, with her, in the same way as before. Was she ready to sing her alleluias?

Mary becomes a great model for us. In her willingness to stay at the tomb, the place of her enormous grief, she is able to receive the good news that Jesus still lives. In our communities we also need to stand in those places where there is enormous grief and sadness, until all the people still living in the tomb—those who see no hope or promise for any kind of abundant living—know hope or see glimpses of joy that come from a living God who knows and cares about them.

March 31, 2013
Resurrection of Our Lord / Easter Evening

Revised Common Lectionary (RCL)
Isaiah 25:6-9
Psalm 114
1 Corinthians 5:6b-8
Luke 24:13-49

Lectionary for Mass (LFM)
Acts 10:34, 37-43
Psalm 118:1-2, 16-17, 22-23
Colossians 3:1-4 or 1 Corinthians 5:6b-8
Luke 24:13-35

First Reading
Isaiah 25:6-9 (RCL)

Following the oracles against the nations, found in Isaiah 13–23, are four chapters that are often titled the "Isaiah Apocalypse." Chapters 24–27, which comprise the apocalypse, are the subject of much scholarly debate. Who wrote them and when? How are these chapters related to their literary and historical contexts? There are no clear answers, but the imagery has long fascinated scholar and preacher alike. Read these chapters in their entirety to get a sense of the gripping devastation and the resilient hope they describe. There are oracles of doom and victory songs. All of them point to "that day" when there will be peace and goodwill and salvation for all people.

Out of the four chapters of the apocalypse, only nine verses out of chapter 25 are found in the lectionary cycle. These few verses hold a significant place there, however, for they are read during Pentecost or on Easter evening. These verses are also alternative readings in Year B for Easter and on All Saints Day. Certainly the verses take on new meanings when read through the lens of the resurrection story.

The first five verses of chapter 25 are a song of praise to Yahweh. The poet recounts all the wondrous things that God has done; God is old, faithful, and sure. While this psalm of thanksgiving is dotted with reminders of desolate cities and the destruction of the ruthless (a reversal of the status quo!), the images of safety and comfort prevail. Note the many metaphors used for God here —God is a refuge to the poor and needy, shelter from the rainstorm, shade from the heat. Each metaphor is a seed from which a sermon can grow.

This outburst of thanksgiving is followed by a description of a wonderful day to come. The terse images provide for the preacher an assortment of rich and poignant pictures of what will be. The vision, like other visions in Isaiah and like many in the Old Testament and New Testament alike, takes place on a mountain. Yahweh will make for *all* peoples a great banquet. The banquet is a common mythological and eschatological symbol in many cultures that lead a hand-to-mouth existence. This banquet is rich with food and wines (this theme is continued in contemporary films like *Babette's Feast* and *Antwone Fisher*). The death that has formerly swallowed men and women will itself be swallowed. Tears will be wiped away from faces, disgrace will be taken "away from all the earth." The people have waited for God (v. 9); now they will be glad and rejoice.

The idea of "waiting" for Yahweh is a common theme through the poetic sections of the Hebrew Bible, both in the Psalms and in the Prophets. The Hebrew word for "wait" is often also translated "hope." The people have waited for God, and they are not disappointed. The text ends on this confident note; they have been saved. It is for this reason, no doubt, that Isaiah 25 has been chosen as a supportive text to the resurrection story. Death has been conquered; tears are wiped away. Salvation can come to all people. The Lord is risen.

This text from Isaiah has an ironic twist, however. In the song of the vineyard (Isaiah 5), Yahweh also waits expectantly. Yahweh waits hopefully and expectantly for justice, but looking around the world sees only bloodshed and violence. Yahweh waits for righteousness but hears only the cries of those who are suffering or oppressed. Yahweh waits. And Yahweh is disappointed. The people who wait for Yahweh, however, are not disappointed; their confidence is not misplaced.

Acts 10:34, 37-43 (LFM)

For commentary on this text, please see the first reading for Easter Day, above.

Psalmody

Psalm 114 (RCL)

Psalm 114 makes an important claim and gives an important witness on Resurrection Day. God's power, seen in the resurrection of Jesus, is a power known by the Jewish community. Many times in their history God delivered them from trial. The psalm delineates some of the saving acts of God that through the centuries have been remembered and told by the people to their children and their children's children.

The psalm begins in verse 1 with the story of Israel leaving Egypt. Their deliverance was miraculous; the sea rolled back so that they could cross into the wilderness. The Jordan River "turned back" so that they could cross over into the land promised to their ancestors. The mountains and hills were dancing at all that was occurring around them. Why did the sea, the river, the mountains and hills do these things? The only answer is that the presence of Yahweh is powerful beyond measure. The people and the earth interestingly are not called to praise but to *tremble*! When have we last "trembled" at the power of a God who can turn rock into water?

Psalm 118:1-2, 16-17, 22-23 (LFM)

For commentary on this text, please see the psalmody for Easter Day, above.

Second Reading

1 Corinthians 5:6b-8 (RCL, LFM alt.)
Colossians 3:1-4 (LFM)

For commentary on these texts, please see the second reading (LFM) for Easter Day, above.

Gospel

Luke 24:13-49 (RCL)
Luke 24:13-35 (LFM)

The two disciples on the road to Emmaus have captured the imaginations of painters and storytellers alike. The story takes place in the evening of Resurrection Day, making it the logical choice for the Easter Evening lection. The two are traveling away from Jerusalem, away from the sounds and sights of the devastation all the disciples felt at Jesus' crucifixion. Their destination was Emmaus, seven miles from Jerusalem. It is not known if there was a city named Emmaus or, if it existed, where it was located. It does, then, make the perfect destination for all who have experienced grief and want another place to be, any place to be.

The disciples are "homilizing" with each other (v. 14); that is, they are having a conversation like we have when we preach a homily to the community. They are talking about their life experiences, and they are trying to understand them in relation to what they have been taught and what they believe.

The story is almost whimsical. Jesus appears as they are walking and begins a conversation with them. He wants to know what they're talking about. They are amazed that anyone would ask that question—what else would anyone be talking about? They tell him how Jesus was handed over to be crucified. They confess their great disappointment; they had thought that Jesus would be the hope of Israel. The disciples then tell the story of Easter morning, how the women went to the tomb and couldn't find the body! Some of the group went to see and found it as the women had said.

Jesus chastises the two, calling them foolish and slow of heart. Didn't the prophets foretell the suffering of the Messiah? Beginning with the writings of Moses and then the prophets, Jesus explains to them all that had been written about himself. As they approach the place where they are staying, it looks as if Jesus is going farther. They hold him back and ask him to stay with them. At the evening meal, he takes bread and blesses and breaks it, and it is in that moment that they recognize him as Jesus the Christ. He disappears, and the two, seeing the postresurrection Jesus, run back to tell the others what happened. This is a story of movement. The disciples are walking along the road alone as the story begins. They are filled with sadness and a lack of understanding. Jesus, unrecognized by them, walks at their side. After breaking bread with the Jesus they now recognize, they get up at once and in that same hour and with great urgency, they retrace their steps to tell the disciples what they have experienced. A single moment has energized them, moved them past their pain and despair to a place of hopefulness. What energizes *us*? What are the moments that have energized you or your community, that have allowed you to "get up" again and make witness to God? When have you last felt the urgency of the two disciples to tell your story?

The LFM text ends with the two disciples going back to Jerusalem to share their news with the others. The RCL text continues. Jesus makes a second appearance to the larger group of disciples. He offers them a word of peace. They are startled and terrified, thinking they are seeing a ghost. Jesus, as he does with Thomas in the Gospel of John, shows them the scars on his hands and feet. He is not a ghost, he is flesh and bone; he asks them for food and he eats a piece of broiled fish. This is the test that he is indeed "real." What are the "real" evidences and manifestations that God lives and works in our own worlds?

April 7, 2013
Second Sunday of Easter

Revised Common Lectionary (RCL)	**Lectionary for Mass (LFM)**
Acts 5:27-32	Acts 5:12-16
Psalm 118:14-29 or Psalm 150	Psalm 118:2-4, 13-15, 22-24
Revelation 1:4-8	Revelation 1:9-11a, 12-13, 17-19
John 20:19-31	John 20:19-31

First Reading
Acts 5:27-32 (RCL)
Acts 5:12-16 (LFM)

As noted earlier, the first readings during the Easter season come from the book of Acts. This takes the worshiping community on an interesting journey through the chronicles of the church in its infancy. It is interesting because on the day of Pentecost, some fifty days later, we "flash back" to the church's birth.

The first chapters of Acts are filled with stories of the disciples and others teaching boldly. God's Spirit falls upon them and inevitably that Spirit brings them to voice. They testify to the good works of Jesus Christ. It seems they are invincible and nothing can silence their witness. In 1:8 we are told that the disciples are called to witness first in Jerusalem, then in all of Judea and Samaria, and then to the ends of the earth. The earliest chapters of Acts take place, then, in Jerusalem.

The readings for this Sunday are especially interesting because the LFM tells the first part of one of these stories, and the RCL tells the last part. Both neglect the middle of this story that is found in Acts 5:12-32. And yet, it is the three together that paint the complete picture of the day that the apostles and the people who held them in high esteem were in Solomon's Portico.

LFM lection (5:12-16). Many were afraid to be with the disciples, but the crowds were growing—men and women who wanted to hear a word from them. And the most compelling part of the picture? Men and women who were ill were carried out to the streets and laid on cots *just so Peter's shadow might fall upon them.* What an incredible snapshot of the power of the earliest apostles! The community thought that just having Peter's shadow cross over their bodies would bring healing! On this Second Sunday of Easter it is amazing to think about the resurrection power that the disciples inherited. It was the legacy of Jesus—through the power of the Holy Spirit they spoke, performing signs and wonders so that the people around them would know new life. What if our churches were so known for their great healing power that people would want just to be in the shadow of them so that their lives could be touched and made whole?

Midsection (5:17-26). In the midpart of the story, we are told that the attention and commotion surrounding the early apostles were threatening to religious officials. The apostles were arrested, but an angel opened the prison doors, brought them out, and told them to go stand at the temple and proclaim. So they went to the temple at daybreak and went on teaching. The temple police were perplexed about the prisoners' release. The police found them out teaching once again and brought them to the council, but without violence because they were afraid of being stoned by the people. It is difficult for us in this country to think about proclaiming the gospel under such hostile circumstances, risking persecution, bodily harm, and imprisonment. But the story raises an interesting question: What value, idea, principle would you go to great lengths to proclaim or defend in the face of such opposition?

RCL lection (5:27-32). The council admonishes Peter and the apostles for their teaching, which has been forbidden; perhaps the motive of the council was jealousy, or perhaps they feared losing the control and power that were theirs. Peter answers, "We must obey God rather than any human authority" (v. 29). When have you experienced a clash between what the gospel calls you to do and what the political or religious authorities call you to do? Where does the courage come from to move ahead, speak, act?

Peter, in his brief recitation of salvation history (vv. 30-31), calls Jesus Leader and Savior. Are these words you use to describe Jesus? What do they mean? Do you have others that are more meaningful to you? Peter says they are witnesses to the story of Jesus. This is a good opportunity to explore with the community the twofold meaning of witness. First, a witness is someone who has seen or heard something. This is passive. But to witness is also to speak about what has been experienced. This is active. To be a witness to the gospel is to pay attention and notice what God is doing in the world *and* to "tell it." Perhaps we should ask ourselves, Is my preaching a bold witness?

It is Gamaliel, a Pharisee and a member of the council, who speaks up and wisely considers the situation that the council is in. If the plan of these men is of human origin, he reasons, the plan will itself die. If the plan is of God, it cannot be overthrown; it will prevail. He tells the council that they should leave the disciples alone. And they did. The disciples did not cease their preaching. It makes us wonder: Is our own preaching dangerous enough, earthshaking enough, challenging to the powers enough, that anyone would want to stop us?

Psalmody

Psalm 150 (RCL alt.)

Psalms 146–150 all begin with *Praise the Lord!* And Psalm 150 brings the Psalter to closure in great doxology. This fits well with the Second Sunday of Easter worship. The community has celebrated the resurrection on Easter Day. But in worship and in preaching, the Easter season continues; this is a time to remember that for which we are grateful. At first glance, the psalm is a disappointment. Unlike many psalms, it doesn't recount the ways that God has been faithful in the past. It doesn't tell us about the life of the psalmist who is worshiping. It doesn't call us out to do the important justice work of God in the world. And so it might seem theologically empty, vacant. But that raises an important question: What is the theological significance of praise?

The psalm answers three questions: (1) *Where* should we praise God? (v. 1); (2) *Why* should we praise God? (v. 2); and (3) *How* should we praise God? (vv. 3-5).

Where praise God? We praise God in the sanctuary and in worship, certainly. But we also praise God in the firmament. That is, we praise God out in the glorious world that has been created for us. Many in your community will know about the revelatory experiences that come from being in and witnessing God's glorious creation.

Why praise God? In many psalms the great deeds of God in the past are rearticulated for the worshiper. Often there is a careful accounting of the Israelites being brought out of Egypt and other similar incidents. But here the psalmist simply uses the phrase "mighty deeds." This simple reminder would bring to the minds of the listeners all the redemptive stories of God's deliverance of their ancestors. Nothing surpasses this greatness.

And praise God how? The psalmist lists many musical instruments—the trumpet, lute, harp, tambourine, strings, pipe, and cymbals. *Everything* that is available to us should be used as we sing and as we dance in praise of God.

So perhaps the psalm serves its own unique purpose. It reminds us that to notice God, to thank God, to praise God, to adore and sing are some of the most important and fulfilling things we can do. This is the heart-work of discipleship.

Psalm 118:14-29 (RCL)
Psalm 118:2-4, 13-15, 22-24 (LFM)

For commentary on this text, please see the psalmody for Easter Day, above.

Second Reading

Revelation 1:4-8 (RCL)
Revelation 1:9-11a, 12-13, 17-19 (LFM)

The preacher might be tempted to look elsewhere in the lections for the seed for Sunday's sermon and bypass the readings from Revelation altogether! But linger here a moment because the weekly readings from Revelation during the season of Easter provide the preacher with an opportunity to address the final book of the New

Testament in ways that will clarify some of the mystery and consequent distancing by many church members who feel unable or unwilling to engage this fascinating material.

Some background material is helpful. Revelation is apocalyptic in nature. The writer uses symbolic language. The reader will notice the constant use of symbols and numbers (4, 7, and 12) to bring a message to the first-century reader. This particular apocalyptic literature is found in letter form. The content, like that of the other epistles of the New Testament, is intended to be read in community. The writer draws sharp contrasts between what is good and what is evil, between God and Satan, and between what is true and what is false. The expectation is that the end time is near. This is consistent with other material in the Gospels where Jesus is expected to return soon. While some communities believe they can find here a timeline for when the world will actually come to an end, it is more likely that the numbering of months and days is intended simply to convey that the days of the world are very few.

Probably written in the first century by someone we otherwise do not know, the apocalyptic genre seems strange and foreign to the contemporary reader, but it would not have been so to the ancient reader/listener. Apocalyptic literature was more common in the ancient world. Inherent in the strange symbols, however, are messages very pertinent and relevant to us: how we overcome systems of evil, how we evaluate the work we do in our local church communities, and what happens when churches become complacent and see no contrast between their Christian commitments and those of the surrounding culture!

It will be good for the preacher to read the book of Revelation from beginning to end to get a sense of its structure and "feel." Knowing the broader context provides some important interpretive clues for understanding the individual assigned lections. For the Second Sunday of Easter we begin at the beginning of Revelation. The RCL invites us to look particularly at 1:4-8 and the LFM at 1:9-19. Together these provide an introduction to both the book as a whole and to the following section in which seven churches are identified, challenged, and affirmed for the work they are doing in the world in which they find themselves.

There are several things to note in verses 1-8. The first verses (1-3) note that the revelation that is coming, what is being uncovered or revealed, is coming from God through Jesus Christ. The revelation is given to John. The words are to be read aloud, and those who hear them are blessed. The blessing ends with these ominous words: ". . . for the time is near" (1:3). There is an urgency here; the words need to be spoken before the end time comes. What kinds of qualities do our words take on when we feel there is an urgency in their speaking?

In poetic language the second coming of Christ is described. Every eye will see him. The section closes with what seems to be some words of assurance: "'I am the Alpha and the Omega,' says the Lord God, 'who is and who was and who is to come, the Almighty'" (v. 8). What kind of thought or feeling is invoked by knowing that God has been and will be forever?

The second part of the introduction (vv. 9-20) tells us that John, who was living on the island of Patmos, heard a voice calling him to write in a book what he saw about the seven churches in Ephesus, Smyrna, Pergamum, Thyatira, Sardis, Philadelphia, and Laodicea. Do not let the difficult place names deter you! Read chapters 2 and 3 to see if any of the descriptions of the seven churches name the realities of your own faith communities. John spoke about each of them:

- The first had a patient endurance and had not grown weary;
- The second knew poverty even though it was rich;
- The third was holding fast to the name of Jesus and had not denied its faith;
- The fourth knew love, faith, service, and patient endurance but also tolerated Jezebel, who claimed to be a prophet but practiced fornication and ate food sacrificed to idols;
- The fifth was known to be alive but was dead; the congregation was encouraged to wake up and strengthen what remained;
- The sixth had little power but had not denied the name of Jesus;
- The seventh was neither hot nor cold. They were lukewarm. They said they were rich and prosperous, but John said they were wretched, pitiable, poor, blind, and naked.

How would you describe your faith community in a single sentence? If the name of the community reflected your community's current reality, what would the name be?

Gospel

John 20:19-31 (RCL, LFM)

The prologue of the Gospel of John begins with the promise of coming light and life. The themes of light, life, and belief are woven throughout the Gospel; they are strong and pervasive. And so, it is disappointing and frightening to come to one of the final stories in the Gospel and find the disciples sitting in a darkened room fearing death. This is not how the Gospel is supposed to end! This story seems to nullify every promise, every vision, every theological affirmation made in the Gospel about Jesus.

The disciples are afraid. Sitting in a room. Visualize the closed door, the closed, locked door. Surprising them again, Jesus appears, fulfilling the promise of presence made so frequently before the crucifixion when he was telling them good-bye. Jesus offers them a word of peace, but the fear and uncertainty they must be feeling will not so easily be quelled. They do experience some relief and joy perhaps when they see the scars on his hands and sides. Do they think that this time he will stay with them?

Jesus says three things to them, seemingly unrelated, and each an important sermon seed.

1. "As the Father has sent me, so I send you" (v. 21). What does it mean to be a "sent" person? What did Jesus mean? Sent out to do what? Are we sent in the same way as the earliest disciples?

2. "Receive the Holy Spirit" (v. 22). What does it mean to receive the Holy Spirit? Will this make them bold, courageous, calm, joyful?

3. "If you forgive the sins of any, they are forgiven them; if you retain the sins of any, they are retained" (v. 23). This seems like common sense, does it not? If we forgive, they are forgiven. If we retain the sins, they are retained. It is not clear whom Jesus is identifying here, but the theological significance of forgiveness is immense. Ministers and priests could well spend time exploring this thorny theological issue. Should we forgive everyone for everything? Is there such a thing as premature forgiveness? Pseudo forgiveness? Is forgiveness something different than forgetting someone's sins? And do *we* forgive, or does God do the forgiving?

Thomas was not with the other ten disciples when Jesus appeared to them. Perhaps he was not afraid and did not need to be behind that locked door! But he does need the same assurance that the others had received; he, too, needs to see the scarred hands and sides of Jesus. And Jesus comes to him and gives him what he needs to understand the promise of presence that he has made to the disciples. What do we know about Thomas? A good exegetical practice would be to explore the Gospel of John for other exchanges between Jesus and this disciple. Do these previous conversations shed some light on what is happening here?

The episode ends; we have heard a story about seeing, hearing, touching, believing. But that story is not ours. Not long after Jesus left the earth, all those who had the opportunity to see and hear and touch him were gone. We are left with the story. The ending of John assures us that this is enough. And for centuries, it has been.

April 14, 2013
Third Sunday of Easter

Revised Common Lectionary (RCL)
Acts 9:1-6 (7-20)
Psalm 30
Revelation 5:11-14
John 21:1-19

Lectionary for Mass (LFM)
Acts 5:27-32, 40b-41
Psalm 30:2 + 4, 5-6, 11-12a + 13b
Revelation 5:11-14
John 21:1-19 or 21:1-14

First Reading
Acts 9:1-6 (7-20) (RCL)

The story found in Acts 9:1-6 serves several purposes. First, Luke uses it to introduce Saul to his reading audience. He is persecutor of Christians *par excellence*. In addition, the story also confirms that although Paul has not had the same experiences as the disciples—either before or after the resurrection—he does have an experience. He is on the road to Damascus when he hears the voice and is blinded. He sees and hears just as the disciples have seen and heard; his ministry is confirmed and he is established as one commissioned to testify for Jesus.

Initially, Saul is not just resistant to the Christian message. He doesn't simply ignore or even passively try to impede its spread. Saul is actively seeking those who are followers on "the way"—the phrase Luke uses to describe those who have been converted to the faith. Saul is breathing threats and murder and travels distances to seek out Christians, binding them and bringing them back to Jerusalem. This scene brings to mind the horror stories of raids, of those who are persecuted hiding silently in attics or in caves underground to keep from being seen or heard by those who are trying to destroy them.

But on the road to Damascus, sixty miles northeast of the Sea of Galilee, Saul is confronted and blinded by a great light, and then he hears a voice: "Saul, Saul, why are you persecuting me?" And in this instant Saul's life is radically changed. The one who has been the greatest persecutor of Christians becomes the most avid follower of Jesus.

Luke plays with the image of light, blindness, and sight throughout his Gospel as well as in Acts (see Luke 2:30; 8:16; 24:16, 31; Acts 13:11; 28:27).

This story is often titled the "conversion of Saul." What is your own response to the word *conversion*? What does it bring to mind? Do you have a conversion story, and is it like Saul's? Or a powerful experience that changed your life forever? There are many ways that people come to the gospel. But the important element of this story, and ours, is that it is God who dramatically changes hearts and minds or who gradually or almost inaudibly coaxes us along as we grow and develop in the faith. Are we converted once? Or over and over again?

This is not the only miraculous thing that happens in the story. Ananias has a vision also. He is called by God to do something very difficult. He sees a vision, and God calls him to go to a street named Straight and look for Saul. God tells him to lay hands on him so that his blindness will be healed. Ananias knows that Saul has done much evil, and he is afraid. This is one of the most difficult life challenges, the calling to be a healer to the one who has been the enemy. But this happens in ministry . . .

Acts 5:27-32, 40b-41 (LFM)

For commentary on this lesson, please see the first reading for the Second Sunday of Easter, above.

Psalmody

Psalm 30 (RCL)

Psalm 30:2 + 4, 5-6, 11-12a + 13b (LFM)

The psalmist has known times of prosperity and believes that he will always know prosperity; he will never "be moved." But he comes upon calamity. In Psalm 30 the crisis is likely some kind of close encounter with death. Perhaps he has had a serious illness, but God has "drawn him up." He has been healed and brought up from Sheol.

The psalm presents us with an important, thorny theological question: Why do we have calamity, struggle, pain in our lives? It is important to have conversations about theodicy, our understandings of suffering, in our church communities so that when disaster hits, the community is ready to engage it. They can do this more effectively, and can help each other more effectively, if they have a theological foundation on which to stand. In this psalm, the one speaking to and about God believes that the suffering he has experienced has been brought about because of God's anger. This is not uncommon in the psalms, and it is not uncommon today. We often hear people who have had tragedy visit them ask, "Why is God doing this to me?"

The psalmist says about God, "His anger is but for a moment; his favor is for a lifetime" (v. 5). Similar phrases find their home in several places in the Old Testament (cf. Isa. 54:7, 8); one wonders if it was a kind of proverb spoken often and in varied settings. There is another phrase used more often and in varied kinds of

Old Testament literature: God is "slow to anger and abounding in steadfast love" (cf. Exod. 34:6; Num. 14:18; Neh. 9:17; Ps. 86:15; Joel 2:13; Jon. 4:2; Nah. 1:3). It raises interesting theological questions about God's "anger." Is there room in your theological framework for an angry God? Or are there things happening in the world that you hope provoke God's anger? What might those things be?

There are several words used for anger in the Old Testament, but the word used in 30:5 can be translated "anger" or "nostril." Why is not entirely clear; perhaps it is because an angry person breathes heavily or perhaps it refers to flaring nostrils. Regardless, the word is used forty times in the Old Testament to talk about human anger. One hundred and seventy times it refers to God. This is a burning, smoking kind of anger at those who are worshiping other gods, those who are treating each other unjustly, some who delude themselves into thinking that they need God no longer.

But there is another thread of tradition in Psalm 30:5, and that is about God's steadfast love for God's people. This is the God who tries to control anger. Jonah knew about this kind of God and did *not* want to send the message of doom to the Ninevites. He knew that God's compassion would win the day, and any message of doom sent to the people would in reality not come to pass. How do we hold understandings of God's anger and compassion together?

This psalm is, in part, a prayer. It is spoken to God (vv. 1-3, 6-12). We often forget what a profound theological statement we are making when we simply pray. We are saying that we believe in a listening God. A caring God. A responsive God. Those are not small attributes!

Second Reading

Revelation 5:11-14 (RCL, LFM)

For a brief introduction to preaching on Revelation, please see the second reading for the Second Sunday of Easter, above.

Following the descriptions of the seven congregations for which there are particular messages, the scene changes to the description of a scroll on which there are words written front and back. The scroll is sealed with seven seals. An angel asks, "Who is worthy to open the scroll and break the seals?" (v. 2). No one in heaven or earth is found worthy, and the one seeing the vision begins to cry. In these first introductory verses, we see similarities to former stories of the tradition, for instance, the story of Noah when there were no righteous people on the earth. Or the story of Abraham who negotiates with God about the righteous people living in Sodom. The one seeing the vision weeps, just as the prophet Jeremiah wept over the plight of his people. But there is one person, the Lion from the tribe of Judah, the Root of David, who can open the scroll. He is the Son of God, the one who is worthy.

In a dramatic reversal in verse 6, it is not the Lion that is seen in the vision, but between the throne and the four living creatures and among the elders there is a Lamb, one that has been slaughtered. This testifies to the reality and irony of the Christian tradition; the one who is worthy is not one who came with the violence of the Lion but one who gave up his own life. This is not the typical conception of a powerful leader, ruler, Messiah.

The creatures and elders sing a new song. The word *new* is found throughout Revelation; there is a new song, new name, new earth, and new Jerusalem. The penultimate chapter of Revelation contains these words: "I make all things new." What does that mean to us as Christian followers of Jesus Christ? What has it meant to you and your community that God has the power to make things new? What "in the world" is God doing that is new?

The new song is about the life that Jesus gave ransomed saints "from every tribe and language and people and nation" (v. 9). The redemption wrought by Jesus is universal. It is for everyone on the face of the earth. The angels, creatures, and elders begin to sing, "Worthy is the Lamb that was slaughtered to receive power and wealth and wisdom and might and honor and glory and blessing" (v. 12). As did the previous unit, this one ends with songs of joyful praise and thanksgiving for the life of the Lamb given so that the earth, and all that is in it, could be redeemed. This is a significant message for the Third Sunday of Easter!

Gospel

John 21:1-19 (RCL, LFM)
John 21:1-14 (LFM alt.)

We read the first verse of John 21, and we can finally exhale. In last week's lection, parts of John 20, the disciples are sitting in a locked room afraid that the fate of Jesus, death on a cross, might be their own. This seems to be a very unfitting ending for the Gospel that begins with a promise of Jesus bringing light and life. The disciples are in a dark room fearing death!

Jesus visits them there and offers them a word of peace. He breathes the Holy Spirit upon them and sends them out into the world to fulfill his mission. And yet, when chapter 20 is over and Jesus has visited the disciples, first without and then with Thomas, they are still in that room. There are some closing words about all the signs Jesus had done, and indications that the story of Jesus is recorded so that others may also know that he is the Messiah. We are left with many questions. What will the disciples do when they leave that room? Go back to the work they had left three years before? Will they face their fears, continue the ministries into which Jesus had invited them? Is the story over?

But when we read the first verse of John 21, no doubt a later editorial edition, our own greatest fears are relieved. The disciples have "left the building" and are out on the Sea of Tiberias. The story takes place at daybreak so light is beginning to come once again into the world. This ending to the Gospel of John is more hopeful—and instructive.

Seven of the disciples are at seaside. At Peter's initiative they decide to go fish. Is this a decision to return to his former profession now that Jesus is gone? They all follow Peter into the boat, but they catch nothing. Jesus, though they do not recognize him, is standing on the beach. Cast your net to the right side of the boat, he tells them, and you will find some. There are so many fish in their net, they cannot pull it in—153 of them! And the disciple whom Jesus loved says to Peter, "It is the Lord!" (21:7). Peter clothes himself and jumps into the sea, and the others bring in the nets overflowing. In this third postresurrection appearance of Jesus, breakfast is shared, bread and fish consumed. Jesus is recognized and the eating, the sharing of the meal, confirms the reality of the resurrected one among them.

The "sidebar" conversation between Peter and Jesus is also interesting here. Why Peter? we wonder. Why does Jesus choose to have this final conversation with Peter? Does John give us this story about a three-part exchange between Jesus and Peter because Peter had denied Jesus three times? Does this story "redeem" Peter? Or is Jesus choosing Peter because he has time and again shown himself the leader of the disciples by asking the challenging and impetuous questions? Was Jesus concerned about Peter's loyalty, or did he see in Peter great potential for being a bold witness for Jesus in his absence? Any of these is possible.

Jesus pulls Peter aside and three times asks him, "Do you love me?"

Each time Peter answers in the affirmative. And the three responses of Jesus to him are . . .

Feed my lambs. Tend my sheep. Feed my sheep.

In both the Old Testament prophetic material and in the Gospels, we are reminded again and again that our love for God and for Jesus is demonstrated by the ways we treat others. We have a strong resistance to this idea. We would rather believe that our strong devotion is shown through beautiful and right worship, our meditative practices, even our own success! But no. It is how we feed and tend the others in the world around us. John again uses the shepherd metaphor to show Peter that it is in caring like the shepherd—being attentive and compassionate, feeding and tending the people in the world around us—that God is well pleased. And miraculously, Jesus is leaving the responsibility of feeding the hungry sheep to his disciples.

April 21, 2013
Fourth Sunday of Easter

Revised Common Lectionary (RCL)	**Lectionary for Mass (LFM)**
Acts 9:36-43	Acts 13:14, 43-52
Psalm 23	Psalm 100:1-2, 3, 5
Revelation 7:9-17	Revelation 7:9, 14b-17
John 10:22-30	John 10:27-30

First Reading
Acts 9:36-43 (RCL)

The early church is increasing in numbers, and its leaders are showing power beyond measure. There is a kind of euphoria as the story is told; there is a crescendo of sorts as the disciples, filled with power at Pentecost, go out into the world to teach, preach, and heal—just as Jesus had taught them.

In the Acts 9 reading for today, our attention is turned slightly from Paul, who has only recently been converted but who is already a threat to the ruling authorities, to Peter. In 9:32-43 Peter performs two healings. The first is of Aeneas, who had been paralyzed for eight years, and then Tabitha, who has died and whom Peter raises from the dead.

The two stories are interesting in their differences and their similarities. In the first, Peter says to Aeneas, "Jesus Christ heals you; get up . . ." (9:34). Perhaps he is teaching those around him that it is the power of God, and not the power of Peter, that heals. When healing Tabitha, Peter has sent all others outside, and though he prays for the power of healing, Peter says simply to Tabitha, "Get up" (v. 40). Perhaps that is because there is no teaching to be done; there is no one else present.

In both stories, however, the healing stories seem to serve the purpose of showing how and why the church is growing in such great numbers. In Lydda, all the residents "turned to the Lord" (v. 35). And in Joppa, "many believed" (v. 42).

Luke is known to have included more stories about women than the other Gospel writers. Often in the Luke/Acts narrative, stories about men are paralleled with or include women. Think of Zechariah and Mary, Simeon and Anna, the shepherd who lost a sheep and the woman who lost a coin, Ananias and Sapphira, Priscilla and Aquila, for instance. But the women do not have the powerful roles of preacher, teacher, and healer. They are often the more passive character; their contributions are more "behind the scenes." Still, Luke notices and preserves for us the stories of women like Tabitha, who was "devoted to good works and acts of charity" (9:36). Her ministry to the widows of the community can remind us of the host of women in the histories of our own faith communities who lived out their calling through silent and often unacknowledged ways. This story about Tabitha is important because it breaks this silence. Unlike other healing stories we know something about the one being healed. The widows bring out garments that she has made for them. We learn that she is generous and compassionate, quietly meeting the needs of those around her. She is identified as a disciple (the feminine form of that noun is used here—the only time in the New Testament!). Who are the Tabithas in the history of your faith community? What are the stories of the women who have labored long in the church's past to live faithfully and to bring the good news to others?

Although this is an unusual healing story, unaccompanied by sermon or theological treatise, still it must have been a relief to the disciples and the church community that Jesus' healing power is still working in the world, healing and bringing wholeness. The followers of Jesus are described as those who "turn the world upside down" (17:6). Certainly this is the case when, through them, God's power is at work bringing those who are dead back to life!

Peter stays in Joppa, and in what appears to be a kind of throwaway line, Luke tells us that he stayed with a certain Simon, who was a tanner. The inclusion of this side note, however, demonstrates that the church is growing in yet another way. Peter is staying with a tanner who is unclean because he deals with the carcasses of dead animals. This may be a precursor to the grand vision Peter experiences in chapter 10 where the boundaries between what is clean and unclean are rendered irrelevant and unhelpful when dealing with the unfolding of the good news of Jesus Christ.

Acts 13:14, 43-52 (LFM)

Anyone who holds an understanding that the early church was free from controversy will have this idea challenged mightily by reading Acts 13. In it, Paul and Barnabas are in Antioch of Pisidia. As in the first chapters of Acts, they continue to preach and speak boldly. They do not shy from controversy, even danger.

On this particular sabbath, nearly the whole city has come to hear them, and the great crowds are threatening to the authorities; the crowds stir their jealousy, and they begin preaching against the apostles. Paul and Barnabas say in return, "It was necessary that the word of God should be spoken first to you. Since you reject it and judge yourselves to be unworthy of eternal life, we are now turning to the Gentiles" (13:46). This is interesting because the words seem to be threatening and punishing.

Since you do not respond to the Christian message, we have taken it elsewhere—to the Gentiles. The words that Paul and Barnabas quote from Isaiah 49:6 are presumably meant to be words of inclusion and acceptance: "I have set you to be a light for the Gentiles, so that you may bring salvation to the ends of the earth" (v. 47). But they take these words and twist them into something ominous. Do we know of other times the church has taken an inclusive and welcoming gospel and turned it into something that disparages and excludes?

The Gentiles, of course, are very pleased to hear these words. The gospel is being brought to them and they are being welcomed into the Christian community. But as the "word of the Lord" spreads, opposition and hostility to it grow. And finally the disciples "shake the dust off their feet," leave the city, and head for Iconium. How do we know when it is time to "let go" and head elsewhere?

Psalmody

Psalm 23 (RCL)

Why has this psalm been the favorite, and even a bedrock of faith, for so many Christians over the centuries? The question is an interesting one, and there may well be several different answers. First, it gives comfort to those who are experiencing difficult, challenging moments in their lives. Many can name the times they were in the "dark valley" and were afraid. Second, it is hopeful, and many strive for the utter and complete confidence the psalmist seems to have in God. Third, from a literary and rhetorical perspective, the psalmist makes use of a single metaphor, the shepherd, and continues to spin out the myriad dimensions of it. That kind of unity is pleasing to a hearer and a listener, something that we could keep in mind as we write our sermons! And last, this is a very personal psalm. The Lord is *my* shepherd. We are drawn to its intimacy.

Using shepherd as a metaphor for a king or for God is common in the ancient Hebrew world and in other ancient Near Eastern cultures as well. But many in our church communities have never lived where there are shepherds, have never seen a shepherd. Are there contemporary metaphors for God that convey the same message of care, trust, and concern?

There are several parts of the psalm that are worthy of exploration. One is the phrase "I shall not want." Living in a consumerist society and having advertisers try to convince us daily that we need more, it is difficult for us to imagine a state of mind where what we have is what we need, where all that is important will be provided by God. How might it be to live in this satisfied state of mind?

Another fruitful sermon theme would be hospitality. The image of God in the last two verses mirrors the ancient Near Eastern perception of the perfect host. The guest is welcomed into a safe space even though there may be enemies surrounding him. The table is prepared. The head is anointed. And the guest is always welcome—even for the length of his days.

The word typically translated "mercy" in verse 6 ("Surely goodness and mercy shall follow me . . .") is the Hebrew word *hesed.* This is a vitally important Hebrew word used throughout the Old Testament to describe the kind of love God holds for us. This kind of love is enduring, loyal. This kind of love sees us through weakness, confusion, despair, temptation, and defeat. It inspires hope and courage. It remains even when we are unlovable or have turned away. It is an "I will not let you go" kind of love.[1]

Psalm 100:1-2, 3, 5 (LFM)

It is always good practice when preaching from the Psalms to read the psalm in its entirety. Often important or challenging verses are omitted from the prescribed lection. The careful reader will usually find that the omitted verses pose thorny theological questions. The reason for the omission of verse 4 is not so readily apparent.

Psalm 100 is pure, unadulterated praise. Interestingly, it provides in different form some of the same imagery as Psalm 23. Here, God is the shepherd and the people are the sheep of God's pasture. It is an active psalm. The people are called to make a joyful noise, worship, sing, know, enter the gates, and give thanks. Also, as in Psalm 23, the God who is faithful loves with an everlasting and steadfast love (see above regarding Psalm 23 for an understanding of the word *hesed*, commonly translated "steadfast love," sometimes "mercy"). Notably absent in this psalm is any recounting of the great deeds that God has done in the past. Missing also is any hint of difficulty or calamity suffered by the worshiping one. This is a call to thanksgiving.

Preaching from a text that is not itself a narrative invites us to think about our own life stories that "surround" the reading. A good question for the preacher to ask would be, When in this community of faith have we had experiences that led us to this kind of praise and thanksgiving for God's faithfulness?

Second Reading

Revelation 7:9-17 (RCL)
Revelation 7:9, 14b-17 (LFM)

The Easter season lectionary in Year C takes us from the first to the final chapters of Revelation. Here we take a moment to pause somewhere in between. The messages to the seven churches have been delivered, and we have not yet entered into the chapters of judgment and devastation. We have not received the picture of the final and glorious restoration of the city of Jerusalem and all nations and all peoples who share the world with us. We are not there—yet—and to keep our faith and to be faithful is hard work. We live day to day with enough glimpses of life as it should be that we keep on.

The unit begins with a vision of a great multitude gathered together. This is a very diverse group of people representing every culture, every race, every nation. These are people who have been through the "great ordeal" (v. 14) or who have experienced persecution. They have known suffering; being a faithful follower of Jesus does not eliminate suffering. These are people who have known hunger or thirst or violence or scorching heat (v. 16). But now God has wiped away their tears.

One of the strong themes in Revelation articulated clearly in this lection is the affirmation that salvation comes from God. There was much pressure during the time of the Roman Empire to believe that salvation, however that was defined, came from allegiance to the empire itself. We are pushed and pulled in similar fashion to believe that what will "save" us are things that do not last and that do not satisfy. The multitudes who are gathered around the throne know who or what deserves their greatest loyalty and allegiance. They know "whose they are." And they are there, standing before the Lamb who has given his life for them.

Gospel

John 10:22-30 (RCL)
John 10:27-30 (LFM)

Reading John 10 in its entirety will give the preacher a more comprehensive understanding of the metaphor of the shepherd that is found in today's lection. In expansive fashion the Gospel writer explores and exploits the metaphor to help define and describe the relationship between Jesus and the people, Jesus and God. Chapter 10 is filled with words that contrast the good shepherd with others. The good shepherd, for instance, enters the sheepfold by the gate. Bandits and thieves climb in through other ways. (Note the way contrast heightens both the energy and understanding in the text. We come to know more about the good shepherd because John contrasts the shepherd with bandits and thieves. A good sermon strategy—using contrast!)

The voice of the shepherd is also contrasted with the voice of the stranger. The sheep follow the former because that voice is familiar. The thieves and bandits come to steal and kill and destroy, but the shepherd comes to give life. The hired hand sees the wolf and, even though the sheep are in danger, runs away. The wolf snatches and scatters the sheep. But the good shepherd cares about and will lay down his life for the sheep. The contrasting images provide a clearer and more powerful picture of the shepherd Jesus is trying to describe. His description provokes anger from the listeners. Many were saying that he had a demon. Others were saying that he did not.

This long excursus about the shepherd is a prelude to today's lection. Now it is winter and the time of the Festival of the Dedication. The Jews gather around him and ask, "How long will you keep us in suspense? If you are the Messiah, tell us plainly" (10:24). Jesus identifies himself as the shepherd; his voice is recognized by the sheep, and they follow. Like the good shepherd, he brings them life. No thief or bandit or wolf will snatch them away from the Father. The lection ends with these words, "The Father and I are one" (v. 30).

Note

1. See Mary Donovan Turner, *Old Testament Words: Reflections for Preaching* (St. Louis: Chalice, 2006), for a fuller explication of the word *hesed* and other important words used in the Old Testament text.

April 28, 2013
Fifth Sunday of Easter

Revised Common Lectionary (RCL)
Acts 11:1-18
Psalm 148
Revelation 21:1-6
John 13:31-35

Lectionary for Mass (LFM)
Acts 14:21-27
Psalm 145:8-9, 10-11, 12-13
Revelation 21:1-5a
John 13:31-33a, 34-35

First Reading
Acts 11:1-18 (RCL)

The story of Cornelius and Peter is told and then retold in great detail in Acts 10 and 11. The repetition indicates that Peter's experience is pivotal and a significant turn in the spreading of the gospel. It is a story of visions and angels and, at the same time, a story that addresses one of the most tensive and volatile issues facing the early church. The issue is one of inclusion, and it illustrates for us the emotional and wrenching decisions the church has always had to make: Does including the new or different mean that we are letting go of the values that have always defined us? Or do the values that define us compel us to be more inclusive and open? That is the crux of much of the turmoil in the contemporary church.

The lection is Peter's retelling of the story of his visions regarding Cornelius. He is meeting resistance; some are upset after hearing that Gentiles are accepting the gospel. And he is telling the story to justify their recent baptism. They ask why Peter was eating with uncircumcised men. Peter answers their questions not through debate or rational discourse. He tells them the story of his vision. So often the explanation for what we believe comes packaged in a narrative. What are the narratives that define your life and your belief in God?

Peter recounts the vision he has seen; a sheet comes down from heaven and on it are all kinds of animals—those with four feet, reptiles, and birds of the air. A voice commands him to get up and eat. But Peter, being faithful to his tradition and what he has learned, replies that he has never eaten anything profane or unclean. The voice answers, "What God has made clean, you must not call profane" (10:15; 11:9). This happens three times. Surely this is one of the pivotal turning points in the book of Acts, but Peter is not initially aware of the vision's meaning. It is only when the three men come to him asking him to go to Caesarea to see Cornelius that Peter begins to understand the enormity of what has happened. He begins to understand that the gospel is available to everyone, Jews and Gentiles alike. It is easy to say the church is for everyone. But the complexities of that statement are encountered and dealt with over time—in arguments, conversations, and council meetings. There seems to be something inherently complicated about inclusion. Is it easier to be insular rather than permeable? Closed rather than open? Static rather than dynamic? Yes, perhaps. But the gospel calls us to travel beyond our comforts and the fixed lines we have drawn in the sand. It is always calling us to increase the size of the circle and make its boundaries permeable. Shouldn't the church be the place that is proclaiming the worth of every person created by God—people of every race, every sexual orientation, gender, and class? Why is the church often the carrier of prejudice and division?

Peter asks an interesting question of those who are resistant to expanding the circle of inclusion. "Who was I that I could hinder God?" Sometimes we do not carry forth the gospel or work tirelessly to bring in the surprising and shocking realm of God to this earth. But at least, this story reminds us, we can try *not* to get in the way of God's miraculous working.

Acts 14:21-27 (LFM)

Again we travel along with Paul and Barnabas. In verses 19-20, and related almost as an aside, Paul is stoned and dragged out of Lystra, left for dead. But Paul gets up and continues his tireless travel to Derbe, then back to Lystra, Iconium, and Antioch. Luke tells us that he is returning to those communities to strengthen the souls of the disciples and encourage them to keep their faith. This raises an interesting question: Why is it that we need so much encouragement to "keep the faith," and why do our souls need to be strengthened? Is it because we get swayed by the world's priorities and find ourselves leaning fully into our culture's individualistic and consumerist culture? Is it because the problems of the communities around us and around the globe seem so insurmountable and we wonder, Where is God? Is it that divisions among us consume our energy and our focus so that other, perhaps more important issues don't get the time they deserve? Can we not sustain our passion about the gospel? Do we need constant reminders that there are things of ultimate value and things of no lasting value?

After appointing elders, with prayer and fasting they then leave these communities to God. At every juncture Paul and Barnabas have to decide: When do we stay and support and encourage, and when do we "let go and let God"? When should we work tirelessly and when do we put things in God's hands? When do we do both?

Psalmody

Psalm 148 (RCL)

The last five psalms in the Psalter (146–150) begin with "Hallelujah!" or "Praise the Lord!" The book of Psalms ends with a rousing call to praise and thanksgiving. Psalm 148 is distinctive in that it doesn't focus primarily on why we should praise or when we should praise. This psalm is about *who* should be praised. The psalmist tells us that the angels, the Lord's host, sun, moon, shining stars, highest heavens, waters above the heavens, sea monsters, the deep, fire and hail, snow and frost, stormy winds, mountains, all hills, fruit trees and cedars, wild animals and all cattle, creeping things and flying birds, kings, all peoples, princes, rulers, young men and women, and the old and the young alike—all are called to praise.

The psalm is beautiful in that it calls all the universe to join in the chorus. And in so doing, the psalmist recognizes that all of these have been created by God. Each has been created purposefully and each contributes to the working of the cosmos. Perhaps this, then, invites us to think of the ways we do and do not hold sacred and thus protect all the varied parts of the beautiful world in which we live.

I believe we rarely ask why it is important to praise God! There are many answers to this question. First, praise invites us to remember all the ways God has been active in our own lives and in our communities. Stories and memories can be brought to consciousness as we give our praise to God for God's agency and participation in our daily lives. Praise says to us, Pay attention to "what on earth" God is doing! Second, praise is a form of thanksgiving. This kind of thanksgiving reminds us of what is really important. In a world that invites us to give thanks for "things," praise to God invites us to give gratitude to the one who created us and gave us important work to do in the world. To be truly grateful for what has been given us results in our not being greedy or stingy with it. And finally, praise is a form of evangelism, of telling the story of God's presence. In so doing, we might invite others to recognize the same redemptive threads in their own lives that bring them both sustenance and hope.

The whole creation is called to join in this mighty praise chorus. Realizing that all of these bear beautiful witness to the name of God may encourage our church communities to take seriously the plight of the earth and compel them to find ways to preserve the environment because it is created by God and thus sacred.

Psalm 145:8-9, 10-11, 12-13 (LFM)

This assigned lection (vv. 8-13) inadvertently divides the psalm into at least three sections; each makes its own contribution to the whole. Preceding the lection, in verses 1-7, the psalmist, using the first person, is recounting his own compulsion to give praise and thanksgiving to God. One generation tells the next of God's gracious and mighty deeds; individuals, like the psalmist, will give voice to God's greatness. What is our own personal testimony in relation to the God whose "greatness is unsearchable" (v. 3)?

In the final section of the psalm that follows the lection, verses 13b-21, we learn something about the kind of God being worshiped. In the form of a "litany-like" list the attributes of Yahweh are recounted. Yahweh . . .

- is faithful and gracious;
- upholds all who are falling and raises up those who are bowed down;
- is just in all ways and kind in all doings;
- is near to all who call in truth;
- fulfills the desire of those who fear him and hears their cry;
- watches over those who love him and destroys the wicked.

These are powerful theological affirmations. Read them slowly to discover the significance of each.

Today's lection, which bridges these two sections, begins with a description of Yahweh that is found in other parts of the Old Testament. Perhaps this attests to the phrase's almost proverbial character. "The LORD is gracious and merciful, slow to anger and abounding in steadfast love." This is a tribute to the patience of God. How have we known God's patience with us? With our communities? With the church? This affirmation about God's patience is followed with "the LORD is good to all, and he has compassion over all that he has made." This is articulated in some communities where almost weekly the minister says, "God is good." And the community responds, "All the time." What do we think about the goodness of God, and how do we reconcile this goodness with an all-powerful God and the all-knowing nature of God? Can God be all these things? How do we reconcile verse 9, regarding God's compassion for every living thing, with the assertion in verse 20 that God will destroy the wicked?

The people will tell of God's glory and power and mighty deeds throughout the earth. How do people in your community tell these stories? What is the understanding of "witness" in your community? Testimony? Evangelism?

Second Reading
Revelation 21:1-6 (RCL)
Revelation 21:1-5a (LFM)

The struggle is over. Evil is no more. Chapter 21, the penultimate chapter in Revelation, brings a picture of the new heaven, new earth, new and restored Jerusalem. Following the description of the last judgment in 20:11-15, these verses renew hopefulness that ultimately God's agency will be demonstrated in creative and redemptive acts of restoration. This is a city where covenant is restored between people and God—God will dwell with them and they will be God's people (v. 3). There will be no more death. No more tears. No more mourning or crying or pain (v. 4).

As in the other parts of the apocalypse, there is an uneasy tension between the newness of the city and dualities or polarities that still exist. Is this a city where all are included, or are the murderers, the fornicators, the sorcerers, the idolaters, and the liars still relegated to the burning lake of fire (v. 8)? The committees who put the lectionary together for us must have themselves been uncomfortable with the exclusive nature of verse 8, helpfully omitting it so that the reading would end with Jesus, the Alpha and the Omega, saying that he will give water as a gift from the spring of life! What are our options when we are faced with parts of the Old and New Testaments that are difficult to understand or even offensive to us? One option, of course, is to ignore them. Another, however, is to wrestle with them on behalf of the community. In the struggle, the preacher's own theological questions will surface and the community will find those questions mirrored in their own thinking about God and faithful living.

This text offers us hope for a better day, for ourselves, for our congregations, for the global community. It is a witness to the Jesus who says again, "I am the Alpha and the Omega, the beginning and the end . . ." During the days and weeks between the resurrection and the coming of the Spirit at Pentecost, the disciples were in a liminal space. Was it true that Jesus would be with them forever, that they would inherit the power of God, that they could go on believing in the Jesus who promised presence? This text is a reminder during the season of Easter and pre-Pentecost that God is constantly creating new out of the old. Can you attest to that in your own life or that of your faith community? What have you seen and heard?

The truth is that while perhaps we can anticipate this glorious day to come, we live in the "not yet." We live in the middle time when all is not glorious. What sustains us?

Gospel
John 13:31-35 (RCL)
John 13:31-33a, 34-35 (LFM)

Though today's Gospel lection precedes what is commonly called the Farewell Discourse in the Gospel of John, "leave taking" is certainly in the air. There is much about "leave taking" in the Gospel stories. There is much "leave taking" in life.

Jesus has taken the role of servant and, teaching them about servanthood, hospitality, and love, he washes their feet. He is troubled in spirit. And suddenly he announces to them, "Very truly, I tell you, one of you will betray me" (13:21). What a shocking statement after such a beautiful and intimate ritual of foot washing! Jesus tells Judas to go and do quickly what he is going to do. And when Judas has left, Jesus speaks to his disciples the words recorded in today's lesson. The first words are about glory, which means honor and a good name. After Judas has left them, Jesus says, "Now the Son of Man has been glorified as God was glorified in him" (v. 31). This is the irony of the Christian story, that the honor, the good name, that comes to Jesus will come through his suffering and death. This ushers in the last advice, or commandment, that Jesus offers to the ones he is leaving.

Last words are important. Perhaps you know this from your own life experience. What were the last words you spoke to a child going off to college? Or moving away from home? Or how intently did you listen for the last words of a loved one who was near death? Certainly, according to John, Jesus knows that his life is coming to an end. Perhaps Jesus is experiencing sadness, the pain of betrayal by someone close to him, and an urgency to say to the disciples the most important words that need to be spoken. This is his last advice, the things he wants most for them to remember. "Little children," he says to them, "I am with you only a little longer" (v. 33). And then, "I give you a new commandment, that you love one another. By this everyone will know that you are my disciples, if you have love for one another" (vv. 34-35).

The call to love each other is not new, of course. In the Old Testament there are calls to love your neighbor as yourself, love the foreigner as yourself. But here the disciples are asked to love as Jesus has loved. They have a model, a standard; they've been shown the way. Following the scene of foot washing, this is a powerful request on the part of Jesus. He is asking them to care for each other as he has cared for them.

We claim that we do not know what God expects of us. We claim confusion about that as a rationalization for keeping firmly in place all that divides us from each other. But here it is clear. This is the new commandment. This is the charge that Jesus leaves with his disciples. And it is simple. And it is complicated and life's greatest challenge. Love one another. This is not a new commandment, of course. But the commandment becomes new as Jesus prepares to give his life for his friends, his disciples, those with whom he shares the world. His kind of love is limitless, steadfast, given of God.

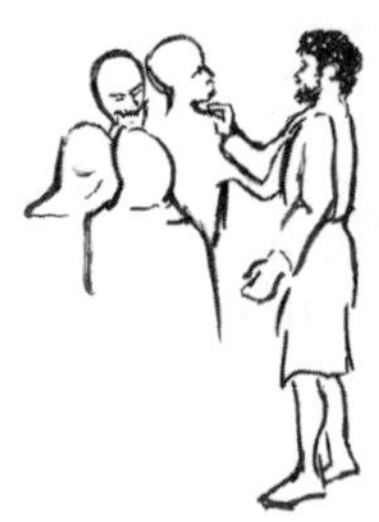

May 5, 2013
Sixth Sunday of Easter

Revised Common Lectionary (RCL)
Acts 16:9-15
Psalm 67
Revelation 21:10, 22—22:5
John 14:23-29 or 5:1-9

Lectionary for Mass (LFM)
Acts 15:1-2, 22-29
Psalm 67:2-3, 5, 6 + 8
Revelation 21:10-14, 22-23
John 14:23-29

First Reading
Acts 16:9-15 (RCL)

Chapter 16 of Acts gives a description of Timothy, whose mother was Jewish; his father was a Greek. Because Timothy was a strong believer with a good reputation, Paul invited him to travel with him.

The geography of their travels is fascinating. In this short chapter Paul visits Derbe, Lystra, the region of Phyrgia, Galatia, and Troas. He and those with him bypass Mysia and Bithynia, which the Spirit did not allow them to enter. Paul receives a vision telling him to go to Macedonia; being convinced that God is calling them there, they set sail from Troas and go to Samothrace, then Neapolis, and then Philippi. While the geographical meanderings seem like throwaway information, they give us a glimpse into the life of the earliest apostles and proclaimers, the builders of the early church. They were travelers, walking the roads endlessly, looking for fertile places for communities of faith to take root and grow. They had little to guide them except an occasional vision. There was no map, no forced itinerary, but something more like a compass—Spirit-led intuitions and a faithfulness and passion for seeing the good news spread from region to region.

Being led by a vision, Paul and his fellow travelers head for Macedonia. A voice has called him there. On this journey they travel to Philippi where they stay for several days and, on the sabbath, go outside the city gates and find a place of prayer with women gathered there. One is Lydia, a woman named for the city of Lydia, which was located in the region of Thyatira. Lydia is living in Philippi away from her home; she is an outsider. People are suspicious of outsiders, of course, and so this may have added to the trauma in her life.

Lydia is often described as a professional woman, a woman who was a "dealer in purple cloth." She has been described as a business owner and, because of her expensive wares, probably a financially successful one. Yet this popular conception of Lydia as a wealthy woman who dealt with expensive fabrics is misleading. A more accurate rendering of *purpurie* is a person who works in the manufacturing of dyed products. Lydia is not the seller of the purple cloth; she is the maker, the producer of it. Textile production was considered mostly women's work and was looked down upon in the public sphere. Lydia's work was most likely a subsistence occupation for herself and her house. This paints a very different picture of her life and of the encounter she has with Paul!

Dye houses had a terrible odor because the process of dying involved the use of animal urine. Thus dye houses were located outside the city gates. The dying was done by hand, which caused a visible stigma.[1] Lydia was marginalized, a migrant worker who, perhaps of necessity, lived outside the city gates in a foreign land. Perhaps because of her status she was open to new understandings, and she gathered with the women and listened intently to Paul.[2]

It would have been customary for women to meet with others who participated in the same trade, so perhaps on this sabbath Lydia is meeting with other women who also dyed fabric. She listens to the teachings of Paul and, as a result, comes to believe. God opens her heart, and she listens eagerly. She and her household are then baptized in the river. Through her persistent appeals to Paul to come home with her, Lydia goes against social convention, which dictated that a woman could be host only to those people she knew. To receive Paul in her home would be to receive Paul in a place that was virtually invisible, hidden from society. For him to enter her household would be to enter a world of otherness, and only someone willing to accept hospitality from another who was marginalized would cross over. Paul refuses to go.

Some say Paul's refusal to go was a modest refusal on the part of a church leader. But was his refusal a hesitancy born from the fact that Lydia was of a different class from his own? Was receiving her hospitality beneath him? Luise Schottroff invites us to think about even another alternative, the possibility that Paul refuses because Lydia is a woman.[3]

Lydia is right to think that her authority to greet, to receive, and to protect the stranger comes from her baptism and relation with Christ. On the basis of her faith and her baptism, she challenges any cultural notion that her house, or she herself, is not fit for visitors. The English translation says that Lydia prevailed upon the visitors to come and stay with her. She calls Paul into account, challenging him with the gospel he himself proclaimed. She had been baptized. And so she "talks back" to the tradition that labels her not fitting (either because she is a marginalized worker or because she is a woman) for visitors.[4] Lydia is a worker, marginalized, strong, voiced, determined—one who challenges discrepancies or hypocrisies when she sees them.

We spend time discussing issues related to race and ethnicity in our church communities, but what we are failing to discuss with equal intensity and frequency are issues of class. Here is where our greater challenge may lie. If the above interpretation is correct, Paul refuses Lydia's offer of hospitality either because she is female or because she is of a class lower than his own. She is a worker. She is "marked" by her profession. And Paul refuses to accept her offer of hospitality.

What is the class structure of your own worshiping community? What classes are welcomed and feel comfortable there? How does your worship and hospitality reflect class bias and assumptions?

Lydia's feast day is August 3. While male figures seem to dominate the story of the early church as told by Luke in the book of Acts, there is no doubt that the careful reader of the narrative will get glimpses of the very important role women played as the church was born and then began to grow and spread.[5]

Acts 15:1-2, 22-29 (LFM)

The fifteenth chapter of Acts doesn't make its way into the Revised Common Lectionary but finds its place in the Lectionary for Mass on this Sixth Sunday of Easter. Is this the case because Acts 15 highlights the process and decisions made at the council at Jerusalem?

The lection highlights one of the problems facing the early church. What should we do with those Gentiles? Following the vision of Peter found in Acts 10, a vision that compelled him to open the door of the church to Gentiles, communities had to deal with the complexity of this kind of inclusion. Do Gentiles need to follow the practices of the Jewish community to make their way into the church? Or not? Of particular concern were two issues: circumcision and the following of the dietary rules and regulations of the Torah. These made up at least part of the unique and particular identity that had been forged in the Jewish community. There were different beliefs and understandings in the church about these things. Some thought Jewish and Gentile Christians needed to follow these laws; some thought only Jewish Christians; some thought neither. This issue and the resulting tensions seemed foundational and needed exploration and discernment before the church leaders could continue on their missionary journeys.

Paul and Barnabas and others were appointed to go up to Jerusalem to discuss these questions with the apostles and elders. The conversation that took place there is important and it models for us some important reminders as we face decisions that mark the contemporary church. In the council meeting Peter stands and speaks about his own *experience* receiving the vision and the resultant decision he made that Gentiles should be included in the church community. He tells stories of the Gentiles receiving the Spirit of God. One voice can make a difference! Paul and Barnabas then report their experiences of traveling and of the signs and wonders God performed in the lives of the Gentiles.

James then turns to *Scripture*, sacred text, to talk about how the words of Peter, Paul, and Barnabas confirm what is written in the Prophets: that all may seek God, even the Gentiles.

This model of critically evaluating Scripture on the basis of our experience, and our experience on the basis of Scripture, is helpful in making the many crucial and important decisions church bodies are called upon to make. In this case, the council decides to fling wide open the doors so that all may know the grace of God.

The lection itself, then, is a copy of the letter sent from the council to all Gentile believers. Many representatives are sent along with the letter so that the word of inclusion can be delivered in print and in spoken word—a word that will calm the fears of the Christian Gentiles. They need only abstain from eating the food sacrificed to idols, eating blood, strangled animals. They are not to commit fornication. These minimal regulations will allow them to be in community with those who do follow Jewish law. This compromise allows for community to be established and grow.

Psalmody

Psalm 67 (RCL)
Psalm 67:2-3, 5, 6 + 8 (LFM)

Psalms 65–68 form a short series where each individual psalm is identified with the title "A Song." Probably used in worship, the words are a call to give praise and thanksgiving to a God who is gracious, who blesses, and who makes God's "face to shine upon us" (67:1). This is an intriguing phrase, one reminiscent of a familiar and oft-cited blessing found in Numbers 6:25.

Requests for God's "face to shine" upon us appear several times in the book of Psalms. In almost all of them, this is followed by a plea for salvation. A beautiful example of this comes in Psalm 80 where the request for God's face to shine appears three times. In each, the psalmist describes the current plight of the people and the passionate desire that God come and deliver them ("Let your face shine, so that we may be saved," 80:3, 7, 19).

The psalmist isn't asking here that just a few people be saved; she recognizes that God's saving power is for *all* nations (vv. 2, 4). As with several other readings during the Easter season, a strong universal theme structures the psalm. It begs the question, How big is our God?

The word *salvation* is found 354 times in the Old Testament. The largest concentration of occurrences is in the book of Psalms (136 times); nearly half the psalms contain the word *salvation*. It is a poetic word, and it is clear that whatever it is, it is something to sing about! The word *salvation* is used to describe the deliverance of the Israelites through the Red Sea. In this instance salvation had a communal significance, though individuals could cry out for salvation also. Most important, salvation has an "of this world" character. The person or community desires to be rescued from whatever is bringing them fear or misery or pain. Salvation could come time and time again when the community or individuals were delivered from their despair.

It is thought by some that the word *salvation* is related to other words meaning "spacious" and "wide." There is in this notion a hopefulness that God can deliver us from what restricts us and oppresses us. We are given room, a liberating space within which we can live our lives. This understanding holds that God actively participates in the life of the community and of the individual, that God hears the cries of our distress, and that God is willing and desirous that we be given a full and wide berth to live out life abundantly.

The psalm begins and ends with the request that God bless us (vv. 1, 7). What does the word *bless* or *blessing* mean? And what are the ways that God has blessed your life, that of your congregation or community? This psalm is an invitation to tell a series of stories recounting the varied ways God blesses. Though the Easter season is coming quickly to an end, it is appropriate to remember the ways that God is actively present with us even in our times of challenge and sorrow.

Second Reading

Revelation 21:10, 22—22:5 (RCL)
Revelation 21:10-14, 22-23 (LFM)

John paints for us the picture of the restored, new Jerusalem. The new city comes down and settles on the earth. It is a city formed and fashioned by God, and with great detail and specificity the city is described to us. As with the description of the building of the ark of the covenant in Exodus, we are given precise information about the shape of the city, how and of what it is made. The tree of life is there and grows on both sides of a river that flows through the city and from the throne of God.

The city is beautiful. The city is redeemed by God, and God's light shines everywhere. There is no need for sun or lamp! Nothing is hidden. There is nothing that causes shame. God's presence is pervasive and undeniable. The city has a permanence not known historically by the inhabitants of Jerusalem. They had known destruction by the Babylonians in 587 BCE and then by the Romans in 70 CE. This invites us to ask ourselves, How do we in the United States mirror these threatening powers that went into Jerusalem and destroyed what was there for convenience and gain? What are the ways we do *not* live up to this image of the new Jerusalem, governed by justice and the struggle for the captives and the oppressed?

At one level, the new Jerusalem has oftentimes been seen as symbolic of the church. To read through this lens, we are invited to ask ourselves how the church is an embodiment of the new heaven and new earth. How is God, or how is Jesus Christ, present in the church, and how does your congregation know the perpetual, indwelling Spirit?

At another level it is interesting to read this text from the perspective of the cities in which we live. What comes to mind when you hear the word *city*? Some of us live in large, teeming cities replete with a multitude of complicated social issues—hunger, poverty, inhumane immigration policies, disparity, environmental racism, violence.

What would a new city look and sound like, and what is the relationship between the building of the new city and God? What is the relationship between the new city and your congregation's calling in the world? Ideally, the city could be that highly concentrated place where people live out their interdependence with each other, but, sadly, that is not what we know.

Gospel

John 14:23-29 (RCL, LFM)

Presence. That is the essence of this part of the Farewell Discourse in John. Jesus promises not to leave the disciples orphaned (14:18), and though the world will not be able to see him after a short while, he will live and the disciples will know that he is there with them. Those who love each other will be keeping the word of God (note how the words *love* and *commandment* are linked here, as they are often in this Gospel). In them both God and Jesus will make their home.

The Holy Spirit will come and remind them of the things that Jesus told them while he was upon the earth. Jesus tells the disciples not to be troubled, not to be afraid because he sends them peace, and he will continue to send them peace even when he is not with them. The Spirit or Paraclete plays an important role in Jesus' teaching and is key in helping the disciples prepare for their life after Jesus leaves the earth. Is there a future to the revelation of God that came through the incarnation? The Spirit is the ongoing presence of Jesus with the disciples in the postresurrection community. The Holy Spirit will come to communities to instruct and witness. It is not the possession of individuals; it comes to the gathered faithful who seek the presence of the Holy One in their midst.

These words must have been confusing to the disciples, and I wonder if they were comforted by them at all! They were becoming aware that Jesus was leaving them, a very troubling reality. And Jesus was telling them that in some way he would continue to be present. It would be helpful and productive for the preacher to think about all the leave takings experienced in his or her life. What was helpful to hear when losing a loved one to death?

John 5:1-9 (RCL alt.)

Interestingly, though we have been working our way through the Farewell Discourse in John during the season of Easter, on this Sunday there is an alternative reading from John 5. This is a healing story about the paralyzed man who was by the Sheep Gate and sitting near a pool. The lectionary assigns only the first nine verses of the chapter, which truncates the reading and dismisses the following nine verses, which delineate the subsequent conversation Jesus has with the one healed and the controversy that arises because the healing took place on the sabbath.

There are some important features of the story, some dimensions that are common and some uncommon for a Gospel healing story. The paralyzed man is sitting in a place where many invalids lay—the blind, the lame, and the paralyzed. Out of all of these Jesus chooses this man because, we are told, he has been ill for a long time. In fact, we as readers know he has been ill for thirty-eight years. We do not know how Jesus knows this is the case. Jesus asks if he wants to be made well, and the man answers that he tries to make his way into the pool for healing but someone always gets in front of him. Jesus heals him—tells him to stand and take up his mat, and he does.

This first part of the story raises interesting complexities for the preacher. The Gospel stories tell us of many miracle healings performed by Jesus. How do we preach on these stories when there are people in our congregations who are ill or disabled and have not been healed? This part of the story tells of a compassionate Jesus who sees a person in need and responds to that need. In this instance the paralyzed man is not only healed but restored to the community of which he can now be a part.

The rest of the story . . . The final verses of this story, which are not included in the lection, give us clues to the purpose the story fulfills in the Gospel as a whole. Only in verse 10 do we find out that the healing takes place on the sabbath. It helps us understand, then, the growing animosity toward Jesus and the consequent plans to kill him. The authorities ask the man why he is carrying his mat on the sabbath. He tells them that he has been healed and that the healing one told him to walk and carry. We realize that the man does not know Jesus! This is not a healing based on the faithfulness of the person being healed.

Later, when they meet, Jesus tells the man to sin no more so that worse things do not happen to him. What is our own understanding of the relationship between sin and disability/illness? What are the understandings in the community that need to be challenged? This story may be a good opportunity to "preach against the text" and to explore theologies of suffering. It is helpful to the community to explore these complicated theological issues before tragedy strikes.

Notes

1. Arthur Sutherland, *I Was a Stranger: A Christian Theology of Hospitality* (Nashville: Abingdon, 2006), 48–49.
2. Ibid.
3. Luise Schottroff, *Let the Oppressed Go Free: Feminist Perspectives on the New Testament*, trans. Annemarie S. Kidder (Louisville: Westminster John Knox, 1993), 132, as quoted in Sutherland, *I Was a Stranger*, 53.
4. Sutherland, *I Was a Stranger*, 56.
5. Ibid., 42.

May 9, 2013 / May 12, 2013
Ascension of Our Lord / Ascension Sunday

Revised Common Lectionary (RCL)	**Lectionary for Mass (LFM)**
Acts 1:1-11	Acts 1:1-11
Psalm 47 or Psalm 93	Psalm 47:2-3, 6-7, 8-9
Ephesians 1:15-23	Ephesians 1:17-23 or Hebrews 9:24-28; 10:19-23
Luke 24:44-53	Luke 24:46-53

First Reading
Acts 1:1-11 (RCL, LFM)

The Gospel of Luke tells the story of the birth, ministry, death, resurrection, and ascension of Jesus. In Luke's second volume, Acts, the reader is reminded that Jesus has ascended to the heavens, and we are told the story of the disciples who experienced his leave taking. This must have been not only a mysterious time, and a joyous one, but a sad one as well. Jesus had been appearing to them after the resurrection—talking with them, instructing them, eating with them. Perhaps they held on to the hope that these experiences would never end. Leave takings are difficult. But Jesus does leave, and trusting that his presence will be with them *somehow,* they devote themselves to prayer so that the promised Spirit will come and visit them. The ascension provides a rightful closure to the postresurrection, earthly experiences of Jesus and the anticipation that God's promised presence will need to come in a different fashion. What are the varied ways you have known the presence of God?

Luke describes the ascension of Jesus in both Luke 24:50-51 and Acts 1:6-11. There are differences between the two. In both, however, the ascension of Jesus follows a commissioning of the disciples. In Luke 24:48 Jesus says to them, "You are to be my witnesses." And in the Acts version of the ascension, Jesus says, "You will be my witnesses in Jerusalem, in all Judea and Samaria, and to the ends of the earth" (1:8).

The story is about a "sending out," but more than that, it is about being empowered for the tasks that are ahead of them. Jesus is gone. They have seen him ascend into the heavens, but there is no time for grieving. For forty days, the account in Acts reads, Jesus had been appearing to them, teaching them, assuring them, and calling them to the work that was left to do. He had taught them to heal and teach and preach and feed the hungry. Now the Holy Spirit will come to enable them to do these same important things.

The first verses in Acts are important because they introduce the reader to some important thematic elements that will be visited and revisited throughout the book's twenty-eight chapters. The presence of the Holy Spirit brings people to voice; the Holy Spirit allows them to testify and brings forth proclamation, testimony, and witness. Over and again in Acts the disciples speak *boldly* because the Spirit is with them, enabling them to withstand resistance, hostility, and imprisonment. They will not be silenced.

What is so important to your own church community that you are willing to engage in this kind of bold speech? Where and when has your community taken a stand? What kind of prophetic word needs to be brought to the wider community? Where does the gospel need to be spoken? These vital questions arise out of the reading for today. As Jesus is ascending, two men appear and ask the disciples, "Why do you stand looking up toward heaven?" (1:11). Instead of waiting for God's kingdom to come on earth, the disciples are to be working to create it. Their eyes are not to be focused above, but on the needs of the world around them—the present world.

Psalmody
Psalm 47 (RCL)
Psalm 47:2-3, 6-7, 8-9 (LFM)

This is an interesting psalm for Ascension Sunday. While the thoughts and emotions of the disciples must have been complicated related to Jesus' final departure from them, the psalm itself is a glorious call to praise and celebration. Verses 6-7 call us five times to sing praises! The psalm is a witness to the greatness and powerfulness of God. Perhaps it is chosen for Ascension Day because God has "gone up with a shout" (v. 5) or because it speaks of the holy throne of God in the heavens where Jesus now resides.

Why should God be praised? Psalm 47 indicates that this is because God, as king over all the earth, is awesome. God subdued the "other nations," has chosen God's heritage, and now sits on the holy throne. Embedded in the psalm is an appreciation of the sovereign God who has given people victory in war and has helped them withstand the onslaught of nations far larger and more powerful. Remembering what God has done in the past and what God is now doing brings doxology.

How is the reading/speaking of this psalm different for us than for the ancient Israelites? They were from a small nation that was celebrating God's deliverance from nations far greater and more powerful than themselves. How do we read this psalm as people who live in one of those great and powerful nations?

As with many other readings during the Easter season, we are reminded that the God we praise is a God of all nations. This does not diminish our respect and appreciation for people of other religious traditions and heritages. Rather, it is a vital reminder that God's love is for all and invites us to think critically about our notions of superiority of self, community, nation. It calls us to ministries of inclusion and peacemaking. It calls us to wrestle with our own apathies, the great and wondrous power of God energizing us for our work in the world.

Why does the LFM omit verses 1, 4, and 5? This is a fascinating question, and the answer could again be the seed of a great sermon!

Psalm 93 (RCL alt.)

Psalm 93 is very similar to Psalm 47. It ushers in a series of six psalms (93, 95–99) that use the metaphor of king to describe God. How easily do we or our communities relate to this metaphor for God? Is it helpful or not helpful? What other metaphors are more comfortable or familiar?

In this psalm God is praised because God is king, has strength, has established and created the world, is steadfast and never moved, is everlasting, has subdued the chaotic waters, and has given decrees that are steadfast and sure. What is your own list of reasons for praising God? What chaos has been subdued, how has God offered you God's strength, how has God been dependable and steadfast in your life or that of your community?

Second Reading

Ephesians 1:15-23 (RCL)
Ephesians 1:17-23 (LFM)

Ephesians has some qualities and characteristics not shared by other letters that we can comfortably ascribe to the apostle Paul. Thus we assume that either it was written late in Paul's career and shows a progression in his thinking, or it was written by a follower of Paul who used some of his language and rhetoric in writing this letter to the churches. Also, in contrast to other epistles, the letter does not specifically address issues and challenges related to a single congregation or church community. It is more of a "floater"—a letter intended to be read and passed on, giving encouragement and counsel to the church in general as it goes through the processes and pain of birth.

This particular lection, read through the lens of Ascension Sunday, brings to the fore the importance of ascension to our theological frameworks. Jesus was resurrected *and* sits at the right hand of God in heavenly places. This is a fitting "ending" for a story that began with Jesus coming from God. Jesus returns to God. We have the picture here of Jesus in the heavens at God's right hand. However, we also know the stories of Jesus walking on the earth, eating with sinners, touching the untouchables. How do our Christologies and understandings of Jesus account for these different, but related, aspects of Jesus? Of Christ?

In this reading from Ephesians' first chapter there is some hymnic, poetic language that stimulates imagination and creativity. In verses 17-18 the writer says that God grants us a spirit of wisdom and revelation and that as we come to know God the "eyes of our heart will be enlightened." In the Old Testament the heart is the seat of emotion. It knows fear, excitement, and joy or pleasure. It is also the very center of the person. The heart can grow soft, tremble, be appalled, or break. It can even die. But more than that, the heart is the lodging place of wisdom and what we think. It is the core of our intellect. It is, then, all that we think, feel, know, and do. When our heart is enlightened, the writer of Ephesians says, we (1) know hope, (2) know the richness of our inheritance as the people of God, and (3) know the immeasurable greatness of God's power.

Our hearts are "enlightened" by our faith, the writer of Ephesians tells us. Consequently, we ask, How does our faith inform our perceptions of what happens in the world—our political views, our relationships with neighbors and strangers? How are our thoughts and behaviors influenced by the faith that we hold?

At the conclusion of this lection we encounter the metaphor of Christ as the head of the church and the church as Christ's body, the fullness of Christ. Does the church we know fall short of that vision—the church as the "fullness of Christ"? When have we been disappointed in the church, and when have we glimpsed the church really being or becoming Christ's body? How do we live with the paradox that both kinds of experiences create?

Hebrews 9:24-28; 10:19-23 (LFM alt.)

The ninth chapter of Hebrews recounts the history of the shedding of blood and sacrifice in relation to Old Testament ritual law and liturgical practice. The high priest would go into the ark of the covenant's Holy of Holies once a year and take the animal's blood offering for himself and for the sins committed unintentionally by the people. This sets the stage, then, for the new covenant by Jesus. A will and inheritance, reasoned the author, are not put into effect, actualized, until a death has occurred. Jesus' death ushered in the legacy of those who were followers and were thus related to him. According to the religious customs Jesus inherited, without the shedding of blood there is no forgiveness of sin.

Christ did not enter a sanctuary made by human hands, but entered heaven itself—appropriate thinking for Ascension Sunday! Christ does not suffer again and again, but he is the great, the greatest, sacrifice that removes our sin. This lection invites us to think about our own understandings of the suffering and death of Jesus, and our community's response to language around the "blood of Jesus." In many traditions and communities the "blood hymns" are popular and the community embraces Jesus' suffering as a sign of hopefulness that they can endure what life is bringing them. In other communities, the blood language in hymnody and in communion or Eucharist is omitted or minimalized. What is true in your community and why? Is this reading from Hebrews comfortable or uncomfortable for your gathered community? Out of comfort or discomfort with a text, a sermon can grow.

If the reader of Hebrews 10 stops at verse 23, the full significance of the three-part imperative of verses 23-25 is hidden. Together the three imperatives are important and bring a fullness to the pronouncement this book's author is making. Being confident that the death of Jesus brought us forgiveness,

- Let us approach with the assurance of clean hearts (v. 22);
- Let us hold fast to the confession of our hope (v. 23);
- Let us consider how to provoke one another to love and good deeds, not neglecting to meet together, but encouraging one another (vv. 24-25).

As a consequence of Jesus' giving his life for us, we are forgiven; we can leave the past behind and have hope for the future. We meet with each other for encouragement and "provoke each other to love and good deeds."

It is the last of these exhortations that is most interesting. What does it mean to provoke each other to love? Does it mean to challenge? Push? Encourage? Is this part of your community's understanding of what it means to "be church"?

Gospel
Luke 24:44-53 (RCL)
Luke 24:46-53 (LFM)

Luke is careful to tie the crucifixion and resurrection of Jesus to the writings of the Law of Moses (Torah), the Prophets, and the Writings (Psalms). By acknowledging these three sections of the Hebrew Bible in verses 44-45, Jesus becomes the fulfillment of all that has been written and foretold. It was important to Jesus that the disciples remember that their beliefs and their work are grounded in tradition, rooted in the past. Our own understandings of Jesus are rooted through the varied lenses of this tradition; it is not possible to unravel or separate the two.

The closing scene of Jesus with his disciples differs from that in the other Gospels. In Luke, the ascension comes in the evening after Jesus has appeared to the disciples on the road to Emmaus and later to the disciples and those gathered with them. While there is a commissioning of the disciples, a "sending out," in Luke there is also a blessing of them and the reiteration of a promise. If they will stay in the city, power will come and rest upon them. But they must wait. It is promising for the preacher to pause here. When should we wait patiently and when should we move forward with the greatest sense of urgency? How is our work in the world a balance between the two—waiting for Spirit, inspiration, understanding, and insight but also being active, proactive, claiming our God-given agency to make a difference in the world?

The final act in the Gospel reading is one of blessing. Jesus blesses the disciples, bestowing on them the gift of hope. And in their joy they return to Jerusalem with joy, and they are seen in the temple blessing God. This is curious. What does it mean to "bless God"?

May 12, 2013
Seventh Sunday of Easter
(if Ascension not observed here)

Revised Common Lectionary (RCL)
Acts 16:16-34
Psalm 97
Revelation 22:12-14, 16-17, 20-21
John 17:20-26

Lectionary for Mass (LFM)
Acts 7:55-60
Psalm 97:1-2, 6-7, 9
Revelation 22:12-14, 16-17, 20
John 17:20-26

First Reading
Acts 16:16-34 (RCL)

Many of the Easter season lections remind us that how we treat each other is of vast, and even primary, importance to God. We have received the commandment to love one another; the resurrected Jesus reminded Peter that the way to show love for him is by feeding and tending his sheep. That our relationships matter is a constant thread throughout the Easter season. And so it is interesting that the Easter season ends with this reading from Acts. It is a powerful narrative about two owners of a slave girl who are exploiting her for financial gain.

The story of Paul exorcising the demon from the slave girl is in substantive ways different from other exorcism stories, and the reader, then, is alerted to the possibility that the inclusion of the story has a different purpose from other healings. Here there is no dialogue with the spirit that inhabits her, and there is no astonished crowd to marvel at the radical transformation that comes over her when Paul orders the spirit to come out. Paul becomes annoyed with the woman's constant crying out. She says, "These men are slaves of the Most High God, who proclaim to you a way of salvation" (16:17). What is annoying about that? And is Paul annoyed that the owners are making a profit off the woman's spirit of divination? We do not know.

This story appears to be another example of the many challenges that come the disciples' way when they are out preaching and proclaiming the good news. They struggle with political and religious authorities. Here they struggle with the slave girl's owners who use her for gain—much like those who engage in human trafficking or in prostitution.

The owners file charges saying that Paul and Silas are disturbing the city, advocating customs that are not lawful in Rome. They speak truth here: the gospel rightly proclaimed does challenge ruling authorities and oppressive systems! Paul and Silas are consequently imprisoned. They are stripped and beaten with rods. We often let our eyes skim easily over these parts of the story, not wanting really to "hear" and "see" the grim and tragic realities of the first proclaimers in the early church. In the night, an earthquake comes, and the prison doors swing open. Paul and Silas are free, but they remain in their cell so that the guard who is in charge of watching over them will not either take his life or be punished. The consideration that Paul and Silas show him is in marked contrast to the ways that the slave owners have treated the slave girl for their own benefit. The story demonstrates the power of the gospel and the ways that the gospel shapes our attitudes and behaviors and considerations toward each other.

The jailer asks, "What must I do to be saved?" (v. 30). Does he mean saved from this terrible, fear-instilling situation he is in? Or does he mean something more? We do not know, but Paul tells him to believe on the Lord Jesus Christ. What does the word *salvation* mean to you and your community? What are we being saved from, and are we always aware of our need to be saved . . . from ourselves? From the need to have "things"? From our complacency? From our self-centeredness?

Acts 7:55-60 (LFM)

These verses from the seventh chapter of Acts relate to us the last minutes in the life of Stephen. The authorities drag him out of the city and stone him, and he prays, "Lord Jesus, receive my spirit" (7:59). Early in chapter 6 we were introduced to Stephen. He was chosen by the twelve disciples to be one of seven men who were of good standing, full of the Spirit and wisdom. He was appointed as a deacon and to the task of feeding widows who were neglected in the distribution of daily food. It is only as the story unfolds that we realize why Stephen was chosen as one of the seven; we become aware of his remarkable character and faithfulness.

Stephen, like many of the earliest disciples, did great wonders and signs among the people; he was filled with grace and with power. As with many others throughout history who have held such great gifts to gather and persuade, he became a threat. In this case, he was threatening to those in the synagogue who could not "withstand the wisdom and the Spirit with which he spoke." This is true for many who are martyrs or who lose their lives for a cause that threatens to change the world and the oppressive systems in it. They charged Stephen with blasphemy because of his proclamations regarding Jesus and took him to the council to be charged. The charge? He will "change the customs." In defense of himself, Stephen outlines a brief, yet detailed, history of the Jewish people, including the call of Abraham to seek out the new land, the birth of the sons of Abraham and the oppression of the Israelites in Egypt, the call of Moses to deliver them, their sojourn in the wilderness (including their building of the golden calf!) with the ark of the covenant (tent of testimony). Stephen knows his tradition! This is a good reminder that the prophetic voice is formed and fashioned by historical and theological knowledge about both the community and its past.

The council becomes enraged; they take Stephen out to stone him. Luke patterns the death of Stephen after the death of Jesus. Like Jesus, in his final minutes he commits his spirit to God (v. 59). And he forgives the ones who are taking his life (v. 60). Stephen becomes known as Christianity's first martyr. I believe we do not like to linger long at this chapter in Acts; we prefer to avert our eyes from Stephen's story because we wonder, *Am I as filled with grace and power? Do I have enough commitment to the story of Jesus to withstand the accusations and resistance that necessarily come to prophets and those who speak truth? Would I ask God not to hold anything against those who are taking my life?* The remarkable qualities of Stephen are remembered on the feast of St. Stephen on December 26, which is "Boxing Day" in the United Kingdom. The name refers to the practice, as legend has it, of nobles and other wealthy Britons "boxing up" and distributing food and other gifts to their servants and to the poor on the day after Christmas. Reminiscent of Stephen's call to be a deacon in the church, Boxing Day was traditionally when the alms box at every English church was opened and the contents distributed to those in need.

The rest of the story . . . We are told that Saul stood at the site of Stephen's murder and the witnesses laid their coats at his feet. On this day, Luke tells us, a severe persecution began against the church. Saul, who later became Paul, was ravaging Christians and their places of worship.

Psalmody
Psalm 97 (RCL)
Psalm 97:1-2, 6-7, 9 (LFM)

Psalm 97 is a psalm of praise that describes and delineates the many qualities of Yahweh the king. This may or may not be a comfortable metaphor for you or your community. It may be fruitful for the preacher to ask, Why or why not is this so? Does the image of the powerful God as king bring comfort to a person or community that is struggling and in despair? Does it provoke faith in a future that, as of now, does not seem hopeful? Did this understanding of God bring courage and sustenance to a group of disciples who had seen Jesus crucified, had fleeting experiences of him postresurrection, but who had not yet had the power of the Pentecost Spirit come down upon them?

The psalm begins not by describing the king but by laying before us the reality that sometimes, maybe oftentimes, God remains hidden from us. Parishioners will be comforted to know that others, even this ancient psalmist, have found that God is surrounded by clouds and thick darkness (v. 2). We cannot fully know God, who many times seems unavailable and silent. And yet this God and God's agency can be seen by the fire and lightning that fill the sky. This God is so powerful that the mountains melt like wax. The psalmist laments that some choose to worship other gods, other things, things that take our time and energy and emerge as our biggest life priorities. This is important—to keep ourselves and our communities focused on what is truly important and what has sacred value.

As in other psalms, the whole earth is called to rejoice in the power of their God whose reign brings salvation and peace and harmony to our world. In other words, the kingship of God is intimately related to our understandings of the kingdom of God on this earth.

A cursory read of the psalm indicates that an important concept in the psalm's twelve verses is "righteousness." Righteousness and justice are foundational for this king's throne (v. 2). The heavens proclaim this king's righteousness (v. 6). The worshipers are assured that light will come to the righteous; joy will come for the upright (v. 11a). And, finally, the righteous are called to give thanks to the holy one (v. 12).

Its current usage makes *righteousness* a difficult word, but it is foundational for both the Old Testament Psalms and the Prophets. We know that there is a strong call to righteousness and justice in many of the Prophets, but it is rarely recognized that this is true of the Psalms as well. Here, the king of righteousness calls us also to be righteous. What does that mean?

The word *righteousness* conjures images of being right, virtuous, noble, moral, upright, or just. It also carries with it some negative connotations of being self-righteous, smug, above the fray, or even rigid. In the Old Testament, righteousness is not just being right according to some kind of legal, ethical, or religious norm. It is, rather, the fulfillment of the demands of a relationship with another person or with God. The righteous person acts in love; we are faithful to God by the way we live our lives with one another.

The one who is righteous tries to preserve the peace and prosperity of the community. In the Old Testament the righteous one delivers the poor and the orphan, helps the blind along the way, supports the weak. It is having mercy for the needy and the helpless. It is not surprising, then, that the rabbis would say, "It is well with the righteous and well with his neighbor." The righteous one would make sure that all is well with those living around her.

If righteousness is living in right relationship with God and neighbor, and if justice is seeking the welfare of the most vulnerable around us, then it is not surprising that the Old Testament prophets and psalmists often speak of justice and righteousness together, as they do here, in the same breath.

An interesting question for those preaching from the LFM is, Why does the lectionary omit verses 3-5, 8, and 10-12 of this psalm? The answer to this question could provide an interesting clue to Sunday's homily.

Second Reading

Revelation 22:12-14, 16-17, 20-21 (RCL)
Revelation 22:12-14, 16-17, 20 (LFM)

It is helpful for the preacher to read the entire epilogue found in chapter 22. The chapter begins with the river of the water of life, which flows from the throne and the Lamb and through the redeemed city. The metaphors of both water and light are woven throughout the last chapter of Revelation. The water provides sustenance for the tree of life, which grows by the side of the river. Nothing accursed will be found there. The servants of God will worship the Lamb. They will see his face and his name will be *on their foreheads*. This is a powerful image of those who follow God; the mark of discipleship is firmly affixed and readily visible to the world. There will be no more night—no need for lamp or sun for the Lord God will be their light—forever. There will be enough water to quench their thirst.

This text provides a good opportunity for the preacher to explore with the community varied understandings of the person of Jesus. We know the long history in the church of councils and commissions and committees that met to decide on issues related to the humanity and divinity of Jesus. Human? Divine? In this text, Jesus describes himself as the Alpha and the Omega, the first and the last, the beginning and the end. He is the root and descendant of David, the bright morning star. He is the one who provides the water of life. He offers grace. What are the understandings of Jesus in the preacher's community? What are the questions about the nature of Jesus? What is grace?

In verse 17 we become aware, as we have many times during the Easter season, that the welcome in the city is for everyone. "Let everyone who wishes take the water of life as a gift . . ." What does this mean for our understandings of exclusivity and inclusivity? Who is in and who is out?

The last chapter underscores the urgency of the message found on the scroll. In verses 7 and 12 we find identical phrasing: "See, I am coming soon!" The author, the one who has seen the vision, wants the community to take the words seriously. There isn't much time left for the community to become faithful followers. Does the contemporary church or your own congregation feel any kind of urgency about their work in the world? What issues should be addressed? What kinds of witness need to be made?

Gospel

John 17:20-26 (RCL, LFM)

The farewell meal and conversation between Jesus and his disciples is related to the reader in chapters 13–17 of John. After the meal, Jesus washes the feet of the disciples in an act that teaches us that the love we have for each other is manifested in the way we serve one another. This is followed by Jesus' teaching, and this section of the Gospel ends with Jesus' prayer to God on behalf of those who are gathered with him. These are the last words of Jesus before we turn to his arrest and consequent crucifixion.

The prayer definitely has a leave-taking flavor. Because he has precious little time left with the disciples, he prays fervently for their well-being in his absence. The prayer in its totality (vv. 1-26) is circuitous and defies a clear or linear structure. One can imagine that these are exactly the kinds of words that would pour forth from someone who is grieving or facing enormous challenge or difficulty, perhaps from someone who can only imagine that the immediate future will bring suffering and loss. The prayer begins with the ominous words, "Father, the hour has come . . ." The music is in a minor key; there is a sense of foreboding, dread, perhaps fear.

The themes that are woven throughout the prayer are related to unity and oneness. God, Jesus Christ, and the Christian community are in a dance with one another—their own kind of trinity. Notice how the three—God, Jesus, and the disciples—are present in all of the following:

- Jesus prays that the disciples will know both God and Jesus (v. 3).
- The disciples belonged to God and now they belong to Jesus (v. 6).
- God gave words to Jesus who in turn gave them to the disciples; they know everything (v. 7).
- The disciples believed that God sent Jesus to them (v. 8).
- Jesus says to God, "All mine are yours, and yours are mine" (v. 10).
- Jesus prays that the disciples are one as Jesus and God are one; he asks God to protect them (v. 11).
- "I have given them your word" (v. 14).
- "As you have sent me . . . so I have sent them" (v. 18).
- "As you . . . are in me and I am in you, may they also be in us . . ." (v. 21).
- "So that they may be one, as we are one" (v. 22).
- "I am in them and you are in me" (v. 23).
- "These know that you have sent me" (v. 25).
- ". . . so that the love with which you have loved me may be in them, and I in them" (v. 26).

What is the essence of these words—this list of ways that Jesus describes and names the relationship between God, Jesus, and disciples? When Jesus longs for a unity and oneness in the community like the one Jesus enjoys with God, what is he longing for? How does that look and act and sound like in a faith community or in the wider community and the world?

The last verses of the prayer which are assigned for today, verses 20-26, are words spoken not only on behalf of Jesus' first disciples but for all those who believe in Jesus through their word. This is a prayer for the generations and for us. The words build upon this intimate relationship between the three and call for unity (v. 21). Were there issues that threatened to divide the disciples and the church communities that were birthed and beginning to grow? Acts and the epistles allude to them. What are the issues that threaten to divide the church today, your congregation? And what does unity look like in the face of them? According to John, it is a unity that is grounded in love—the kind of love God has had for Jesus and for us (v. 26). This is complicated business—love that binds us together even when there is no unity on issues, questions, and priorities. Can a splintered and divided church bear witness to God's love?

What is your prayer for your community of disciples? For your denomination? For the church at large? The ending of the prayer ("Righteous Father, the world does not know you, but I know you; and these know that you have sent me," v. 25) acknowledges that the disciples' work in the world is not immediately accomplished; it is not easy. The forces that do not know God and that work against the work of the Spirit are here identified as "world." But Jesus and those who follow will continue to bring words of love to a world in need of it.

May 19, 2013
Day of Pentecost

Revised Common Lectionary (RCL)	**Lectionary for Mass (LFM)**
Acts 2:1-21 or Genesis 11:1-9	Acts 2:1-11
Psalm 104:24-34, 35b	Psalm 104:1 + 24, 29-30, 31 + 34
Romans 8:14-17, 22-27 or Acts 2:1-21	1 Corinthians 12:3b-7, 12-13 or Romans 8:8-17
John 14:8-17 (25-27)	John 20:19-23 or 14:14-16, 23b-26

First Reading
Acts 2:1-21 (RCL)
Acts 2:1-11 (LFM)

Pentecost. An answer to prayer. The birth of the church. A mystery bound in speaking and listening. Red flame and wind. A festival that ushers in a season of Ordinary Time.

Jesus has sent the disciples to Jerusalem to wait for the coming of the Holy Spirit. Luke tells us, warns us, about the violent demise and ending of the one who betrayed Jesus, and the disciples choose his replacement. Now the disciples and the women are devoting themselves to prayer. They seem expectant. Jesus has told them that the Holy Spirit will come upon them to teach them and encourage them in his absence. When we worship in our communities, are we as expectant and hopeful that the Spirit will visit us?

It is in this context that the day of Pentecost comes, a celebration fifty days after Passover. With imagery that engages our senses of sight, sound, and touch, Luke describes the coming of the Holy Spirit upon the disciples and those gathered with them. We hear the sound of a violent wind. Tongues as of fire appear among them. The sound of the wind is joined by the sound of other languages as the Spirit gives them the ability to speak. The Jews from all nations are amazed that those who have gathered, who are all Galileans, are speaking, and yet they all hear what is being said in their own languages. This is the miracle of Pentecost—being able to hear each other beyond our differences!

What are the evidences of the Spirit of God being present among those in your community? When does the Spirit create new bridges of understanding between people diverse in background or language? When does the Spirit provoke and when does it mend?

The disciples and the women are not drunk, as those who are watching and hearing them suppose. The Spirit has come upon them. The RCL reading includes the sermon Peter preaches to those who are gathered. Peter calls upon the Hebrew prophet Joel, making Joel's vision foundational for his Pentecost preaching. Joel had prophesied that God's spirit would be poured out on *all flesh*. There would be prophesying and proclamation. There would be dreams and visions about the future, a stirring of imagination and creativity—among *everyone* in the community, sons and daughters, old and young, and servants. The dream and the vision can come from anyone; they can come from unexpected places. When has an inspired word come in your community from a child, from someone often ignored or unnoticed, from the visitor or the stranger?

Genesis 11:1-9 (RCL alt.)

This story is the final narrative in the primeval history of the world (Genesis 1–11), which is made up of the legends about the beginnings of the earth, the flood, and finally our story for today—the tower of Babel. The story about Babel is the culmination of the stories of the disobedience of Adam and Eve in the garden and God's search for righteous people that eventuated in the flood. In this story, the whole earth has one language, the same words. They live together in one place, and they say to each other:

- Come, let us make bricks (v. 3);
- Come, let us build ourselves a city with a tower in the heavens (v. 4);
- Come, let us make our name for ourselves (v. 4).

They do this in an effort to keep themselves from being scattered (v. 4). The people want to stay the same, be the same. That is their motivation. In response to the people's plan to build the tower, God says, "Come, let us go down, and confuse their language there, so that they will not understand one another's speech" (v. 7). Clearly, this action is a consequence of the people's desire to build the tower to heaven. The story does not seem, however, to be one about the people's pride, but a response to the people's desire to build a single "name," to be the same in language and identity. It is an effort to create something for themselves and by themselves, and an effort to keep themselves from being scattered across the face of the earth. Their desire to go "upward" is to keep them from going "outward." Their identity does not come from the relationship they have with God. It comes from what they themselves can create out of a single community of "likeness." God takes this opportunity to create diversity. The God who is known as a gathering God becomes the scattering God;

God's desire is to have God's people across the earth, speaking different languages. Ultimately, what will unite them is not their desire for fame and power, but their dependence on the God who created them regardless of the language they speak, the cultures they form and fashion, the color of their skin.

This story read through the lens of Pentecost takes on new dimensions. God has scattered the peoples across the globe. They cannot easily talk with each other; even a superficial unity is not present. But the spirit comes hovering over this chaos—just as it did in the creation story—and a miracle happens. Those who speak differently can still hear and understand each other. We are invited to ask, How is this story important in our congregations or in the wider community where there is great diversity in nationality, race, and culture? If our primary allegiance is to God, can we work together for the world's common good, or are the barriers and walls between us so high there is no ladder tall enough to help us transcend our differences?

Psalmody

Psalm 104:24-34, 35b (RCL)
Psalm 104:1 + 24, 29-30, 31 + 34 (LFM)

Both the RCL and the LFM focus on the second half of Psalm 104. Interestingly, they both omit the first half of verse 35: "Let sinners be consumed from the earth, and let the wicked be no more." Clearly, those who put the lectionary together for us wanted us to avoid this sentence and all its theological complexity!

The first half of Psalm 104 extols the God who created the world and subdued chaos so that all that was created could come into being. There is a grand cataloging of all the wondrous creatures that populate the earth because God brought them into being. The psalm is a prayer from one who knew God's greatness, God's honor and majesty and light. Springs flow, food is grown because God has made it so.

In today's reading, the psalmist describes earth's creatures and the interdependent relationship they have with their Creator. Note the phrases in verses 27-30: "They all look to you to give them their food" (v. 27); "When you open your hand, they are filled" (v. 28); "When you hide your face; they are dismayed" (v. 29); "When you send forth your spirit, they are created . . ." (v. 30). This is the relationship not exhibited in the Babel story in Genesis 11, where the people believe that their identity, their name, will come from what they themselves achieve. The psalmist describes "earth creatures" who acknowledge and celebrate the ways that God nurtures and provides for them. The greatness of God brings them to praise and doxology.

Second Reading

Romans 8:14-17, 22-27 (RCL)
Romans 8:8-17 (LFM alt.)

Again the RCL and LFM engage the same chapter but different verses in their designated lections. In Romans 8 we see the duality of flesh and Spirit drawn out before us. The letter's wider social context helps us understand this text, and others like it, that have influenced the church's inability to have conversations or engage in healthy dialogue about our sexualities.

It is helpful, however, to broaden our understanding of "flesh" beyond our sexual selves to see it as that part of us which is selfish, engaged in our own welfare, thus our consumerist and independent natures. The Spirit delivers us, redeems us, from this kind of living! In contrast, the author describes a person of the Spirit—one who lives through righteousness. Righteousness is living in good relationship with God and neighbor. We are called from living in the flesh to living in the Spirit with the other children of God—those who have been created and who are beloved of God. We are called from being solely concerned about our individual selves to being concerned about community.

This is an appropriate reading for Pentecost Sunday! In Romans 8 we are told that we can set our minds on the Spirit, which will bring us peace and life. We can be "in the Spirit," the Spirit of God dwelling in us. All who are led by the Spirit of God are the children of God.

Those on whom the Spirit fell at Pentecost were ushered out into the world; there was resistance to their words and there was suffering. God's Spirit continued to be with them, not just on the day of Pentecost but as they moved out into their ministries, strengthening them in their weakness. The world was groaning, waiting for the words that the first disciples gave them. In them were the words of life.

1 Corinthians 12:3b-7, 12-13 (LFM)

The Corinthians text offers the preacher a radically different view of the Spirit from that found in Romans 8. Here Paul tells us that the Spirit comes to each of us differently, giving us different gifts, all of which can be used for building the realm of God. The phrase used here is often translated the "common good." This phrase has been used in the past decades to describe work that acknowledges the value of every person; that seeks to remedy the conditions that oppress the most vulnerable among us; and, in our own faith tradition, that proclaims that we are one network, one web, one people. The well-being of one affects the other. If one is not free, we all are not free.

The Corinthian text is an affirmation of all kinds of Spirit-given gifts, and inherently it issues a warning to us not to value one gift over another. There is no hierarchy of gifts! God blesses each of us differently but values us the same.

Acts 2:1-21 (RCL alt.)

For discussion of this text, see the first reading, above.

Gospel

John 14:8-17 (25-27) (RCL)
John 14:14-16, 23b-26 (LFM)

As we have noted earlier in the Easter season, the Gospel of John is unlike the Synoptic Gospels in that parables and many of the narratives present in the latter are absent in

John's version. Instead, John's Gospel is filled with teachings from Jesus that name and describe who Jesus is in relationship to God and to humanity. The Gospel lesson for today is one of these.

In John 14:6 we find the very well-known statement of Jesus, "I am the way, and the truth, and the life. No one comes to the Father except through me." Many have rightfully struggled with or heartily embraced these two sentences, seeing in them a disparagement of other world religions, an exclusivist notion that only in Jesus can one come to know God. The thoughts and feelings about these two sentences will differ in varying congregations and traditions. Jesus seems to be saying here that in his intimate, several-year relationship with the disciples, they have had the opportunity to see what God "looks like." They have seen him reach out to the needy, the most vulnerable in the world around them. They have seen compassion and a speaking of truth. You have watched me and listened to me, Jesus is saying to the disciples. What you have seen and heard—this is the way to God. This is living that is "of God."

This statement by Jesus ushers in the conversation he then has with Philip, the conversation that is part of the RCL reading for today. Philip says to Jesus, "Show us the Father" (v. 8). Jesus responds by telling Philip to look again with new eyes, to remember what he has experienced as he has traveled with Jesus: "I am in the Father and the Father is in me" (v. 10). And if you cannot believe this, Jesus says, then believe in the works themselves. Believe in the works I have done; what I have done among us is the way to God. As Jesus says farewell to the disciples, he is trying to create in them a community of believers who remember who he was and what he did, a community that will be empowered by the presence of the Spirit in its life.

This conversation continues with a call to the disciples to continue the works that Jesus himself has done (v. 12). If they believe in Jesus, they will continue *to do* what he has done. Ultimately, that is because the God who lives in Jesus lives in them also. In Jesus we can see how God lives life; we have been given a model, a teacher, a mentor, a guide. We have been given the way to life that is satisfying, enriched, abundant.

The LFM for today also emphasizes this responsibility on the part of the disciples. Jesus says, "If you love me, you will keep my commandments" (v. 15). Belief in Jesus, belief that he has come from God, will result in a certain kind of shaping and forming of the ways we live our lives. The world will not want to see this (v. 17)! Disciples of Jesus will not always walk in ways the world understands. There will be something distinctive about their talk and their walk that can be troubling to the status quo and the powers that be. The Rev. Dr. Martin Luther King Jr., in a speech on the University of California, Berkeley, campus in the 1960s, called the students to be as "maladjusted as Jesus"! He was calling them not to adjust themselves to the world's ways, but to walk in the distinctive ways of Jesus.

The last verses of both the RCL and LFM for today offer us, no doubt, the reason why these assorted verses from John 14 are chosen for Pentecost Sunday. Jesus assures the disciples that the Advocate, or the Helper, the Holy Spirit, will come to be with them in his absence when he has gone. The Holy Spirit will continue to teach them and be with them to guide them. He bids them not to be afraid but to hold some measure of peace that God will continue to be with them. This is not the kind of peace the world offers, Jesus says to them, but a different, more lasting kind of peace. In our contemporary world, from where or from whom do we receive seductive offers of peace that are less satisfying, have less "staying power" than the peace that comes to us from the abiding, indwelling presence of God?

John 20:19-23 (LFM alt.)

Interestingly, the LFM invites the preacher on this Pentecost Sunday to go back to the evening of Resurrection Day, the first part of the reading for the Second Sunday of Easter. The disciples are sitting in a room; it is getting dark, and they are afraid. As we have noted before, this is a chilling ending to the Gospel of John, which has promised the reader a story that will bring them light and life. Now the disciples are in a darkened room fearing death!

But Jesus comes to them and shows them his hands and side. He offers them a word of peace and then sends them out into the world. He breathes on them the Holy Spirit. In a quiet and more intimate way than the rush of the wind and chatter of different voices on Pentecost, the Holy Spirit is given to the disciples to dispel their fear and their grief. This is the softer underside of Pentecost, but one to which most in the congregation can attest and give witness.

Time after Pentecost / Ordinary Time
Trinity Sunday through Lectionary 16 / Proper 11

Eric D. Barreto

At this point in the liturgical calendar, the tinsel and glitter of Advent and Christmas will be for many of us a distant memory. The contemplation of Lent and the high mark of Easter are probably quickly fading from our memories. Spring has come and gone. The heat of summer descends and our communities will start to disperse. Families will go on vacations. Children will go to camp. The outdoors will beckon us. Life seems to slow down a bit. And yet, in the midst of these summer days, the lectionary texts draw us into matters of great concern for us today.

Several key themes will arise again and again. First are the many surprises that emerge when God meets God's people. Unexpected individuals on the margins of societies will be graced with God's presence. The broken will be made whole. The whole will be drawn to walk alongside the broken. Second, we will learn about the challenges and blessings of discipleship. What are the costs of following Jesus? What do we risk when we accept God's claim to be our eternal parent? What abundant gifts does the path of discipleship include? What do we do when the road on which Jesus leads us is marked with potholes and precipitous ditches on each side? What do we do when we don't know which way to go? How do we follow Jesus today? Finally, the texts will emphasize the bonds and composition of Christian community. We do not live lives of faith in isolation from others. We need one another in these difficult days. Of course, as fragile and sinful people, we will invariably harm one another. How, then, does Christian community embrace and embody the reconciliation God so willingly offers us?

We often joke that the Christmas holiday keeps creeping ever earlier on the calendar. We lament when decorations start lining the store shelves as fall is only beginning. But we might forget that the celebration of the birth of Christ does not really close when the calendar enters a new year. Similarly, we often forget that every Sunday is Easter morning, a celebration of the resurrection of Jesus Christ, the Savior of the world. In these summer months, these texts can evoke anew these festive high points, reminding us that even in "Ordinary Time" God is still doing extraordinary things. My encouragement would be to allow your preaching to invite people to join God in this quotidian but extraordinary work.

May 26, 2013
Holy Trinity Sunday
First Sunday after Pentecost

Revised Common Lectionary (RCL)
Proverbs 8:1-4, 22-31
Psalm 8
Romans 5:1-5
John 16:12-15

Lectionary for Mass (LFM)
Proverbs 8:22-31
Psalm 8:4-5, 6-7, 8-9
Romans 5:1-5
John 16:12-15

We all know that the Trinity stands as a central confession of our faith. It binds Christians across a plethora of other denominational, confessional, and cultural differences. But the Trinity is also confounding to clergy and laity alike. Complex theological terminologies are befitting such a profound theological conclusion but also prove difficult for most of us to comprehend.

So the challenge is to proclaim this indispensable point of faith but help your hearers integrate trinitarian faith in their daily lives. Rather than a point of theological trivia, what might a quotidian experience of a trinitarian God living in eternal relationship look like? What difference does this all make, not to the theologian whose livelihood hinges on such minute matters, but to the ordinary person of faith? After all, in the end, her faith hinges on such complex matters, too!

Gospel
John 16:12-15 (RCL, LFM)

Unlike the end of Luke and again at the beginning of Acts, the Gospel of John does not close with a narrative account of Jesus' ascension. Nevertheless, there is a theological concern throughout the narrative of John that grapples with Jesus' absence. What happens when Jesus is no longer with us as he once was? How do we continue to follow God when Jesus, our guide, is no longer with us in the same way?

Our passage is lodged within a larger set of instructions following the Last Supper. In this series of "farewell discourses," Jesus teaches his followers the shape of Christian community (chs. 13–17). As chapter 16 opens, Jesus promises that persecution will come their way. The road will not be easy. He warns them of these impending difficulties so that they may draw strength in the midst of these afflictions. He comforts them with the knowledge that he has sought to protect them from these realities as long as possible (16:4b) but also with a promise of an "Advocate" (NRSV) or "Companion" (CEB) who would step into the breach Jesus' absence would leave. What will the Companion do? The Companion "will show the world it was wrong about sin because they don't believe in me. He will show the world it was wrong about righteousness because I'm going to the Father and you won't see me anymore. He will show the world it was wrong about judgment because this world's ruler stands condemned" (16:9-11 CEB). In other words, in the verses leading up to our passage, Jesus made a promise not to leave Christians alone in a world dominated by misapprehensions about the basic building blocks of life and faith: sin, righteousness, judgment (see 16:8). The Advocate will correct a world that holds a skewed vision.

Having pointed to the effects the Advocate will have on the world, our passage turns internally to the workings and complexities of Christian communities. How will our lives together take shape if Jesus is not physically present to show us the way? Will we be left alone to figure things out?

As our passage begins, Jesus acknowledges that the work of shaping Christian communities is not brought to completion during his earthly ministry. The disciples simply cannot bear the full brunt of Jesus' teaching while he is still with them. Thus believers, even those closest to Jesus during his ministry, are not done learning how to live their faith, but neither are they alone in their search for truth. Moreover, the Spirit is not an independent agent apart from Jesus. The Spirit is not a new boss who will run things her way. Instead, there is a mutuality in the work of God, Jesus, and the Spirit. The Spirit is characterized by truth, a truth dependent on the relationship of these divine actors.

And what greater, more complex, more mysterious truth is there than what the future might hold? With the horizon of all possibility, the future holds both promise and peril, both of which the community John writes to has probably experienced already. The Spirit will speak truth about "the things that are to come" (16:13). What things? Certainly, in the context of John's narrative, Jesus meant the travails of Jesus' last days along with his resurrection. But for John's community as well as communities of faith today, this glimpse into the future through the Spirit is an invaluable gift. The Spirit is a living assurance that God knows full well what the future holds. And what does the future hold? Nothing more than the glorification of Jesus. These are brief but powerful words. They seek to capture the ineffable work of the Spirit, who Paul will elsewhere declare can intercede for us in ways we can't possibly verbalize (Rom. 8:26).

Thus it is important to remember the purposefully symbolic language John's Jesus employs. As he explains in 16:25, "I have said these things to you in figures of speech." These are profound truths that Jesus wants to communicate, but in John he is well aware that such knowledge would be too weighty for the disciples at that moment (16:12) or simply incomprehensible without the proper hermeneutical lens. It is only in the wake of his death and resurrection that Jesus' seemingly cryptic sayings will be fully understood.

In Jesus' gentleness with his followers, we may see a model for talking about complex, difficult, but true theological insights. Doctrines like the Trinity are not solely cognitive but profoundly experiential. We not only *know* or *believe* that God is three in one, but we experience the relationality of God and thus gain new insight into who God is. In the case of the promised Paraclete, we experience the comfort and wisdom of the Spirit and catch a glimpse into the unplumbable depths of God.

In short, the Trinity will remain a dusty dogma and not a robust guide to faith unless we help others see the presence of the Triune God, not just in worship and other churchly activity, but in the extraordinary ways that God's love, grace, and forgiveness inject our seemingly ordinary lives with meaning. Such is particularly true when Christians reflect on the Spirit. Many of us are more at ease with the first two persons of the Trinity, but the Spirit remains largely abstract. Too often, the Spirit is an afterthought in our theology. Therefore, help others recollect when the Spirit has guided them into truth. Help others recollect when the Spirit has helped shine a light on what belongs to God. As Gail O'Day has noted, "Through the promise of the Paraclete, the Fourth Evangelist is able to portray Jesus' death, resurrection, and ascension not as the end, but as the beginning of a new era in the life of the believing community."[1] That community's life is composed not just by believers gathered around a common faith but also by God's Spirit who embodies God's care and compassion in our midst.

First Reading
Proverbs 8:1-4, 22-31 (RCL)
Proverbs 8:22-31 (LFM)

What is wisdom? What are its characteristics? How do we know wise advice when we hear it? In our passage, wisdom is not a notion or a trait so much as a living being, an extraordinary outgrowth of God's original creative acts. Traditions of Wisdom personified as a woman were a way to express how God continues to shape and reshape the world even beyond the primeval days of creation. In Proverbs 8, Wisdom calls all of God's children to heed God's call.

Wisdom is God's first act of creation according to verse 22, a precursor upon which all the rest of creation is established. She precedes the separation of the waters, the crafting of hills, and the dawning of the first day. Wisdom was witness to the birth of a world, but even more she was a partner with God in the original creative act. Even at the dawn of creation, God was not alone. The passage concludes, "I was daily his delight, rejoicing before him always, rejoicing in his inhabited world and delighting in the human race" (Prov. 8:30-31). Whenever God creates, Wisdom is there with great celebration. Wisdom delights in God's creation and we are invited to follow her lead.

Proverbs is certainly not imagining the Triune God of the Christian faith. We would also be mistaken simply to equate Wisdom and the Holy Spirit. Nevertheless, Proverbs speaks important truths. It demonstrates that the people of God have long sought models for understanding the great expanse of God's glory and work in the world. It demonstrates that feminine imagery was never foreign to our understanding of who God is. It demonstrates that reflections about the character of God and reflections about everyday life were never far apart. Wisdom in Proverbs is not an ontological abstraction but a reflection on the goodness, beauty, and, yes, wisdom we find in the world God created.

Psalmody
Psalm 8 (RCL)
Psalm 8:4-5, 6-7, 8-9 (LFM)

Psalm 8 is a musical, lyrical praise of God's greatness. The primary characteristic of God in this psalm is God's creative touch in the world. God is a God who creates but who remains deeply connected to God's creation and God's children.

The psalm moves from the highest heavens down to the earth. At every point, humans praise God's holy name. When God is enthroned in the loftiest heavens, even the "babbling of babies" proclaims God's greatness.[2] The psalmist continues to reflect on the luminous bodies that populate the skies, causing him to wonder why God is concerned with us, mere specks of dust, while these great bodies grace the farthest reaches of space. And yet God is concerned. In fact, as in the Romans passage in the second reading below, God grants us a share in God's glory and a share in God's dominion over the world. We may be mere specks in the universe, but we are specks imbued with God's love. It is thus more than appropriate for the psalm to begin and close in the same way: "O Lord, our Sovereign, how majestic is your name in all the earth!"

Who, then, is the God we worship? God is a God who creates but never deserts us, who is enthroned high above but always at our side.

Second Reading
Romans 5:1-5 (RCL, LFM)

As Katherine Grieb has argued in her marvelous commentary on this letter, Romans is a "narrative defense of God's righteousness."[3] God is the primary subject of this influential composition, and it is the surety of God's promises that Paul hopes to defend. If God is faithful and righteous, then how can the God of Israel embrace the Gentile world without breaking God's commitments to Israel? This is the primary question driving the theology of Romans. In the end, Paul hopes to spark a new imagination in a congregation he has never met. What if God's saving of the world must include going to "the Jew first and also to the Greek" (1:16)? These themes are first enunciated in Romans 1:16-17, the thesis of the letter. In preaching Romans, setting an exegetical and theological anchor at these crucial verses is key, lest the letter become only a way to reflect on human salvation rather than God's righteousness.

Our passage follows an extended discussion about Abraham, the progenitor of all people of faith, whether Jew or Gentile. When Abraham believes, God reckons it to him as righteousness.[4] As descendants of Abraham in faith, we too can have faith that will be reckoned as righteousness.

The opening of chapter 5 then characterizes the quality of such a life of faith and righteousness. However, notice that God brackets our pericope. In verse 1, it is peace with God through Jesus Christ that is our ultimate gift, while verse 5 concludes by pointing out that "God's love has been poured into our hearts through the Holy Spirit that has been given to us." With these brackets, it becomes evident why these verses are included in the lectionary for Trinity Sunday. They are evidence of the interworkings of the Triune God.

What might we say about this important text? One option is to focus on the paradoxical reasons for boasting that Paul lays out. On the one hand, "we boast in our hope of sharing the glory of God" (5:2). This is a hope that rests solely on God's work through Jesus Christ (v. 1) but means sharing in some significant sense the glory and greatness of God. After all, what more glorious state is there than peace with God (v. 1)? On the other hand, however, Paul also claims we can boast in our sufferings. How can he boast both in God's glory and in suffering? In the life of Jesus, these are not mutually exclusive but interdependent. Suffering, Paul claims, does not end in dejection or disappointment but with hope because of God's undying love.

Focal Points for Preaching

One way to celebrate Trinity Sunday is not so much to dwell on the how or what of the Trinity but on the why and the wherefore. Seminary education in the West around the Trinity usually focuses on ontological and philosophical rumination, which, while incredibly valuable, often requires a great deal of translation in parish ministry. Latina/o theologians have ably grappled with trinitarian thought not just as a philosophical abstraction but as a quotidian reality. As Oswald John Nira writes, "Contemporary Latino/as understand and celebrate the Trinity through the experience of community."[5] Theologies from marginalized social locations are an ideal place for us to dislodge our typical patterns of thinking when it comes to the Trinity. Here the work of African American, Asian American, and other global theologians will prove most helpful. In short, wonder together with your communities how the Triune God moves where you are. In what ways do your local congregations experience the Trinity? In what ways is the Paraclete a palpable presence in your midst?

Notes

1. Gail R. O'Day, "The Gospel of John," in *The New Interpreter's Bible*, ed. Leander E. Keck et al. (Nashville: Abingdon, 1995), 9:776.
2. Patrick D. Miller, note on Ps. 8:2, in *The HarperCollins Study Bible*, ed. Wayne A. Meeks (New York: HarperCollins, 1994), 805.

3. A. Katherine Grieb, *The Story of Romans: A Narrative Defense of God's Righteousness* (Louisville: Westminster John Knox, 2002).
4. This conclusion is based on Gen. 15:6 and is repeated three times in Romans 4 (vv. 3, 9, 22).
5. Oswald John Nira, "Trinity," in *Hispanic American Religious Cultures*, ed. Miguel A. De La Torre (Santa Barbara: ABC-CLIO, 2009), 2:558. See also Zaida Maldonado Pérez, "The Trinity," in *Handbook of Latino/a Theologies*, ed. Edwin David Aponte and Miguel A. De La Torre (St. Louis: Chalice, 2006).

June 2, 2013
Lectionary 9 / Ninth Sunday in Ordinary Time / Proper 4 (RCL)
Solemnity of Corpus Christi (Body and Blood of Christ) (LFM)
Second Sunday after Pentecost

Revised Common Lectionary (RCL)	**Lectionary for Mass (LFM)**
1 Kings 18:20-21 (22-29), 30-39 or 1 Kings 8:22-23, 41-43	Genesis 14:18-20
Psalm 96 or 96:1-9	Psalm 110:1, 2, 3, 4
Galatians 1:1-12	1 Corinthians 11:23-26
Luke 7:1-10	Luke 9:11b-17

The texts of the RCL and LFM diverge significantly this week as the former moves into the season after Pentecost and the latter first celebrates the Body and Blood of Christ. While acknowledging that Protestants and Catholics will likely be focusing on different texts this Sunday, I nonetheless will treat these texts together in the hope that pairing these texts in conjunction will prove exegetically beneficial no matter which text a preacher will proclaim.

Of course, the themes of these texts are diverse in some significant ways. The RCL readings share a common thread of theological reflection on the worship of the God of Israel by individuals and communities beyond the bounds of Israel. In our passages, God does not express a mere tolerance for difference but a distinct embrace of diversity. God welcomes all who come to worship God. The LFM readings, of course, revolve around the observation of the feast of Corpus Christi. Bread, wine, and the enigmatic priestly king Melchizedek bind these texts together. When holy meals are shared, God is present, and people are changed. Despite these different emphases, I note below the ways in which openness to the other, to the foreigner, is a critical trait of the God of Israel, a God who welcomes us all to the table no matter who we are.

Gospel
Luke 7:1-10 (RCL)

This Gospel reading, along with next week's, together form a narrative pair in Luke. The stories are meant to be read in conjunction, the one enlightening the other and vice versa. Thus, part of the homiletical challenge will be to bridge two weeks' worth of sermons that together work to say something about the world-changing power Jesus exerts in the Gospel. Luke will often pair a story about a man with a woman. In this case, the contrasts extend even beyond gender. On one side, you have a powerful centurion, beloved by the local Jewish community but still a leader of the invading Roman force. He exhibits great faith when he comes to Jesus, as we will see. In the second story, we learn of a grieving widow. Her son's death, as I will discuss in next week's commentary, is a devastating blow both emotionally and economically. Her community mourns alongside her. Nowhere is her faith highlighted by Luke or Jesus, only her grief. Both receive what they sought, even if in the case of the grieving widow, she was well beyond a reasonable hope that her life and that of her son would be restored. In both cases, Jesus restores life where death and illness prevail. In both cases, unexpected individuals receive these free gifts.

One of the striking features of the story of the healing of the centurion's servant is that the centurion and Jesus never meet face-to-face. All their interaction occurs through the means of intermediaries. First, it is the local Jewish leaders who ask for Jesus' help. The centurion, they say, "is worthy of having you do this for him" (7:4). Jesus sets out, apparently without much hesitation, though his contemporaries would not have blamed him for having some suspicions and concerns. After all, entering the house of a Gentile could potentially make Jesus unclean.[1] Plus, a centurion is the enactor of the raw force of Rome that both has dominated the people of Israel and will be Jesus' executioner. Jesus has a number of reasons to resist assisting this centurion even when he is commended by the local leaders. And yet Jesus accompanies them. But on his way, another set of intermediaries enters the scene.

The centurion sends friends to stop Jesus from coming to his house. He recognizes that he is unworthy to host Jesus, a rather extraordinary display of humility and submission for a Roman military leader. His humility, however, does not foreclose his recognition of the power and influence he has as a military officer. He recognizes the same power and influence in Jesus, believing that if Jesus merely speaks the word, his servant will be healed. Jesus is dazzled by this centurion's faith, marveling that such faith is not even found among God's chosen people. How strange it is that a foreigner, a Gentile, a centurion is so highly commended for his faith. Actually, as we will see in the other texts this week, perhaps this notion is not so strange. The foreigner and the stranger are as welcome at God's table as anyone else is.

But what was the content of the centurion's faith? What did the centurion believe fundamentally? He believed and recognized, I think, Jesus' power over the forces of death. As a military officer, he likely understood well how powerful raw force can be. He recognized such power in Jesus but with some significant differences. Military might cannot heal the sick or raise the dead. Imperial power cannot gain the affections of a people, only their fear. Jesus' exertion of power contravenes the order of the day by healing both the servant of a centurion and the son of a widow, both the enemy of Israel and the prophetic image of the marginalized for whom God cares most. Jesus brings good news to all people, both powerful and weak, both rich and poor.

Preaching on this text will necessarily raise questions about the connection of faith and miracles. Justo González notes, however, "The juxtaposition of these stories shows that the common notion that miracles are necessarily connected to faith is not correct. The centurion had great faith, and his slave is healed. The woman has no expectation to see her son again, and does not even appeal to Jesus for help; and her son is returned to her. One miracle is based on the centurion's faith; the other on Jesus' compassion. Miracles or the lack thereof are not necessarily a measure of the faith of believers."[2]

Perhaps this text can open up a vibrant conversation about the nature of faith. Is there a way in which both the centurion and the widow have faith? The centurion's faith is bold, willing to reach out to Jesus through a number of trusted intermediaries. Due to the bitter hostilities between Israel and Rome, Jesus should have no part in healing a centurion's servant. But the centurion asks nonetheless. He has faith. In contrast, the widow's faith is rocked by grief and sorrow. Her hope is muted, dampened by the loss of both husband and son. As we will see next week, Jesus has compassion on her and her plight. I think she too had faith, even if it was not like that of the centurion. How might we help people see themselves in all these varieties of expression of belief?

Luke 9:11b-17 (LFM)

When I'm teaching the Gospel of Luke, I will often compare it to the HBO show *The Sopranos*. It's a strange comparison, I admit, but let me explain. It always seemed to me that the main characters in *The Sopranos* did little else but eat when they weren't, you know, engaging in organized crime! Invariably, the show always drove me to eat. Perhaps the two have little else in common, but *The Sopranos* and the Gospel of Luke share an abundance of scenes around tables and food, both of which are sites of great cultural, personal, and religious significance both in antiquity and today.

This is, of course, not the first time that God has fed God's people in the wilderness. Both the NRSV and CEB obscure the link between this story and the provision of manna in the wilderness by translating *erēmos* in verse 12 as "a deserted place" and not "wilderness," the latter evoking the story of Israel's long sojourn after the exodus. The translation is not incorrect, but we might miss an important connection in the history of Israel. From the first, God has been a God of provision and abundance, a God upon whom we can rely for our daily bread.

This is also not the first time that Jesus has asked his disciples to do the extraordinary. Just a few verses earlier, Jesus sends the twelve out on a mission that reflects the kind of ministry with which Jesus has already been engaged. Luke 9:1-2 reads, "Jesus . . . gave them power and authority over all demons and to cure diseases, and he sent them out to proclaim the kingdom of God and to heal." This sending anticipates a second mission endeavor that Jesus will empower in chapter 10 when he sends out seventy or seventy-two followers with a very similar set of instructions (see comments on the Gospel for Lectionary 14 / Proper 9, below). Just prior to our pericope, however, the disciples return to Jesus with news of the success of the mission. It was just as Jesus had told them: the sick were healed, demons were cast out, the gospel was proclaimed in both word and deed (9:10).

As is often the case in Luke, Jesus and his disciples are followed by a crowd of followers. Jesus spends the day doing precisely what he asked the disciples to do: healing and proclaiming the gospel.[3] At the close of the day, the disciples recommend dispersing the crowds so that they might get something to eat. Jesus instead suggests that the disciples feed them. They respond in a way that suggests their memories are short. Despite having successfully healed, exorcised, and preached, they are confounded by Jesus' request. So he takes the mere five loaves and two fishes, blesses and breaks them, and then gives them to his disciples. All are fed and satisfied, and in the end twelve (!) baskets of food remain.

Eucharistic overtones certainly reverberate throughout this story. There are striking parallels between this scene and Luke's account of the Supper in 22:14-23 and even Paul's account in 1 Corinthians 11, especially in the pattern of taking, blessing, breaking, and giving the meal. These patterns are also echoed in Jesus' self-revelation on the road to Emmaus in 24:28-35 where the two disciples only recognize Jesus when he shares bread with them. In other words, in Luke some of the distinguishing characteristics of Jesus are generosity, hospitality, and abundance. In the feeding of the five thousand, the miracle is one of bounty, not just sustenance. God's provision of bread and drink is characterized by abundance. This miraculous meal is not cobbled together. Jesus does not have to water down the mix to stretch the provisions. Instead, all eat their fill and plenty is left over.

Of course, in a culture where we throw away so much edible food, such an image is easily misunderstood. Our sense of abundance too often verges on waste and resembles excess. We live in a culture where our "stuff" has become our "stuffing."[4] Our "stuff" is not just decorative ornamentation in our lives but the very center of our being and our identity. This is not the image of abundance the twelve baskets of food represent. Instead, this abundance rests on God's providence, not our industry; trusts God's graciousness, not our fruitful endeavors; relies on God's hospitality, not our acquisitiveness. As Augustine once preached, "Is the one who multiplied the loaves in the hands of the distributors not the same one who multiplies the seeds in the earth, and from a few grains can fill barns? However, since this miracle takes place every year we are not surprised by it. Yet the reason why we are not awed is not that it is not wonderful, but that it is repeated so often."[5]

In a world divided between people who waste and people who yearn for the basics of life, this story is vital for us. The narrative is a reminder that the breaking of bread among believers is not an empty ritual but a powerful embodiment of our deepest convictions about a God who gives us our daily bread, who took flesh in Jesus so that his body might be broken and his blood shed for our sakes. Encourage your hearers to remember this story every time we join in the Lord's Supper. Encourage them to remember a God who nourishes in the wilderness and always has that much more to give us.

First Reading

I Kings 18:20-21 (22-29), 30-39 or I Kings 8:22-23, 41-43 (RCL)

First Kings includes a scene we could easily label a divine smackdown or a clash of the titans. Baal is the divine villain and opponent of our hero Elijah. Elijah finds himself largely abandoned by the people. He reports that he alone remains faithful to the one true God while Baal has a whole retinue of 450 prophets. On the basis of numbers alone or even a poll of public opinion, the God of Israel is losing this contest. Elijah, however, proposes a contest of sorts to demonstrate the sole supremacy of the Lord. With care and precision, the prophets of Baal prepare an altar and beg for fire from heaven. There is, of course, no response. In contrast, Elijah constructs an altar and commands that it be soaked and surrounded with water. When his lonely voice calls out to God, "then the LORD's fire fell; it consumed the sacrifice, the wood, the stones, and the dust. It even licked up the water in the trench" (18:38 CEB).

So should we try this amid our ecumenical partners? Should different Christian traditions create a contest to test God's allegiances? Probably not! The story is not really about a popularity contest or a show of force alone. It is a reflection of a people's commitments. Where does our trust lie?

The alternate reading for the RCL brings us to Solomon's dedication of the temple. Especially striking are verses 41-43 where claims of particularity and universality overlap. Even as Solomon prays over a temple for Israel, he imagines a temple whose doors and thus worship are open to people from around the world. What may seem at first a conflict between the exclusivism of Elijah's conflict with the prophets of Baal and Solomon's openness to the people of the world in the temple of the God of Israel is quite in line with the opening confession of Solomon's prayer: "There is no God like you . . . , keeping covenant and steadfast love for your servants . . ." (8:23). Those servants may come from anywhere in the world as they acknowledge the one God of the universe.

Genesis 14:18-20 (LFM)

The figure of Melchizedek is shrouded in some mystery among exegetes, but this has also produced a great deal of interest and curiosity among interpreters.[6] Genesis tells us very little about him save that he was somehow a priest of God even though the priesthood of Israel was yet to be established! He was also a king, though there is even some uncertainty about his capital city. Is Salem a reference to Jerusalem or some other city? Also strange is the encounter he has with Abram. Melchizedek gives a blessing to Abram in both word and deed. He speaks words of blessing but also provides a gift of bread and wine, symbols of hospitality then and now.

As noted above, interpretive traditions around this story are varied and complex. However, Hebrews 7 takes pride of place among Christian interpretations. There Melchizedek's name is interpreted. Verse 3 even makes the claim that he has no genealogy and thus is a priest forever. Jesus, according to Hebrews' reading of this story and Psalm 110:4 (see psalmody, below), is precisely a priest in the order of Melchizedek. With no beginning and no end, Jesus is priest forever and ever.

In the end, however, much mystery remains in this strange tale of an otherwise unknown priest and king. Many have sought to understand this story, leading to a number of interpretations. What remains, though, is the blessing of Abram, the recognition that the Most High God had made him a parent of many nations.

Psalmody

Psalm 96 or 96:1-9 (RCL)

The psalm, like Solomon in the first reading, calls the whole world to worship the one true God, the one true Creator, the only God among a litany of mere idols. This is a word of praise that ought to emerge not just from Israel but from all the peoples of the world, whom the psalmist invites to "bring an offering, and come into his courts" (v. 8). The psalm then moves to a word of judgment in verse 10, though it has been a subtext of the psalm leading up to this point. There is a real God who creates, and there are mere, mute idols. But notice what follows this explicit word of judgment in verse 10. Joy! The grateful response of the normally chaotic sea! Fields exult! Silent trees "sing for joy" (v. 12)! That is, when God's judgment comes, we certainly tremble but not in fear. God's presence inspires awe in God's people no matter where they call home.

Psalm 110:1, 2, 3, 4 (LFM)

Hebrews 7 draws on this passage in seeking to comprehend how Jesus becomes the eternal high priest. In its original context, the psalm was likely a royal psalm perhaps used in ceremonies enthroning a new king. The psalm thus links the Lord to the earthly king the Lord has assigned. God promises to vanquish the king's enemies. The king will be heralded by a people grateful for their victories in the Lord. Verse 4 concludes with even more concrete certainty. Like Melchizedek, this king's reign will know no end, for God is sure and steadfast in God's commitments. In the psalm, therefore, Melchizedek is a powerful symbol of God's covenants and God's perfectly consistent promise keeping. God keeps the promises God makes. This is a confession we celebrate every time we break bread and drink wine together as people of faith.

Second Reading

Galatians 1:1-12 (RCL)

Like modern letters, ancient epistles followed some basic conventions. When letter writers diverge from these conventions, we are supposed to notice. As Galatians opens, we learn who the addressee and recipients of the letter are (1:1-2), and we read a quick word of greeting (vv. 3-5). Verse 6 should next include a thanksgiving section, but Paul subverts the expectations of his first audience by launching an impassioned tirade rooted in his love for this community. In the opening to Galatians, Paul wonders aloud and with some ferocity how everything could have gone so wrong in this community.

Even in his greetings, Paul begins to establish the theological foundations of the case he will make to this beloved but frustrating community. In verse 1, Paul describes himself as an apostle who was "sent neither by human commission nor from human authorities, but through Jesus Christ and God the Father, who raised him from the dead." In next week's second reading, Paul will draw on his own biography to demonstrate this very point. If he was sent by God and not humans, then the gospel he proclaimed is nonnegotiable and absolute, not one among many other gospels.

After skipping the expected thanksgiving, Paul's language is even more pointed. There is only one gospel, the gospel of Christ, and the Galatians are turning from it. Twice in verses 8 and 9, Paul wishes for individuals to be cut off from God if they were to preach "another gospel." The fact is that, for Paul, there is not "another gospel" and thus straying from this divine revelation is the basest folly.

1 Corinthians 11:23-26 (LFM)

The Lord's Supper is unlike any other meal. In today's churches, this is perhaps more evident than in the practices of the earliest churches. In Corinth, the Supper had become a moment for community revelry and fellowship. In some ways, this is consistent with the spirit of the words of institution Paul recollects in our pericope. After all, these words and this meal are meant to bind Christian sisters and brothers together in the new covenant in Jesus' blood. The Greek verbs and pronouns in the passage are all second-person plural. That is, they assume that it is a community of people gathering around the table. At the same time, Paul reports that the solemnity and propriety of the Supper have been lost among the Corinthians. Instead of a moment of unity, division reigns at the Supper as some indulge and others go hungry (see 11:17-22). Thus when Paul reminds the Corinthians of the words that institute the Supper, he does so with the fracturing of this community at the forefront of his mind. He is not writing a theology of the Supper so much as he is reminding these Christians about Jesus' words in order to align their communal practices with their deeply held belief in the good news. This pericope contains one of the handful of times that Paul directly quotes Jesus in his letters (see also 1 Cor. 7:10; 9:14; 1 Thess. 4:15). As in the beginning of Galatians, Paul wants to ensure that the Corinthians understand that these words are a revelation from Jesus Christ, not the concoctions of charismatic church leaders. Therefore, the words are sure, as are the aims of this meal. This meal is powerful (see 11:27-32), for there we meet God and one another.

Focal Points for Preaching

The God of Israel is both particular and universal in reaching out to the people of the world. God has chosen a particular people for the sake of the wider world. God is truly the God of Israel and the rest of the world. Whether you are celebrating the Second Sunday after Pentecost or the Solemnity of Corpus Christi, these are important themes to carry forward after the celebration of Pentecost. God's love is not generic but particular, not exclusive but inclusive. It is precisely here where the texts of the LFM and RCL meet. It is precisely where these different lectionaries inform one another in powerful ways. Even as we preach different texts, there is a unity of spirit that binds us: the table of God is inclusive, calling for all of us to share in the bountiful gifts of bread and wine that represent the self-giving love of God through Jesus Christ.

Notes

1. In fact, only once does Jesus enter Gentile land in the whole Gospel of Luke. See Luke 8:26-39 and the commentary on Lectionary 12 / Proper 7.
2. Justo L. González, *Luke*, Belief: A Theological Commentary on the Bible (Louisville: Westminster John Knox, 2010), 98.
3. As I will discuss more extensively in the commentary for Lectionary 14 / Proper 9, for Luke healing and proclamation are two sides of the same coin and not two discrete acts of ministry. When we proclaim, we heal. When we heal, we proclaim.
4. See Eric D. Barreto, "'To Proclaim the Year of the Lord's Favor' (Luke 4:19): Possessions and the Christian Life in Luke-Acts," in *Rethinking Stewardship: Our Culture, Our Theology, Our Practices*, ed. Frederick J. Gaiser (St. Paul: Word & World, Luther Seminary, 2010), 65–76.
5. This is a translation by Justo González of Augustine's Sermon 130, On the Multiplication of the Loaves 1, in *Luke*, 115.
6. For a fascinating account of the numerous interpretive traditions that arose around Melchizedek, see James L. Kugel, *Traditions of the Bible: A Guide to the Bible as It Was at the Start of the Common Era* (Cambridge: Harvard University Press, 1998), 276–93.

June 9, 2013

Lectionary 10 / Tenth Sunday in Ordinary Time / Proper 5

Third Sunday after Pentecost

Revised Common Lectionary (RCL)

1 Kings 17:17-24 or 1 Kings 17:8-16 (17-24)
Psalm 30 or 146
Galatians 1:11-24
Luke 7:11-17

Lectionary for Mass (LFM)

1 Kings 17:17-24
Psalm 30:2 + 4, 5-6, 11-12a + 13b
Galatians 1:11-19
Luke 7:11-17

The literary figure of the "widow" is a powerful biblical image. A widow in ancient cultures lived on the edge of existence. Without a husband to provide her financial support, she could quickly fall into debilitating poverty. If she were left without a son, her situation was that much more precarious. Scripture turns to widows as exemplars of those most marginalized, neglected, and threatened by the wider culture. Nearly all of this week's texts evoke these experiences of liminality and threat, but they also confess that God is aligned precisely with those who are marginalized, neglected, and threatened by the wider culture. Where is God to be found? Look to the widow.

Gospel

Luke 7:11-17 (RCL, LFM)

As is often his pattern, Luke pairs the story of a man with that of a woman. In the contrasts these parallels draw, we learn something of Luke's theological agenda. As Luke 7 opens, Jesus encounters a centurion beloved by the surrounding Jewish community. This centurion seeks the healing of his servant. That is, this healing involves an individual of some power but also renown who is looking for the restoration of a beloved servant. Even though he is a representative of the brutal force of Roman imperial power, he is beloved by his Jewish neighbors, and Jesus recognizes the depth of the centurion's faith (7:9). In short, a number of the reader's expectations are turned upside down in this first healing. This pattern will continue as Luke draws Jesus to the town of Nain.

In contrast to the centurion's power, we find a grieving widow now bereft of her son. Without a husband or a son to provide financial support and social protection, a widow in the ancient world faced nearly unavoidable calamity. Such calamity is in the background of the hopeful word of James 1:27: "Religion that is pure and undefiled before God, the Father, is this: to care for orphans and widows in their distress, and to keep oneself unstained by the world." Similarly, we might turn to Psalm 68:5: "Father of orphans and protector of widows is God in [God's] holy habitation." In short, widows are symbols both of utter vulnerability but also of those most in need of God's care. God lives on the margins of our world.

Vulnerable and exposed, Luke's unnamed widow must have been experiencing manifold griefs. The death of her son is inexorably her social and financial death as well. It is probably this profound grief that draws Jesus' compassion in verse 13 and impels him to touch the bier or coffin that contains her son's dead body. This is a bold action already. Dead bodies were considered ritually unclean, and contact with them or anything linked with them should have brought uncleanliness upon Jesus. Instead, Jesus subverts the normal order of things. Where death previously ruled, now life returns.

But notice whose life is really restored in this narrative. It is the widow and not her son who is the primary concern of the story. Jesus has compassion for her, not him. His concern is not primarily the death of this son but the cruel repercussions of his untimely demise. Notice also that when her son returns to life, "Jesus gave him to his mother" (v. 15). The effect of the healing is certainly the resuscitation of this son, but the end of his healing is not his life but hers. He is brought to life, but it is truly her life that is saved.

The contrasts with the story of the centurion's servant, which I wrote about last week, are again instructive. While the centurion boldly comes to Jesus asking for his restorative touch, the widow of Nain does not ask for Jesus' help directly. Instead, Jesus notices her plight and has compassion on her. In a sense, it is her tears that stand as a plea to Jesus. After all, the first words Jesus speaks to her are, "Do not weep." Her "healing" is precipitated not by her faith so much as Jesus' compassion for her difficult state and the depth of her despair.[1]

Why does she not reach out to Jesus directly? Perhaps she has already let go of the dim hope that her son would be given back to her. Perhaps her future is so dark that she cannot imagine another way out. Perhaps all she can do in this moment of despair is grieve for her son and for herself. Perhaps there is nothing left for her to do but to face death. But Jesus intrudes into this scene of death and hopelessness, sees in the widow's tears a cry of anguish God has long promised to heed, and boldly brings her from death into life. In other words, for Luke, resurrection is not just the resuscitation of a dead body but the invigoration of people and their communities in God's righteousness and justice. Who better to receive this gift than a widow on the very brink of death?

Why, then, are the crowds afraid? Fear (*phobos*) is a rather common reaction to God's actions through Jesus and his followers in Luke-Acts (e.g., Luke 1:12, 65; 2:9; 5:26; 7:16; 8:37; 21:26; Acts 2:43; 5:5, 11; 19:17). The fear imagined here is not mere terror but, instead, the proper response to God's holy presence and activity. The fear imagined here is less dread than awe. After all, the crowd reacts with fear and then glorifies God, voicing their certainty that God has not deserted God's people.

Certainly, God has acted by bringing breath back into the body of this man. But more than that is the life God has breathed into the widow. Here, Jesus embodies the great prophetic ideal of caring for the widow and the orphan. After all, what is a prophet but someone empowered by God to discern the present and see God's future, to see tragedy but deliver the promise of God's compassion and care?

Plus, consider what this miraculous restoration of her life suggests about God's commitments to God's promises. As the people conclude, "God has looked favorably on [God's] people!" (7:16). How do they know this? Most likely, they see God moving in the extension of compassion and mercy to a widow on the very brink of social death. If God will reach out to those most on the margins, will not God also keep all the other promises God has made? If God can do what is most difficult, what will be impossible for God?

Luke prepares us for this powerful scene earlier in the narrative. First, Mary's song of God's justice (1:46-55) promises that God will act to shift the world in great reversals. God has lifted up the lowly and fed the hungry. All these things, Mary sings, God does "in remembrance of [God's] mercy, according to the promises [God] made to our ancestors" (1:54-55). That is, these acts of radical reversal are not a detour for God but precisely the way in which God has always acted. Second, Jesus himself points to a foreign widow in his inaugural sermon in 4:25-26. His ministry will move in unexpected ways just as God sent Elijah not to someone in Israel but to a foreign widow. God's activity in the world is bold and committed to those most neglected in the world.

Moreover, the widow of Nain becomes an exemplar of God's compassion for the least among us, most strikingly in the story of the "widow's mite" (Luke 21:1-4). Unfortunately, the addition of chapter breaks in the text keeps many readers from noticing an important introduction to the story of the faithful widow who gives what little she has. In 20:47 Jesus denounces religious leaders who "devour widows' houses." When the very next scene includes a widow whose house is being devoured as she gives all of the little she has, Jesus is not commending every poor person to give everything they have to religious institutions but is condemning a place that was intended to bring glory to the God who sides with the poor and the broken but is now a site for abuse of those who can least afford it. As the rich give from their excess and call themselves holy, they miss the widow's plight, a plight God has called us all to alleviate.

First Reading
1 Kings 17:17-24 (RCL, LFM)
1 Kings 17:8-16 (17-24) (RCL alt.)

Each of the Gospel writers looked to the texts of the Hebrew Scriptures to provide a way to come to understand the meaning of Jesus' life. Matthew will often list specific prophecies that Jesus fulfills. Luke's allusions are often subtler and more literary. They tend to have Jesus and those around him take on the garb of an ancient story. Specifically, Luke often turns to the stories of Elijah and Elisha for inspiration, for theological frameworks to structure his account.

The alignment of the Gospel and first readings in the lectionary about widows brings to the forefront how Luke interweaves these tales. In fact, Luke 4:25-26 has already alluded to this story in 1 Kings. But to what end?

As 1 Kings 17 opens, we learn that a great famine has gripped the land. God sends the prophet Elijah to Sidon, a Gentile area, to find a widow who will provide Elijah's sustenance. Earlier in the narrative of 1 Kings, Sidon had been home not to a desperate widow but to Jezebel (16:31).[2] The widow and her son are on the brink of death, having only a bit of grain and oil to share as a last meal. Elijah, however, promises that neither will run out until God ends the great drought.

That promise is seemingly challenged in our passage. The son is gripped with a deadly illness and dies. The promises God made through Elijah seem suddenly empty. But Elijah intercedes on behalf of this child and his mother. When the boy is healed, Elijah "gave him to his mother" (v. 23). This is language Luke 7:15 intentionally echoes. The life of this widow and the life of her son are inextricably intertwined. One cannot live without the other. Neither can survive without the care of God.

How unexpected to find God's prophet in Sidon, the land of the Gentiles, the home of the devotee of Baal, Jezebel. How unexpected that he would turn to the poorest and the hungriest to find sustenance in the midst of a great famine. How unexpected is this all unless we remember how God acts. According to the authors of 1 Kings and the Gospel of Luke, this is precisely how God chooses to act.

Psalmody
Psalm 30 (RCL)
Psalm 30:2 + 4, 5-6, 11-12a + 13b (LFM)
Psalm 146 (RCL alt.)

The lectionary invites us to imagine Psalm 30's prayer on the lips of the widows of Zarephath and Nain. Verse 3 is particularly poignant as the psalmist praises God for bringing life in the midst of death. Again, in the case of both widows, the death of their sons was tragic as these two women would have lost clearly beloved children. Equally tragic, however, is that the survival of both women rests on the care of their sons. Not only are these sons brought back from Sheol, so also are these two faithful women. Their joy is reflected in verse 11 where mourning is exchanged for dancing, the dress of grief for clothes of praise.

Like nearly all the other passages this week, Psalm 146 evokes the plight of widows and confesses God's care for them along with strangers and orphans. The main theme of this psalm is the persistence of God's justice. While it seems like the powerful of this world will always sit on their thrones, verses 3-4 speak of their assured fall. In contrast, God "keeps faith forever" (v. 6). This conviction is exemplified by a God "who executes justice for the oppressed; who gives food to the hungry" (v. 7). There is an additional resonance in verses 7-8 with Luke's text. These verses are powerful predecessors of Mary's song. Together, Psalm 146 and Mary sing a duet of justice. God sides with those who are most in need.

Like the faith of these widows, the hope enunciated in both Psalms 30 and 146 is neither fatalistic nor facile. Hope in these cases does not rest on the continuation of a life devoid of pain and tragedy. Indeed, the psalmist has tasted the bitterness of death, known the cruelty of death's sting. The psalmist is not naïve. The psalmist hopes because, in the midst of great struggle, God has nonetheless been faithful.

Second Reading
Galatians 1:11-24 (RCL)
Galatians 1:11-19 (LFM)

Paul opens Galatians with a barrage of ferocious concern. He subverts epistolary customs as I discussed last week and even invokes the possibility of being cursed in order to start the letter with a tone of exasperation. Remember also that last week's second reading alluded to Paul's own experience as an apostle sent and commissioned by God alone. The gospel he proclaims therefore is from God, not from humans. In fact, he claims in verse 12 to have received a direct "revelation of Jesus Christ."

Here we must tread with some care. Readers tend to harmonize this revelation with Paul's Damascus-road experience. Of course, Paul never tells that particular story in his extant letters; only Acts records the details of Paul's call to be a missionary for the gospel (Acts 9:1-19; 22:6-21; 26:12-18). Paul may be referring to the same event, but we can't be certain. Pauline biography, however, is not really the point. What Paul is emphasizing is the character of this gospel. By claiming it as a revelation of Jesus Christ, Paul can claim direct access to this gospel and thus persuade the Galatians to hold to it without swerving into other so-called gospels.

Next, Paul will then delve into his own biography, not for the sake of retelling his life story, but for a larger theological point. Presumably, they know his story as he likely shared in the proclamation of the good news. But he recalls his own life story to make a point about the character of God and God's gospel. Paul's life is a vivid, living example that human authority does not rest over us; only God calls, only God sends, only God grants authority. Paul's life is a vivid, living example that the good news is not ours but God's alone. Paul's life is a vivid, living example that God can turn a persecutor into a spiritual sibling. Like Paul's rhetorical ploy as the letter opens, God surprises us at every turn.

Focal Points for Preaching

The treatment of widows today will often continue to take a place of prominence in our communities. For some, the experience of a precarious financial and social situation will be familiar. Not so for others. How then can we think about a God who sides with ancient widows, with people most at threat of ruination by a neglectful culture? Even as you preach about the plight of the ancient widow, help your hearers wonder where modern-day widows continue to live on the edge of existence, at the corner of our concerns. Who is neglected in our midst? If we wish to find God, that is precisely where we ought to look.

Notes

1. See Justo L. González, *Luke*, Belief: A Theological Commentary on the Bible (Louisville: Westminster John Knox, 2010), 98.
2. See Choon-Leong Seow, "The First and Second Book of Kings," in *The New Interpreter's Bible*, ed. Leander E. Keck et al. (Nashville: Abingdon, 1999), 3:128.

June 16, 2013
Lectionary 11 / Eleventh Sunday in Ordinary Time / Proper 6
Fourth Sunday after Pentecost

Revised Common Lectionary (RCL)
2 Samuel 11:26—12:10, 13-15 or
1 Kings 21:1-10, (11-14), 15-21a
Psalm 32 or 5:1-8
Galatians 2:15-21
Luke 7:36—8:3

Lectionary for Mass (LFM)
2 Samuel 12:7-10, 13
Psalm 32:1-2, 5, 7, 11
Galatians 2:16, 19-21
Luke 7:36—8:3 or 7:36-50

Simply put, forgiveness is difficult to receive, even more difficult to dispense. Forgiveness is especially difficult when the powerful take what they want and the powerless are trampled underfoot. This week, the lectionary is an exercise in contrasts in sin and forgiveness. On the one hand, we hear the story of a woman Luke calls a "sinner" who receives Jesus' forgiveness. We do not know why she is called a sinner, but her marginalized position is evident in the disdain with which Simon the Pharisee dismisses her. On the other hand, two powerful kings—David and Ahab—reach out into the world with avarice and with disastrous results. Their forgiveness takes a very different shape, though it comes with a very high price for both of them.

Gospel
Luke 7:36—8:3 (RCL)
Luke 7:36—8:3 or 7:36-50 (LFM)

The story of the woman who anoints Jesus is a striking reminder of the *theological* importance of what scholars refer to as the "Synoptic Problem." That is, the way Luke tells this story differently from both Mark and Matthew says much about what he hoped to demonstrate in its telling. It also reminds us of the dangers of unconscious harmonization. Matthew, Mark, and Luke each approach the story of Jesus with a distinctive theological perspective and agenda. The lectionary here calls us to focus on Luke and his unique take on this story. To get a sense of Luke's angle of vision, let's first turn to Matthew and Mark's parallel narrations.

In Matthew 26:6-13 and Mark 14:3-9, an unnamed woman approaches Jesus and gives him an extravagant gift while he is at the home of a man named Simon. She breaks open a wildly expensive jar of ointment, covering his head. In both Matthew and Mark, some grumble about the wastefulness of the gift; Matthew 26:8 specifically identifies the grumblers as the disciples. In either case, they complain that the jar of ointment could have been sold to help the poor. But Jesus retorts that this unnamed woman has done him a great service by preparing him for his burial. She therefore becomes a critical hinge as these two Gospels turn to Holy Week, and Jesus himself declares that her acts will always be memorialized.

The Lukan account is similar but contains some striking shifts. Most telling is the placement of the story. Instead of leading into Jesus' crucifixion, Luke's account is quite early in the narrative. Thus placed and narrated, Luke's story does not prepare Jesus for his burial, for the cross still remains far down the road. In addition, Jesus' host is identified by name but also by sect; he is a Pharisee. Yet another difference is the identification of the woman who anoints Jesus. In Matthew and Mark, she is anonymous yet later praised by Jesus for her faithfulness. In contrast, Luke identifies her directly as a "sinner" (7:37), and her final gift is the forgiveness of her sins (7:48), not the promise that her actions would be remembered.

Unfortunately, a number of commentators have sought to fill in the gaps in this story. Many have sought to identify the woman's "sin," usually settling on some sort of sexual promiscuity. Worse still, the close placement of this story and the listing of Jesus' benefactors in the first verses of chapter 8 have led some to theorize—with no real exegetical rationale—that the unnamed sinner was Mary Magdalene. Thus some have concluded that Mary was this unnamed sinner and more specifically a former prostitute. This senseless maligning of Mary Magdalene is something preachers ought to confront with vigor. By placing these stories together, the lectionary provides a valuable opportunity to reverse this vicious libel.

Where, then, does Luke's redaction of this powerful story lead us? Most of all, the story is another instance of Jesus fulfilling his call to reach out to the marginalized. We may miss Luke's aims if we look to identify the "sins" that he chooses not to name. Instead, by deeming her a sinner, she is marked as a social outcast. It is her social status that is described with this label more than her "sins" as we typically understand them. In short, she is exactly the kind of person with whom Jesus tends to breaks bread.

With boldness, this unnamed woman enters a social space fraught with danger for her. Repeatedly, tables are centers of cultural negotiations for Jesus in Luke. Her courage stands in sharp contrast to the shoddy hospitality the supposedly righteous Pharisee offered Jesus. Simon thinks he has no need for Jesus' presence, really; he sees no reason to welcome him into his house as an honored guest. In contrast, a "sinner," a person with little standing in her community, a woman with no power or voice, recognizes Jesus for who he is. Her gratitude is in direct proportion to her identification as a "sinner." In contrast, the Pharisee's lofty social position means he thinks he has little use for Jesus' forgiveness.

Jesus cements this contrast with a brief image of two individuals with significant debts. One of the debts is tenfold the other. That is, both are deeply indebted. Both are grateful for being saved from insolvency. But Simon recognizes that the one with the greater debt will love the one who forgives that much more.

And yet we never hear the woman speak. She is never named by Luke. Jesus addresses her directly only once but otherwise speaks *about* her, not *to* her. In Luke's account, we no longer hear that her prophetic act will resonate throughout time. Plus, her vital role in preparing Jesus for the cross is muted in Luke's account.

Both the history of interpretation of this passage and its redactions should lead preachers to treat this woman's story with much care. That individuals whom our current culture deems "sinners," "deviants," or "a little strange" are yearning to hear a word of inclusion means that we too must be willing to break bread with them. That there will be many who hear us preach this story who never feel they "fit in" in their families, their cultures, or the church suggests that the inclusive embrace that accompanies forgiveness and acceptance remains good news today.

But we might also remember the role of Simon in this story. After all, he did invite Jesus into his home, and Jesus accepted the invitation. Jesus certainly ate with tax collectors and sinners, but Pharisees were not excluded from his social calendar. What might it mean that Jesus will eat with anyone who asks, whether Pharisee or "sinner"? Some in your congregation may recognize themselves primarily not in the woman who anoints Jesus' feet but in the righteous host who neglects his honored guest. Forgiveness extends also to those who miss when God draws near. Such individuals may not treasure this forgiveness as much as the "sinners" among us, but that forgiveness is no less valuable, no less costly.

In the end, we might return to Jesus' tale of the debtors and wonder aloud who he imagines owed a greater debt: the righteous host or the sinful interloper. Both have great debts. Both are in need. Do both love Jesus equally in the end?

The high cost of forgiveness leads into our first readings.

First Reading

2 Samuel 11:26—12:10, 13-15 or 1 Kings 21:1-10, (11-14), 15-21a (RCL)
2 Samuel 12:7-10, 13 (LFM)

The story of David reaches a troubling nadir in this pericope from 2 Samuel. Ensconced in the comforts of his home and the safety of the city, David becomes enamored with Bathsheba, the wife of Uriah the Hittite. He conspires to kill Uriah by ordering that he fight in the front lines. With Uriah's murder, David is free to take Bathsheba as his own. Crimes committed by the powerful, especially a monarch, will usually go by unpunished. As Richard Nixon famously quipped, "When the President does it, that means that it is not illegal."

The prophet Nathan is tasked by God to confront David, to speak truth to power. Speaking in a parable, Nathan tells the story of a rich man with "many flocks and herds" (12:2) who, despite his abundance, opts to take the one precious lamb of a poor man to host a dinner for a guest. Of course, David reacts with wrath and demands justice. Only then does Nathan reveal the meaning of the parable: "You are the man!"

Both lectionaries excise the most difficult condemnations of David in 12:11-12. There God promises that David's wives will be taken like Uriah's wife, not in secret but in full view of everyone. Grieved, David seeks repentance, but the judgment has already fallen: David's life will be spared but the child Bathsheba now carries will be struck dead.

This is distressing. Why should others pay for David's crimes? There is no easy way to explain this seemingly unjust outcome. Perhaps, however, what we have in these verses is a very realistic consequence. When the powerful use their position for wicked purposes, others usually pay the cost: family, friends, children, loved ones. No sin is ever really personal, for these acts—especially those committed by the powerful—leave in their shadows broken homes and lives. And yet, even in these situations, forgiveness and reconciliation are possible though they come at a heavy price.

Striking parallels emerge in 1 Kings 21. We hear of Naboth who owned a vineyard held by his family for generations. King Ahab wishes to own the land and offers Naboth what seems to be a fair price. Ahab does not appreciate the value of the land, however; an inheritance is simply not for sale. A conspiracy between Jezebel, Ahab, and local elders leads to Naboth's downfall, and Ahab seizes the land as his own.

In both cases, the powerful seek to own what is beyond their grasp. Power corrupts in such a way that the rest of the world appears to be ready for repossession. And yet God stands on the side of the dispossessed, not the powerful.

Psalmody
Psalm 32 or 5:1-8 (RCL)
Psalm 32:1-2, 5, 7, 11 (LFM)

A penitential psalm, Psalm 32 dwells in the tensions of forgiveness. Grief and happiness, regret and a sense of joyful deliverance are interwoven. After an expression of the joys of God's forgiveness, the psalm then explores the pitiful life of the impenitent sinner (vv. 3-4). The effects of sin are comprehensive, attacking both the body and one's inner will. Verse 5 marks the transition from this state as the psalmist brings his sins before God. After the psalmist reiterates the protective care of God, the instruction of the reader is more direct. There is some debate among scholars around the identity of the "I" in verses 8-9. Some argue that the psalm speaks from God's perspective, as God exhorts the hearer to follow God's counsel and escape the "bit and bridle" that accompany sin. Others argue that here the psalmist continues to speak, enjoining the hearer to learn from his missteps but also the blessed state of forgiveness he now enjoys.

Psalm 5 echoes many of these themes but with more focus on the external danger of the enemy. This psalm is a sharp reminder that living in God's care does not ensure freedom from enemies, whether spiritual or human. The confidence of Psalm 5 rests on God's character. God is a God of justice and righteousness who cannot abide with the destructive powers of evil. God's allegiances are thus clear for the psalmist.

Second Reading
Galatians 2:15-21 (RCL)
Galatians 2:16, 19-21 (LFM)

It is always vital to remember that Paul's letters are contextual and occasional. That is, Paul here is not primarily reflecting on the abstract notion of justification. Don't picture a theologian contemplating profound questions about God and humanity. Instead, imagine the daily work of a pastor to help create Christian community among people torn apart by dissension and confusion. The work and ministry of the latter are no less theological or profound than those of the former.

The theological and contextual reflections in these verses emerge in light of the conflicts with Peter that Paul describes in 2:1-14. Paul confronted Peter when he refused to share a table with Gentiles, a problem analogous to the conflicts around fellowship apparently present in the Galatian churches. The conflict with Peter itself rests on a larger argument at the beginning of Galatians. Paul insists that the gospel he proclaimed to believers in Galatia is wholly reliable and authoritative not because its human proclaimers (whether they are the Jerusalem elders, Peter, or Paul) are reliable or authoritative but because of the divine origin of the good news (see Gal. 1:11-12).

Our verses are theologically dense but also central to much of Christian theology. How are we made right before God? To what implications does that status lead in Christian community? Interpreting verse 16 is particularly important. What exactly does Paul mean by "works of the law"? We might understand it best by examining its contrast: "faith in/of Jesus Christ." The translation of this phrase is highly debated by scholars. Is Paul here pointing to Jesus' faithfulness to God as the means and source of our righteousness (the faith of Jesus)? Or is Paul here pointing to our faith in Jesus as the means by which God makes us right (faith in Jesus)? In the end, Paul is arguing that our relationship with Christ has many dimensions. First, we lean on Jesus' faithfulness in his own life. Second, we believe in the saving power of Jesus' faithfulness exemplified in his life, death, and resurrection. Last, as Paul concludes in 2:19-20, Christ transforms our life by granting us a new identity, an identity that Paul argues in the rest of Galatians takes form in Christian community.

In short, the problems Paul addresses here are about the shape of the Christian communities just as much as they are explorations about salvation. As Luke Timothy Johnson has concluded, "At one level, Paul's argument is soteriological: How has God saved them? At another level, it is ecclesiological: What sort of community displays the reality of that salvation?"[1]

Focal Points for Preaching

These texts invite us to reflect on the nature of forgiveness, both divine and human. The temptation is that the preacher may universalize her or his experience of deliverance from guilt. Some who hear you will need to be freed from their pride but not everyone. Some people who hear the promise of forgiveness contained in these texts will have already been broken by the world and deluded into thinking that they will always fall short of God's standard. Forgiveness for them does not mean submission so much as a grateful embrace of God's valuing and love of them. Both kinds of forgiveness are extremely difficult to embrace. The texts this week provide incredible language to verbalize these struggles and engage these powerful feelings. Invite others to join the tensions and joy, sorrow and deliverance we find in Scripture.

Note

1. Luke Timothy Johnson, *The Writings of the New Testament*, 3rd ed. (Minneapolis: Fortress Press, 2010), 293.

June 23, 2013
Lectionary 12 / Twelfth Sunday in Ordinary Time / Proper 7
Fifth Sunday after Pentecost

Revised Common Lectionary (RCL)	**Lectionary for Mass (LFM)**
Isaiah 65:1-9 or 1 Kings 19:1-4, (5-7), 8-15a	Zechariah 12:10-11; 13:1
Psalm 22:19-28 or Psalms 42 & 43	Psalm 63:2, 3-4, 5-6, 8-9
Galatians 3:23-29	Galatians 3:26-29
Luke 8:26-39	Luke 9:18-24

What does it mean to be a disciple, a follower of Jesus? The texts this week lay out the many paths discipleship takes but also the many pitfalls we might face along the way. Discipleship is not like taking a test and getting the right answer. It is not about knowing the right stuff. Instead, following God means drawing near to the broken, the marginalized, and the suffering. After all, that is so often where God has chosen to meet us.

Gospel
Luke 8:26-39 (RCL)

When Jesus enters Gerasa, it is the first and last time in the Gospel of Luke that Jesus goes beyond the ancient borders of Israel and enters a strictly Gentile area. Beyond the geographical note in verse 26, several other symbolic markers indicate that Jesus has entered a different world. The man Jesus encounters is not just possessed but consumed with demons, as we will later learn (8:29-30). He is nude and makes his home among the ritual uncleanliness of tombs. Moreover, the presence of swine and their herders only confirms the Gentile character of the area.

That the man is profoundly possessed is confirmed by the negotiation the legion of demons initiates with Jesus. They beg to be transferred into a herd of pigs. When Jesus grants the request, the demons drive the herd into the lake where the pigs are drowned. The demons thus return home by reentering the chaotic waters.

The reference to "legion" must have evoked the Roman Empire's military arm in the minds of Luke's earliest audiences. In subtle ways, Luke tends to indicate that the forces now ruling the world have the backing of Satanic forces. Notice, for example, how during Jesus' temptation in Luke 4:6 Satan offers him the kingdoms of the world, kingdoms whose authority has been granted to him. The power that Jesus wields over this legion of demons is thus not solely spiritual but profoundly political. In this Gentile region, Jesus' power over the forces of chaos, death, and destruction is unquestioned. The residents of Gerasa find themselves disrupted by this exercise of power.

There are two rather distinct reactions to this exorcism. The locals react with abject fear and ask Jesus to leave. Why? Their fear may be rooted not in the holy awe the faithful feel toward God but in the disruptive influence Jesus inevitably effects. The formerly mad are made well, and economic systems are at risk. Even though one person is healed, Jesus represents a threat to this Gentile city, especially to its social and economic order. Prior to the arrival of Jesus, the herd of pigs was still a viable investment, but, more importantly, the lines of demarcation between the whole and the broken were crystal clear. The healing of the former demoniac is a blessing for him but a disruptive shift in relationships in this town. As Justo González concludes, "The demons that Jesus conquers are not only those of disease and death, but also those of isolation and exclusion."[1]

Thus the reaction of the erstwhile demoniac is to beg Jesus to allow him to follow in his steps. Why would he want to stay among people who maligned him and not with the one who made him whole? Unlike the disciples whom Jesus asks to leave everything to follow him (5:11, 27-28; 6:12-16), the former demoniac is instructed to tell others in his hometown what God has done for him. That is, even as Jesus now returns to Israel proper, he has left a disciple back in Gerasa who is commissioned to proclaim the good news of Jesus' healing touch and his power over all the dark forces troubling the world.

In Luke, the forms of discipleship are not universal. Some leave everything behind; others stay home. Both, however, share the good news of what God has done and will do. In addition, the passage serves as an initial step toward a worldwide mission, a mission foretold by the many songs of Luke 1–2. This is a movement of God's Spirit that promises to "turn the world upside down" (Acts 17:6).

Luke 9:18-24 (LFM)

Luke 9 grapples with two central themes in the Third Gospel: the identity of Jesus and how one's confession of Jesus' identity informs discipleship.[2]

Rumors are running rampant about who Jesus might be. What is his true identity? In fact, just a few verses earlier (vv. 7-9), Herod asked these very questions. Herod's wonderment is a stark reminder that Jesus posed a political threat to the powerful of the time. For Luke, Herod's interest is not primarily spiritual but about the repercussions of Jesus' identity for his own grip on power. Even Herod recognizes that how we respond to these questions of identity have far-reaching implications for how we lead life in a broken world.

Is he one of the prophets who has returned? Is he Elijah or even John? In these verses, Peter makes an astounding confession: You are the Messiah, that is, the anointed of God. Even as Peter correctly deduces whom God made Jesus to be, his confession is undercut. He, along with the disciples—who, remember, will run in fear as Jesus faces his execution—have other expectations of the Messiah, expectations that don't include suffering and affliction. Many in our congregations will understand the bitterness of shattered expectations.

What would this confession have meant for Luke and his earliest audiences? Messianic expectations in the Jewish world of antiquity were incredibly complex and certainly not homogenous. For Luke, however, Peter's confession that Jesus is the anointed of God likely evoked the anointing of Israel's kings. Anointing with oil was a symbol and sign of God's favor over an individual called to be an agent of God as king and ruler. Thus Peter's confession is bold and profoundly political. No one else can make a claim to rule, for God has chosen one and only one anointed.

But the power Jesus wields is unlike any human power we know. His is not a reign that rests on "shock-and-awe" tactics. He does not require the services of an armed mass of soldiers or the coercive power of law and order. Instead, the Messiah of God becomes the recipient of all such cruelties and violence. The Messiah is rejected and afflicted, not regaled and uplifted.

Peter's confession is not just cognitive or an act of understanding. Instead, Jesus insists, it is another step on the long, difficult road of discipleship. Speaking those words means embracing that the Messiah will not rule as a king normally does. Speaking those words also means embracing that same road of suffering. Following Jesus means taking up one's cross.

After such a long time, the power of the cross has been blunted by its ubiquity in our churches. For residents of the Roman Empire, a cross was a symbol of shame, a cruel form of execution reserved for the worst of insurrectionists, and a reminder of Rome's claim to absolute power. How incredible then is it that we adorn churches and our necks with a symbol so representative of unchecked power and unrestrained injustice! Following the path of the cross means being willing to sacrifice our lives for the sake of others. More importantly, however, it means that God through Jesus has chosen to taste the depths of despair and abandonment, to feel the pain of rejection and exclusion, and to experience death in its cruelest forms.

In the end, therefore, it is not Jesus' ontology or identity that is most important here. Jesus here deflects expectations away from himself to the suffering he would endure and thus that his followers would also have to bear. A suffering Messiah means that his followers must follow in his difficult footsteps. Discipleship is not a matter of comprehension, of making the right theological confessions. Discipleship is a way of life that will demand all that we have and a bit more. Discipleship is also a promise, however, that God will save us from death and from our deepest afflictions.

In both of these texts from the Gospel of Luke, we notice one of Luke's distinctive theological contributions to the New Testament. Luke often trades on radical reversals. From Mary's prophecy that the powerful would be brought low and the lowly lifted to places of prominence to Jesus' preference for breaking bread with the dregs of society, Luke's Jesus and his followers inhabit a "world turned upside down" (Acts 17:6) and inside out. Jesus' actions among the marginalized, destitute, and neglected reveal God's predispositions and God's work of liberation in a world marked by violence, oppression, and suffering.

First Reading

Isaiah 65:1-9 (RCL)

Isaiah trusts that the God of Israel is a God who keeps promises even when keeping them does not make sense from our perspective. God, Isaiah hopes, reaches out to children who seek to flee from God, children who seek to create their own paths through the world only to invent cruelty and folly everywhere they go. Such actions should create a permanent cleavage between a holy God and a sullied people. And there is certainly judgment and wrath on the part of God. The price of faithlessness is great. But God's promises yet remain. Jacob and his ancestors will continue to follow God and rest in God's care.

1 Kings 19:1-4, (5-7), 8-15a (RCL alt.)

Even the greatest prophets can only bear so much. Under the threat of Jezebel's ire, Elijah flees into the wilderness. We can imagine Elijah voicing the recurring cry of the psalms. Where are you, God? Save me from my enemies! In the wilderness, he is ministered to by an angel who sustains his body. Braced for the journey, Elijah travels for forty days and nights. All this sustenance was preparation for a radical moment of God's self-disclosure. The mere presence of God is awe inspiring and frightening. The world literally shakes before God's presence.

Zechariah 12:10-11; 13:1 (LFM)

Christians cannot help but read the christological echoes of these brief verses in Zechariah. They are particularly resonant with Luke's account of the cross. Luke 23:48 notes that those who witnessed Jesus' execution leave in mourning and grief over the end of an innocent man's life. Zechariah comprehends that grief can be restorative and mourning reviving. New life can emerge where death has been observed and felt most deeply. "On that day" of mourning, cleansing waters will come as well.

Psalmody

Psalm 22:19-28 (RCL)
Psalms 42 & 43 (RCL alt.)
Psalm 63:2, 3-4, 5-6, 8-9 (LFM)

Faith is never solely an individual matter and always deeply imbedded in the dynamics, possibilities, and difficulties of life in community. Psalm 22 imagines the fullness of such a community. As J. Clinton McCann Jr. concludes, "This community of the faithful from all times and places sounds like neither Israel nor the church, both of which would and can be terribly parochial and exclusivistic. . . . The poet's exuberant vision is not a mistake but a challenge, a call to enter the reign of God."[3]

Faith is never a matter of unabated confidence. Psalms 42 and 43 give voice to those dark moments when we yearn for God's presence even though God seems most distant. Psalm 42 begins with the image of thirst. That feeling of insatiable need one feels on a hot day is like that when God seems most absent. Fortunately, we are not left alone in our despair. The psalmist remembers moments of glorious worship, observes the power of creation in thunder and the waves. Simply, we are not left alone. Even when God seems to have deserted us, we too can give voice to our despair and lean on our trust that God is faithful.

Faith is never a journey with a set destination. Images of thirst and need continue in Psalm 63. In contrast to Psalms 42 and 43, the tone of this psalm is one of rejoicing. God is the only salve that can heal us, the source of refreshing waters that can sate any thirst.

Second Reading
Galatians 3:23-29 (RCL)
Galatians 3:26-29 (LFM)

The tone of Galatians is harsh. Paul's frustration with these communities bubbles over at several points, including the opening of chapter 3 when he wonders aloud, "Who has bewitched you?" (3:1). In an effort to return them to the path of the gospel, Paul points to the spiritual exemplar of Abraham, whose *faith* was counted as righteousness (3:6-7) even before the advent of the law (3:17). Moreover, God made promises in response to Abraham's faith to all of his descendants; predating the law once again, these promises cannot be nullified by the law.

Now, what does Paul mean by the law here? As we move through chapter 3, it sounds like the law has no place in the life of the Christian. However, Paul clarifies starting with verse 19 that the law has a function. After all, God was the author of the law and thus the law itself cannot be "opposed to the promises of God" (3:21). The law and the promises are not working at cross-purposes. Thus Paul does not object to the law per se but to seeing the law as a means toward righteousness. That is not what God intended, according to Paul.

We thus arrive at our text. The law, Paul explains, was a disciplinarian (a *paidagōgos* in Greek) until the arrival of Christ. As Richard Hays has explained, this disciplinarian was not a teacher so much as "a slave in the Greco-Roman household who supervised and guarded children. . . . The *paidagōgos* . . . was not a member of the family, and when the child grew to a certain age, his services were no longer required."[4] In other words, the function of the law as a disciplinarian has now passed. We are no longer bound to it in this way, for we are in a new relationship. We are now children of God. We are now partners with Christ.

Paul concludes with a beautiful statement of equality in Galatians 3:28, a verse properly used to advocate for justice and equal treatment no matter one's gender, race, ethnicity, or social status. Notice especially the purposeful allusion back to the Genesis creation accounts in the last pairing of "male and female" (3:28). This is a re-creation of God's children as God had always intended.

What the verse is not, however, is the end of difference. Paul here does not imagine that our differences have come to an end, but he does invoke something even more radical.[5] Our differences are no longer barriers to relationships. It is not expunging our differences that can change how we relate to one another, but Christ's gift of making us one but not the same.

Focal Points for Preaching

Faith does not come easily to us if we are honest with ourselves. There are many reasons to doubt and wonder if God is who God claims to be. In preaching these texts, give space to verbalize these uncertainties. Allow these texts to provide a fresh language for expressing these frustrations and models of faithful questioning. The path of discipleship is not paved by our assurance or our sure knowledge. Instead, following Christ means trusting in the darkest moments, seeing God in the eyes of those most neglected by the world. But following God is also how believers find spiritual sustenance and imagine a world of inclusion and justice.

Notes

1. See Justo L. González, *Luke*, Belief: A Theological Commentary on the Bible (Louisville: Westminster John Knox, 2010), 98.
2. In his *The Gospel of Luke*, The New International Commentary on the New Testament (Grand Rapids: Eerdmans, 1997), Joel B. Green writes, "Luke's presentation of the inseparability of christology and discipleship reaches its acme in the tightly woven sequence of this narrative unit" (366).
3. J. Clinton McCann Jr., "The Book of Psalms," in *The New Interpreter's Bible*, ed. Leander E. Keck et al. (Nashville: Abingdon, 1999), 4:765.
4. Richard B. Hays, "Galatians," in *The New Interpreter's Bible*, ed. Leander E. Keck et al. (Nashville: Abingdon, 1999), 11:269.
5. See Denise Kimber Buell and Caroline Johnson Hodge, "The Politics of Interpretation: The Rhetoric of Race and Ethnicity in Paul," *Journal of Biblical Literature* 123 (2004): 235–51.

June 30, 2013
Lectionary 13 / Thirteenth Sunday in Ordinary Time / Proper 8
Sixth Sunday after Pentecost

Revised Common Lectionary (RCL)	**Lectionary for Mass (LFM)**
1 Kings 19:15-16, 19-21 or 2 Kings 2:1-2, 6-14	1 Kings 19:16b, 19-21
Psalm 16 or 77:1-2, 11-20	Psalm 16:1-2a + 5, 7-8, 9-10, 11
Galatians 5:1, 13-25	Galatians 5:1, 13-18
Luke 9:51-62	Luke 9:51-62

The theme of discipleship, of the contours of life walking alongside Jesus, continues this week. The price we might pay for confronting the powerful is costly indeed but incomparable to the free gift of grace God offers us all. In the subtle allusions to the call of Elisha in Luke's narrative, we learn that this is a life always on the move and always ready to proclaim the good news at an instant. That good news in Galatians is shaped by freedom, an important but often misunderstood value. This is a freedom according to Psalm 16 that not even the specter of death can restrain.

Gospel
Luke 9:51-62 (RCL, LFM)

Luke 9:51 marks a critical narrative and theological turning point for the Third Gospel. This verse closes Jesus' ministry in Galilee—which began in 4:14 as he emerged from his time of testing in the wilderness—and inaugurates what scholars call the "Travel Narrative." Though Jesus "set his face to go to Jerusalem," it takes a long time to get there. The Travel Narrative runs from 9:51 until 19:28 in a circuitous route that we would be hard pressed to explain unless we blamed a faulty GPS. Perhaps the road is long, however, because Jesus has much to say and do on the way to Jerusalem. Perhaps also this section of the Gospel is meant to evoke the character of the life of Jesus' disciples. The road of discipleship is long and strenuous. Additionally, these nearly ten chapters contain a great deal of material unique to Luke, including some of Jesus' most memorable and distinctive parables, like the parable of the good

Samaritan (10:25-37; see commentary on Lectionary 15 / Proper 10, below) or the parable of the prodigal son (15:11-32). In other words, much of what makes Luke's narrative voice theologically distinctive is found in the Travel Narrative.

There is something about roads that seems to resonate with Luke's imagination. First, of course, is the evidence of Jesus' long journey that Luke inaugurates here. Plus, he's already been living the life of an itinerant, migrant preacher. More striking, however, is that in Acts the followers of Jesus are known most often not as "Christians" (see Acts 11:26) but as adherents to "The Way" (see Acts 9:2; 18:25; 19:23; 22:4; 24:22). The same Greek term can be translated as either "way" or "road." For Luke, it seems, following Jesus means going places. It means going where people are so that they might hear the good news. In addition, the metaphor of the road or the way points to a living, moving faith. Such a faith will not be confined by provincialism and a limited imagination but steps boldly into the world. Like the apostle Paul in the closing verses of Acts, this is faith that is unhindered.

But this is not a faith that leads Jesus down an easy road. Indeed, a critical part of his itinerary will be an unjust trial resulting in the execution of an innocent man. This is a road marked by Jesus' confrontations with political and religious authorities. In a sense, the indication that Jesus set his face toward Jerusalem is not just cartographical but a profoundly political choice. He is headed toward Jerusalem to decry "the powers of oppression."[1] In his trial and execution, Jesus' message seems to have been defeated by the blunt force of those powers of oppression. But this is not the end of the road for Jesus, as we know. In fact, Luke already augurs Jesus' ascension in verse 51 when he refers to Jesus being "taken up." This is not a way for Luke to minimize the importance of the cross in the story of Jesus' ministry but an early reminder that his faith will not return empty. Even as he is taken up on the cross, God will receive him in the clouds (see 24:50-53; Acts 1:6-11).

With his face set toward Jerusalem, Jesus only continues to draw would-be followers (vv. 57-62). These pleas point to how compelling Jesus' message was and is; people were, and today still are, willing to leave their lives behind to follow him. But Jesus' responses are full of insight into the path of discipleship I wrote about last week. First, Jesus explains that following him is not an assurance of comfort or safety. He tells one would-be follower that the Son of Man would find no home on this road. The journey of obedience never ceases for Jesus, for he has no home save to reign at the right hand of God. Second, discipleship calls for the correct prioritization of what's important in life. After Jesus calls someone to follow him, the called disciple asks to return to grant his now-dead father the rituals due to a beloved parent. Jesus instructs, "Let the dead bury their own dead; but as for you, go and proclaim the kingdom of God" (v. 60). Jesus does not promote abandoning families or eschewing the proper paying of respect for the dead. What he is illustrating are the high demands of the call to follow him, especially at this particular moment of importance. Moreover, Jesus' call does not end because we cannot drop everything. "Go and proclaim!" he says to the would-be disciple (v. 60b). Third, Jesus makes yet another radical claim. Another would-be follower asks for a moment to say a final good-bye to his family and friends. Jesus retorts, "No one who puts a hand to the plow and looks back is fit for the kingdom of God" (v. 62). A singular focus is required on this path.

Of course, we cannot deal with this passage and not grapple with the strange request of the disciples to vanquish a whole town of Samaritans (vv. 52b-56). Their plea is in response to the Samaritans' rejection of Jesus "because his face was set toward Jerusalem" (v. 53). The rivalries between Samaria and Jerusalem may be in play. Simple dislike and distrust may lie behind the Samaritan rejection. If Jesus' posture toward Jerusalem is political, however, the Samaritans' rejection may be strategic. They may see in Jesus a rabble-rouser whose punishment may redound on them if they are seen as collaborators. Whatever their reasons, Jesus "rebukes" his disciples but without a full explanation. Why? Luke here anticipates the parable of the good Samaritan just one chapter hence (10:25-37; see the commentary on Lectionary 15/Proper 10, below). While the Samaritans are depicted as villains and enemies by the disciples and have rejected Jesus, a Samaritan nonetheless will become an exemplar of a faithful walk.

What is evident is that these verses mark a clear turning point in the Gospel of Luke. Something significant has changed. So significant is the change that disciples join Jesus on this road only by leaving everything behind. In these radical calls, a sense of eschatological urgency drapes this scene. So also the confrontation between the power of God and the forces that then ruled the earth begins to take center stage. The question for readers and hearers is, How do we follow in such a time as this? When the gospel calls for all we have, when the Gospels call for us to confront powerful institutions and oppressive forces, how will we respond?

First Reading
1 Kings 19:15-16, 19-21 or 2 Kings 2:1-2, 6-14 (RCL)
1 Kings 19:16b, 19-21 (LFM)

The call of God can arrive in unexpected ways. In the wake of God's stunning encounter with Elijah (19:11-12), God commands the great prophet to appoint new kings but also, perhaps even more importantly, a new prophet: Elisha. The balance between the anointed king—a monarch entrusted with great power and wealth—and the mouthpiece of God—the prophet who both anoints kings and condemns their crimes—is a powerful narrative and theological current in 1 and 2 Kings. At core, we find a vital question we still struggle to answer today: How does God grant power, especially to those who are in political positions? But a second question is never too far behind: Who will speak when the powerful fail? God answers both these questions as God appoints both kings and prophets, both rulers who defend the status quo along with their positions of power as well as rabble-rousers who call these same rulers into account when they act only in their own best interests.

Luke 9:57-62 echoes Elisha's call in the account of a number of hopeful followers of Jesus. Elisha himself wishes to say the proper good-byes and follow Elijah. But the call is unique and the time is ripe. Something is changing. Knowing this, Elisha slaughters his oxen and feeds his people, perhaps as a recognition of the new path he is about to follow. God's calls today are no less unexpected and no less radical. What would it means for us to have the compass of our lives changed in an instant?

Elisha's faithfulness to Elijah continues as 2 Kings begins. Even as Elijah prepares for a dramatic departure from the earth, Elisha stays close behind. In these final moments together, Elisha makes a bold request for "a double share of your spirit" (2:9). Having granted Elisha this share in the prophetic mantle, Elijah is welcomed into the heavens, and Elisha can only exclaim, "The chariots of Israel and its horsemen!" (2:12). These verses are a portrait of faithfulness to a teacher, prophet, and friend.

Psalmody
Psalm 16 (RCL)
Psalm 16:1-2a + 5, 7-8, 9-10, 11 (LFM)
Psalm 77:1-2, 11-20 (RCL alt.)

The life of faith in God is dotted with dangers and snares. Psalm 16 encapsulates the trust that faith requires. But that trust is hard earned. Faith is confidence but not ease. Instead, faith rests on the Lord who "is my chosen portion and my cup" (v. 5). As J. Clinton McCann Jr. writes, "Thus Psalm 16 articulates the experience of life and joy, not apart from suffering, but in the midst of it. For those who entrust their lives and futures completely to God, suffering and glory are inseparable."[2] The final contrast in this psalm is between life and death. God shields the psalmist from Sheol or the Pit, which in ancient Jewish imagination was a place of shadows and the dead. It was not hell, for it was not a place of punishment, but neither was it a place of eternal reward. The apprehension voiced in the psalm is not of a fearsome eternal destiny in the afterlife but that the psalmist's life would be cut short. In contrast to the frights of death, faith leads the psalmist down a path of joy and "pleasures forevermore" (v. 11). In other words, the psalmist has faith that God will save his life and fill it with every good thing.

Psalm 77 expresses this same confidence of faith by rooting it in the long history of God's awe-inspiring interaction with the world. All of creation reacts to the very presence of God. No other deity matches up to the God of Israel. No one else has been so faithful to a people. That is, faith rests not on blind hope but on the assurance of God's consistent grace in the protection of God's people.

Second Reading
Galatians 5:1, 13-25 (RCL)
Galatians 5:1, 13-18 (LFM)

Galatians reaches its theological and narrative climax in these verses. Paul couches his specific advice to the local community in a reflection on Christian freedom. Like the lectionary, however, we tend to separate these two by skipping over verses 2-12. To be sure, questions around circumcision are not of primary concern in today's Christian communities. We may therefore make a case that we focus on Paul's theological reflection and let loose his specific pastoral advice to this particular people. However, we will too easily insert our own often narrow definitions of freedom if we do not root our study in Paul's own context.

Paul's central concern in this letter is that the Galatian community continue to reflect the gospel of Jesus Christ. He is troubled that some in the community have convinced others that circumcision and a certain perspective on the law are prerequisites of God's grace. The only prerequisite is Christ and Christ alone. Of course, Paul here is not assailing circumcision and the law themselves. After all, they are central components of the relationship between God and Israel. What Paul is concerned with is that their importance has been misunderstood by some. Circumcision and the law for Paul are not vehicles of grace. Christ and Christ alone is our hope of salvation.

Thus Paul calls the Galatians to live into the miraculous freedom that God has granted us. We are free from sin and death, but that freedom is not for our own sakes. Freedom is not for the individual. Freedom is a matter of the neighbor and the other. We are made free not so we can live we as please but so that we might love one another. This freedom ironically binds us to one another. This freedom is radical and thus a path to slavery to the needs of others.

Remember, however, that in Galatians these are not abstract reflections for Paul. His aim is not to write a treatise on Christian freedom but to address the very present concerns of a community threatened by divisiveness. The question for modern interpreters, then, is how we point out and struggle against the false chains that prevent our embrace of God's free gift of grace and constrain us from exercising the freedom to live for the sake of others.

Focal Points for Preaching

One of the challenges preachers face this week is, of course, rather common when seeking to make sense of ancient documents in a very different world today. What does the ancient world have to do with our world today? How do we enter into some understanding of the long-standing conflict between Jews and Samaritans? Are there any real analogues to our world today? That is, can we imagine a people so despised that we would be willing to rain down fire from heaven upon them? How do we enter into some understanding of the psalmist's fear of the finality of death? How do we enter into some understanding of Paul's radical notion of freedom, a freedom that flees from easy libertinism and embraces our commitments to our sisters and brothers? If we can but help people today understand these strange and yet familiar notions, then they too may be inspired by God to leave all things behind to follow Jesus.

Notes

1. See Justo L. González, *Luke*, Belief: A Theological Commentary on the Bible (Louisville: Westminster John Knox, 2010), 131.
2. J. Clinton McCann Jr., "The Book of Psalms," in *The New Interpreter's Bible*, ed. Leander E. Keck et al. (Nashville: Abingdon, 1999), 4:738.

July 7, 2013
Lectionary 14 / Fourteenth Sunday in Ordinary Time / Proper 9
Seventh Sunday after Pentecost

Revised Common Lectionary (RCL)

Isaiah 66:10-14 or 2 Kings 5:1-14
Psalm 66:1-9 or Psalm 30
Galatians 6:(1-6), 7-16
Luke 10:1-11, 16-20

Lectionary for Mass (LFM)

Isaiah 66:10-14c
Psalm 66:1-3, 4-5, 6-7, 16 + 20
Galatians 6:14-18
Luke 10:1-12, 17-20 or 10:1-9

Discipleship is not solely a matter of right belief. Discipleship calls us to walk on a particular path and live in ways that counteract and protest against the assumptions of a broken world. The texts this week provide a variety of portraits of discipleship. In every case, however, God surprises those who would follow the path of faith. God will send us to unexpected places, to unexpected people. God will then ask and empower us to do the unexpected: to love, heal, and preach the good news that death and cruelty will no longer prevail over us.

Gospel
Luke 10:1-11, 16-20 (RCL)
Luke 10:1-12, 17-20 or 10:1-9 (LFM)

At the beginning of Luke 9, Jesus empowers the twelve disciples to do something radical. He asks them—but also grants them the ability—"to proclaim the kingdom of God and to heal" (9:2). In essence, he asks his closest followers to act like him. Think of this as the ultimate WWJD ("What Would Jesus Do?") moment. It makes some sense for Jesus to send out his inner circle to emulate his ministerial practice. But in our passage, Jesus takes it one step further. He now endows seventy or seventy-two followers to work in pairs and prepare his path on the road to Jerusalem. How? By healing and proclaiming the good news. For Luke, these are not two separate and distinct activities but two sides of the same coin. The kingdom of God has drawn near. How do we know? Because the captives are liberated, the blind are made to see, the downtrodden are uplifted (cf. Luke 4:18-19). The advent of the jubilee year promised in Jesus' first sermon is being proclaimed, enacted, and embodied by Jesus' followers. Clearly, there is a model for faithful discipleship in these verses, but one that is bound to disrupt our easy assumptions about a life of faith.

The first exegetical matter to note is that the manuscripts of Luke do not all agree on the number of followers Jesus commissions: seventy or seventy-two.[1] In fact, text-critical criteria are difficult to apply in this situation as the case can plausibly be made for both readings. If we wonder what the symbolic import of the number might be, we find a number of texts in the Hebrew Bible that mark seventy as potentially significant. One important example is the numbering of the seventy nations of the world in the Hebrew text of Genesis 10. To complicate matters, however, the Greek text of Genesis 10 in the Septuagint actually lists seventy-two nations! Which tradition might Luke have relied on in composing this scene? The NRSV opts for seventy, though commentators will not always agree with this conclusion.[2]

Why does this matter exegetically and homiletically? In both cases when Jesus sends out a coterie of followers to proclaim and embody the work of the reign of God, the number of people he sends is not incidental. For Luke, these numbers are ripe with meaning. Most likely, Luke imagines that the seventy or seventy-two represent the fullness of the world and its peoples. As Jesus sends out these commissioned followers, he already augurs that this kind of work will continue until the very ends of the earth (see Acts 1:8). This is a reign with no bounds, whether national or ethnic. All will hear even if some will not listen.

Like the disciples in chapter 9, the seventy are instructed not to prepare for the journey. They are not to make hotel reservations or take extra supplies with them. They should even avoid greeting anyone on the road. Such seemingly rash actions only make sense if we note the eschatological urgency ringing this commissioning. The time is short and "the laborers are few" (10:2). These are crucial moments, and the work the seventy are called to embrace is a matter of life and death. In other words, there is no time to prepare for this journey. The need is too great for the seventy to gather what they need. Instead, Jesus calls them to rely on the generosity of those whom they would touch with the good news and the healing touch of God. Two times, Jesus specifies that those who are sent are to eat whatever is set before them (vv. 7, 8). First, of course, this highlights Luke's focus on hospitality and table fellowship. Wherever people gather and eat, significant social and theological commitments are displayed. In this case, the seventy commit to God's providence and sustenance through the kindness of others. They also commit to breaking bread with anyone who is willing. Second, this commandment may anticipate Peter's vision of clean and unclean animals in Acts 10. In both cases, the instruction to eat whatever is set before you is not really about food but about human relationships. Those who do the work of God will be fed because God is faithful; indeed, "the laborer deserves to be paid" (v. 7). Even more important is that the universal scope of the symbolically important number seventy and this commitment to eat whatever is set before you point to the worldwide mission

Luke envisions. Eating what is offered us is an acceptance not just of mere sustenance but of the ways and lives of those who feed us. For Luke as for us, breaking bread is a moment of great intimacy and connectivity.

The reciprocity of relationships Jesus promotes here cuts both ways, however. Those who welcome the seventy will see in a tangible way the drawing near of God's reign. Again, how do we know that God's reign has drawn near? Jesus himself provides the response in Luke 4. In contrast, those who refuse to see and hear will hear the good news but not understand and will see these followers shaking the dust off their feet. Moreover, Jesus prepares them for the dangers and obstacles they will face. He acknowledges, "See, I am sending you out like lambs into the midst of wolves" (10:3). The road is dangerous and fearsome. There is great risk involved in following Jesus.

Despite these great risks, the seventy return with confirmation of God's work in their midst. The stunning success of these unprepared but thoroughly equipped proclaimers and healers is a reminder that this is God's work and not theirs (see 10:20). That this is God's work is further emphasized by the fact that this is a manifestly cosmic conflict. The opponents in this war are Satan, "the power of the enemy," and "the spirits." Played out on a human plane, these cosmic conflicts break human lives and cause havoc wherever they go. And this is the essence of the good news. Those cosmic powers, though seemingly invincible, cannot compare to the power and grace of a loving God who through humans speaks the good news and heals our wounds.

First Reading
Isaiah 66:10-14 (RCL)
Isaiah 66:10-14c (LFM)
2 Kings 5:1-14 (RCL alt.)

When this section of Isaiah was composed, Israel likely found itself having just returned from exile. They had previously lived on the edge on faith, far from home but especially the temple where the one true God chose to dwell. Now that they are home, the city represents God's care for God's people. Joy and mourning are held closely together as our reading begins. After all, the exhortation to rejoice with Jerusalem in verse 10 would have sounded a dissonant chord in the ears of Israelites in Babylon. How can this be? Verse 11, however, points to the mournful doubts that must have burdened Israel. Jerusalem, God says, will be a nursing mother whose milk satisfies the thirst of disappointment and despair. The image of a mothering city continues in the following verses but quickly morphs as it is God who takes on the maternal role directly and not just through the image of the city of Jerusalem. God will comfort God's people with a nursing breast and the security of their home in Jerusalem. These verses provide an important homiletical moment to highlight the ways in which depictions of God in the Bible can take both masculine and feminine forms. Scripture is equally comfortable calling God Father and Mother. The mother's comforting breast brings assurance, not of reward in some future afterlife but of joy on this side of life. "You shall see . . . ," God promises. As Gene M. Tucker concludes, "God's word spoken through the witness of his servant Isaiah cannot come to an end, until of course God is all in all."[3]

In 2 Kings, the grace of God extends well beyond the boundaries of Israel. This famous story narrates a powerful general seeking the healing touch of God's prophet Elisha. Someone accustomed to giving orders is now asked to follow the seemingly inane instructions of a foreign prophet. So striking is this narrative that it becomes for Luke a model upon which Jesus builds his ministry (Luke 4:27). The God of 2 Kings and Luke alike is a God who subverts expectations and turns the world upside down so as to show God's grace in all its splendor.

Psalmody

Psalm 66:1-9 (RCL)
Psalm 66:1-3, 4-5, 6-7, 16 + 20 (LFM)
Psalm 30 (RCL alt.)

Words of praise do not emanate from humans alone as Psalm 66 begins. The psalmist calls upon the earth itself to bear testimony to God's goodness and greatness. And yet the praise of God in this psalm is not rooted in God's original creative act so much as how God has moved nature in order to accomplish God's purposes. That is, creation still responds to God's original creative act. The psalmist points to two particular instances. First is the miraculous parting of the waters in Exodus 14–15 while the second is similar but likely points to the fulfillment of God's promise of the land in Joshua 3:14-17 as Joshua leads Israel into the land of Canaan after crossing the Jordan River. In both cases, natural structures will not inhibit God and God's people. If anything, these potentially roiling waters become a path of salvation for God's people. In short, God's goodness knows no bounds.

Psalm 30 contains the praise of a grateful worshiper whose prayer has been answered. Delivered from great danger, the psalmist rejoices while acknowledging that in those dark moments God's presence may seem distant. God can become angry and the night may envelop us, but the psalmist can nonetheless declare that God's favor and the joy that comes with such favor are never-ending.

Second Reading

Galatians 6:(1-6), 7-16 (RCL)
Galatians 6:14-18 (LFM)

Galatians, like many of Paul's letters, concludes with pleas and exhortations. In this case, these are final instructions for a community at the edge of losing its way. Though they seem to be merely practical admonitions appended to the letter, these instructions are as theologically significant as the reflections on freedom in last week's second reading. Easy to neglect, these concluding words often contain Paul's most direct instructions but also the embodied communal practices that are his primary concern as a pastor to these churches.

Isolated verses in the opening of the chapter may seem at first glimpse to be an individualist's manifesto. To a Western eye, verses 4-5 seem to speak of a rugged individualism characterized by self-reliance. Nothing could be farther from the truth for Paul. The scope of verses 1-10 continues the recurrent Pauline theme of communities of faith being a vibrant site of God's work in the world. The freedom Paul described in Galatians 5 is one that ironically binds believers that much closer together and thus requires our commitment to one another.

Paul's closing words are brief but a rather full encapsulation of the message of the letter. These final verses also provide a helpful reminder of the letter-writing process of the ancient world. Paul typically would have dictated his letters to an amanuensis who would record and even edit as he spoke. It was also conventional, however, for the person speaking the letter to conclude the letter in her own hand. Paul does exactly that in verse 11, but this interlude is more than mere convention, I think. He writes with a passion that he wants to see reflected in the very shape and size of the letters he writes. The closing is as impassioned as the letter's furious beginning. There, Paul flouts letter-writing conventions by eschewing a thanksgiving section (see 1:5-6). Here, he embraces convention but with the same aim: to catch the undivided attention of his audience.

Why? Perhaps because in verses 14-16 we find the very essence of the good news in this letter. The cross, a site of shame and death, is the center of our faith. What a strange thing upon which to boast! But for Paul, the paradox of faith is Jesus' power in weakness, life in the wake of death. The call of faith is not just to observe the cross from afar but to participate in its repercussions for the world. Verse 15 then brings us back to one of the main concerns in Galatians. Circumcision or lack thereof steps aside as an unswerving marker of God's approval. Instead, we see God moving in our presence in the "new creation."

Focal Points for Preaching

Too often Christians are paralyzed by their faith. Perhaps more precise is to say that too often Christians live in their minds. That is, we have tended to think a great deal about our faith but too rarely have followed its implications in the ways we move in this world. There is a good reason for this reluctance to turn faith into action. After all, a vital confession both ancient Judaism and Christianity shared is the God-centeredness of our salvation. Simply put, we neither merit nor earn God's grace. God is kind to us unilaterally and beyond all measure.

This does not mean, however, that God's grace does not impel and inspire us to move and to act. God's stunning grace does not mean that a life of faith dwells only on the things we know or believe. Instead, faith will move us. God will inspire us to take seriously the claims of the good news that healing and teaching, believing and acting in response to that belief are commensurate but also inextricably intertwined. Simply put, we cannot believe unless we act on that belief and in response to God's call to step out into a broken and complex world.

Notes

1. See Bruce M. Metzger, *A Textual Commentary on the Greek New Testament*, 2nd ed. (New York: Deutsche Bibelgesellschaft/United Bible Societies, 1994), 126–27.
2. See e.g., Joel B. Green, *The Gospel of Luke*, The New International Commentary on the New Testament (Grand Rapids: Eerdmans, 1997), 409.
3. Gene M. Tucker, "The Book of Isaiah," in *The New Interpreter's Bible*, ed. Leander E. Keck et al. (Nashville: Abingdon, 1999), 6:552.

July 14, 2013
Lectionary 15 / Fifteenth Sunday in Ordinary Time / Proper 10
Eighth Sunday after Pentecost

Revised Common Lectionary (RCL)

Deuteronomy 30:9-14 or Amos 7:7-17
Psalm 25:1-10 or Psalm 82

Colossians 1:1-14
Luke 10:25-37

Lectionary for Mass (LFM)

Deuteronomy 30:10-14
Psalm 69:14 + 17, 30-31, 33-34, 36a + 37 or 19:8, 9, 10, 11
Colossians 1:15-20
Luke 10:25-37

At their core, questions about discipleship wonder what God wants and hopes for us. What shape should a life pleasing to God take? Our texts this week set forward that such a life is characterized by joy and abundance, not burden and limitations; justice and righteousness for all and not a select few.

Gospel
Luke 10:25-37 (RCL, LFM)

Most preachers will likely be unable to avoid engaging one of the best-known stories in all of Scripture. Even people who have never read the Bible, even people who wouldn't even know where to find the Gospel of Luke, even people with no knowledge of the texts of Scripture know what a "good Samaritan" is. This story has enormous cultural resonances and for good reason. It is a marvelous story. At the same time, preachers may assume that all that can be said about this story has been said. Fortunately, the parables of Jesus are rich and complex. They challenge us in ways we would never expect. The parables continue to speak to us because they both arise from a particular cultural context and speak to overarching human problems and situations.

What we most need is to highlight how radical and unsettling these parables were in their original contexts. Though the widespread cultural notion of the good Samaritan means an audience more ready to hear this story, we also have tended to domesticate this story and thus lose its prophetic edge. How might we hone how we tell this story to reveal once again how truly revolutionary Jesus' teaching in this passage is?

In every case in the Gospels, the literary frame around the parable is a critical clue for how we read these texts. In the Gospels, Jesus does not deal out parables willy-nilly. The parables in the Gospels are not abstract nuggets of teaching but contextual stories responding to some precipitating event or question. So what is the particular context of this famous parable?

The pericope begins with a legal inquisition of Jesus. The lawyer's aims are not to learn something from Jesus but to "test" or "challenge"[1] him. The lawyer asks an important question revolving around a key verb ("do"), which will reoccur in the narrative: "'Teacher,' he said, 'what must I do to inherit eternal life?'" (10:25). That is, what actions lead to a life that God will honor with the gift of eternal life? Jesus turns the question back on the lawyer and his expertise. What does the law say? The lawyer responds that what we must "do" is "love." Verse 28 should conclude the scene with Jesus confirming the lawyer's correct legal opinion.

But remember, the lawyer is not looking for enlightenment so much as a sparring session. The lawyer retorts, "Who is my neighbor?" In essence, he asks how wide he must cast the net of love in his world. In the eyes of God, who counts as my neighbor?

To answer this question, Jesus weaves a powerful story with a poignant question—not a moral or some direct instruction to the lawyer—of its own at its end. This is a story we know well. Much has been said and written about the conflicts between ancient Jews and Samaritans, but most helpful in the interpretation of this passage is the previous mention of Samaritans in last week's Gospel reading. There, we already saw Jesus rebuking the casual violence some of the disciples were willing to dispense. Apparently, the division between Samaritan and Jew was so great in the eyes of the disciples that they had no reason to hesitate to bring down fire from heaven. In short, when it is a Samaritan who follows God's law, this would have been rather shocking to Jesus' first audience. One analogy might be to imagine a cultural enemy today doing the right thing while we blithely neglect the needs of some stricken person. This cognitive dissonance is exactly what Jesus is tapping into.

Furthermore, we would do well to remind ourselves of the travails of ancient travel. As is still true today in many parts of the world, roads in the ancient world were potentially dangerous and lonely places. That an individual traveler would meet the fate described in verse 30 would not shock ancient people. Neither would the behavior of the priest and Levite be entirely shocking. After all, Jesus specifically identifies the beaten traveler as "half-dead" and thus well on the way to a ritually unclean state. Plus, "half-dead" indicates a rather dire state. There are significant religious and personal risks the Samaritan will eventually take upon himself.

What ultimately sets the Samaritan apart? Luke reports he was moved by "pity" (NRSV) or "compassion" (CEB). His compassion drives him to care for all the needs of an individual on the brink of death.

As the story closes, Jesus asks an important question: Who acted like a neighbor? In other words, who exemplified the fundamental command God gave God's people to love one another? With some chagrin, I imagine, the lawyer has to admit that it was the despised Samaritan who acted in a way shaped by a God-given imagination about the other. Imitate the Samaritan, then, Jesus concludes. Again, the shock of this conclusion can only be replicated by inserting our own political and cultural enemies in this admonition.

As Justo González concludes, "Jesus' final injunction to the lawyer, 'Go and do likewise,' does not simply mean, go and act in love to your neighbor, but rather, go and become a neighbor to those in need, no matter how alien they may be."[2] In the case of the anonymous man half-dead in a ditch along the road, we are called to help anyone in need whom we meet. Their name, their identity, their ethnicity, their faith are all irrelevant. We know nothing of this unnamed individual, at least partly because much of the world beyond our friends and families are strangers, strangers whom God calls us to love.

First Reading

Deuteronomy 30:9-14 (RCL)
Deuteronomy 30:10-14 (LFM)
Amos 7:7-17 (RCL alt.)

Christians for too long have misread the function and purpose of the law. Especially in our reading of Paul, we tend to pose law over against grace. We too often assume that law is a way that humans try to gain God's favor; grace assumes that only God can choose to grant us this favor. But this easy binary—like so many others—is misguided. The first reading provides a valuable glimpse into Jewish reflection on the meaning and function of God's law. Instead of a burden, the law is a delight and a means by which God visits us with unmerited grace.

In the Gospel reading this week, Jesus recognizes the truthfulness and efficacy of the law. It is a true expression of God's hopes for the world. What Jesus challenges is not the law so much as human efforts to narrow the scope of God's care for the world. "Who is my neighbor" is a question posed by someone whose hardened heart precludes loving others as God loves them. In contrast, the passage in Deuteronomy imagines that "the word is very near to you; it is in your mouth and in your heart for you to observe" (Deut. 30:14).

But what happens when these good commandments are neglected? Amos was a prophet in a divided and deteriorating land. The image of the plumb line is a symbol of uprightness and fidelity to God. Amos records God's judgment here of a people who have chosen the wrong paths, and the consequences are monumental. What should we make of such harsh words of judgment? We ought to help others understand that for God love and judgment are not opposites but are intertwined. God cannot abide with injustice. God cannot simply tolerate the oppression of others. It is not that these people have believed the wrong things but that these twisted beliefs have led to a land and a people characterized by "poison" and "wormwood" (see Amos 6:12).

Psalmody
Psalm 25:1-10 (RCL)
Psalm 82 (RCL alt.)

Psalm 25 imagines God as a wise teacher, a loving instructor, a gracious guide. In each case, the teacher is both compassionate and firm, gracious and wise. The psalmist does not imagine God's instruction as a burdensome set of dictates from which we stray at our own peril. Instead, it is a way of life that the psalmist calls "paths of . . . steadfast love and faithfulness" (25:10).

But how do people of faith respond when those paths are marked by injustice? Psalm 82 gives voice to the voiceless. It is a way for the wronged and the oppressed to demand God to be who God is. The psalmist here speaks in frustration to a God who seems unmoved by the plight of "the weak and the orphan" (82:3). Such a call for justice is an indispensable expression of faith.

Psalm 69:14 + 17, 30-31, 33-34, 36a + 37 or 19:8, 9, 10, 11 (LFM)

The Psalms grant us the freedom to cry out to God and expect God's response. In Psalm 69, the psalmist finds himself in great distress (see vv. 1-3). He feels assailed on all sides (vv. 4-8). The psalmist's pleas continue to dot the rest of the prayer to God. Why does the psalmist cry out? Because he believes God is faithful, will hear his supplication, and will respond (v. 33).

Psalm 19 revels in the delight of walking on God's path. Our relationship to God via God's commandments is deemed "perfect" and "sure" (v. 7), "right" and "clear" (v. 8), "pure" and "true" (v. 9). In the end, the psalm is a sensuous comparison of the law to gold and honey. God's commandments are far more valuable than anything we know. God's commandments are not like mere food that provides sustenance but a delightful, even indulgent, extravagance. What would a life of faith that revels in God's commandments look like if it were understood as a delight and not a mere burden to bear?

Second Reading
Colossians 1:1-14 (RCL)
Colossians 1:15-20 (LFM)

Colossians has traditionally been known as one of Paul's prison letters. Purportedly written from one of his many imprisonments, this scenario adds an insightful glimpse into these letters' instructions. However, many scholars today believe that Colossians was not written by Paul himself but by one of his followers. Nonetheless, Colossians remains a vital resource for preachers today, especially in its provision of indelible images of the Christian walk, two of which I will discuss below.

The letter's theological core is found in 2:6-7. Christ has changed us in radical ways, but Christ has also given us a new and firm foundation. We are rooted to Christ and to one another. For this reason, we can trust God and live by faith. The implication for the Colossians is that they ought not allow anyone to deceive them to think otherwise.

1:1-14. Colossians begins with the traditional conventions of ancient letters. After listing the addressee and addresser in verses 1-2, the writer then turns to a thanksgiving section; this section starts preparing the ground for the writer's exhortations. In particular, notice his appeal to a long-lasting hope whose true home is heaven (v. 5) but also the repeated emphasis that their faith arrived from the very first moment they heard the good news (e.g., v. 6). What shape has that faith now taken? The writer expresses thanks for their transformed lives, starting in verse 9. The thanksgiving section concludes with a particularly potent image in verse 13.

Jesus performed a great rescue mission, saving us from the tyranny of darkness, and has now "transferred us into the kingdom of his beloved Son" (v. 13). The ramifications of this new citizenship are singular and monumental: "redemption, the forgiveness of sins" (v. 14). That is, we do not await redemption. We do not await the reign of God. The reign of God is now and with us.

1:15-20. From the kingdom in which we now dwell, Colossians now turns to the sovereign of that kingdom. What is the character of the one who rules this present kingdom? First, there is an intimate, inseparable relationship between the Jesus who walked on this earth and "the invisible God" (v. 15). So inseparable are the two that Jesus himself takes an active, determinative role in the very creation of all things "visible and invisible" (v. 16). Even the most powerful forces this world knows are not self-generated but infused with God's creative touch through Jesus. Furthermore, Jesus walks before us, having conquered death through the resurrection and sin through his death. In the end, Colossians notes, when we see Jesus, we see the invisible God. Note, however, that all these christological confessions are not abstract theological thoughts. Instead, Colossians here wants to say something about the tenor of our relationship with God right here and right now by confessing the gracious, powerful, divine identity of Jesus of Nazareth.

Focal Points for Preaching

Life in Christ should be joyous and full. When worship becomes rote and dry, when prayer transforms into dull mumbles, when our life is not filled with joy, then we have likely lost the way. Of course, this does not mean that life will be free of pain, that prayer is easy, or that worship will not sometimes bore us. After all, the story of the good Samaritan makes no sense if the possibility of finding yourself at the brink of death after a vicious mugging is not tangibly possible. The world is too cruel, too broken for Christians to dwell in naïveté or false cheerfulness. In the same way, the troubles and distress of the psalmist do not mark him as faithless. Protesting and railing against God, the psalms demonstrate, are an exercise of faith, not a detour around it.

The texts this week together argue that God's commandments, decrees, laws, and the like are not arbitrary rules meant to keep us in line. Instead, they are expressions of the very character of a God who is just and patient but also full of wrath and fury against evil and injustice. Moreover, we embrace these laws in grateful response to God's care for us. And in the end, these commandments call us to a life of service to those who are most marginalized, a life of compassion to those most downtrodden, a life of loving the unlovable. This is the very essence of God's calling on our lives: to be like that good Samaritan who shatters all our expectations by living out God's call to justice, not the world's call to self-preservation.

Notes

1. A translation suggested by Joel B. Green, *The Gospel of Luke*, The New International Commentary on the New Testament (Grand Rapids: Eerdmans, 1997), 428.
2. See Justo L. González, *Luke*, Belief: A Theological Commentary on the Bible (Louisville: Westminster John Knox, 2010), 139–40.

July 21, 2013

Lectionary 16 / Sixteenth Sunday in Ordinary Time / Proper 11

Ninth Sunday after Pentecost

Revised Common Lectionary (RCL)

Genesis 18:1-10a or Amos 8:1-12
Psalm 15 or Psalm 52
Colossians 1:15-28
Luke 10:38-42

Lectionary for Mass (LFM)

Genesis 18:1-10a
Psalm 15:2-3a, 3b-4, 5
Colossians 1:24-28
Luke 10:38-42

The book of Hebrews ends with a catena of exhortations, the first set of which calls Christians to "keep loving each other like family" (Heb. 13:1 CEB). Specifically, Hebrews 13:2 encourages, "Do not neglect to show hospitality to strangers, for by doing that some have entertained angels without knowing it" (NRSV). Encounters with strangers in need of food and shelter are moments of great meaning in Scripture. The intimacy of the provision of our basic needs, especially to or by people with whom we have no bonds, invites us to reflect on the nature of our relationships with one another and with God. What kind of God calls us to open our homes and share our food with strangers? What kind of God might show up at these potentially dangerous but also potentially blessed moments? In what ways is hospitality a practice of faith?

Gospel

Luke 10:38-42 (RCL, LFM)

The conflict between Martha and Mary has led to more than a few bouts of exegetical speculation. Is the story lifting up women by inviting them to sit and learn at the feet of Jesus like his male disciples? Is the story critical of women, forcing them to sit silently at Jesus' feet while the one woman who speaks is censured by Jesus? Is the story an exercise in contrasts between the active and contemplative lives? Does it make sense to identify individuals in our churches as "Marys" and "Marthas"? How do we understand this story, especially in the wake of the resonant tale of a Samaritan embracing his neighbor despite the hearers' prejudices?

The first place to start is, of course, with last week's Gospel reading. The parable of the good Samaritan immediately precedes the story of Martha and Mary. Both contain a number of common themes that encourage us to read the texts in tandem. Of course, they both draw on practices of hospitality and caring for the needs of others. Both involve journeys of some kind (vv. 30, 38).[1] At the center of both narratives is Jesus' instruction about the intersection of faith and caring for the needs of others. Most importantly, in both cases, Jesus shatters his hearer's expectations. In the preceding parable, a villain becomes a hero. In this story, the rigid rules of hospitality are turned inside out not because those rules are no longer relevant but because the very presence of Jesus demands a radical rethinking of even our most ingrained cultural instincts.

What, then, is this story about? Many presuppositions about the "point" of this story have led to a number of exegetical mistakes. For example, Loveday Alexander has accurately pointed to a number of narrative features in the pericope that indicate that this is not really a story of a triangle between Mary, Martha, and Jesus but a dialogue between Martha and Jesus.[2] These are the two primary actors in the story and where most of our attention should focus. Indeed, it is Martha, not Mary, who plays an active role in this narrative. She is the only one of the two sisters who speaks and questions. These narrative dynamics suggest that reading this story primarily as a sibling conflict is inaccurate. Instead, the story centers on the conversation between Martha and Jesus.

Furthermore, and related to this first correction, assuming that this is a "women's" story might narrow our exegetical vision and lead to flawed theological conclusions about this story. Specifically, is this story fundamentally and solely about women's activities in the world? Too often, preachers and scholars alike have found in this story an instructional guide for women's spiritual lives and service. Of course, we underestimate the dynamics of gender at our own peril. Such questions of identity are never too far below the surface of the Gospel narratives, and also the testimony of the Scripture, for that matter. However, some readings of this passage have too easily devolved into gendered stereotypes about the role of women in a household. Might it instead be a complement to the story of traveling men in the good Samaritan parable, a story meant to teach something about the radical faith Jesus proclaims?

When Martha demands Jesus' assistance in encouraging Mary to help minister to her guests (the word used by Luke is *diakonia* in verse 40 and is translated as "tasks" in the NRSV; cf. Luke 8:3), does he really rebuke her? Does he highlight one form of ministry over another? Notice in verse 40 that Martha is distracted or anxious because of her ministering to her guest. So when Jesus rejects her request, he does not thereby reject her ministry. After all, he has been dependent on precisely such *diakonia* since at least Luke 8:3. Instead, as Alexander suggests, "It is the story of a hostess who 'misses the point' of her hospitable activity, and invites its auditors to see the implications of this in a situation where the guest—and the point—is Jesus himself. It is paradoxical rather than paradigmatic, deliberately overturning its auditors' expectations about 'good' and 'bad' behavior—which means that using the story to set up a new code of behavior is to repeat the mistake."[3]

Or, as González concludes:

> The parable of the Good Samaritan calls for a radical obedience that breaks cultural, ethnic, and theological barriers. The story of Mary and Martha is equally radical. First of all, we often do not realize that the first one to break the rules is Jesus himself. He is the guest, and against all rules of hospitality he rebukes Martha, who is his host. And Mary too breaks the rules. Her role as (most probably) a younger sister, or as one living in the house of her sister, is to help her in her various chores. Instead, she just sits at the feet of Jesus and listens to him.[4]

González goes on to note that it is "radical obedience" that links both of these stories. Thus the object of neither narrative is to provide a normative set of behavioral characteristics. Instead, they posit a radical imagination of care and compassion that exceeds the cultural boundaries of the time. The two stories in tandem both highlight radical hospitality as an exemplar of faithfulness but also relativize hospitality within the radically changed world Jesus brings about. Whether we are dealing with long-standing ethnic strife or the niceties of proper hospitality, Jesus makes a bold claim: the reign of God has upturned the tables and established a new order of things. It is this radical obedience that shatters our expectations and upends all the rules for the sake of the marginalized, oppressed, and broken whom Jesus calls us to embrace.

How, then, might we preach this text? Initially, we ought to highlight the radical ways in which an ancient reader's expectations would have been subverted by the story of Martha and Mary. Also important is to avoid falling into old, misguided interpretive patterns that lean on gendered stereotypes about women and purportedly "women's work." Finally, therefore, we can invite people to reflect on the forms of *diakonia* any of us might embrace that fill us with anxiety or distraction. How easy is it to miss sight of the presence of Jesus even as *diakonia* is our aim? How do we know when the time is ripe to follow the Samaritan's example? How do we know we have lost our way as Martha did even while she was serving Jesus?

First Reading
Genesis 18:1-10a (RCL, LFM)
Amos 8:1-12 (RCL alt.)

God is a God of promises, radical promises, unbelievable promises, but promises that cannot be broken. In the first reading, God visits Abraham and Sarah in the form of three visitors. Like Martha, Abraham quickly sets out to prepare a fulsome hospitality. These are strangers to him, and he may simply be embracing the ancient practices of hospitality. After all, without hotels and rest stops, travelers often relied on the kindness of strangers for food and shelter along the way. Nonetheless, he seems to sense that these are not typical sojourners.

After consuming the meal Abraham and Sarah have prepared, one of these three strangers makes an incredible promise. Sarah will have a son. Genesis will continue the story in the coming chapters. Both Abraham and Sarah seem unconvinced that their elderly bodies can do such a thing. The promise comes under threat a number of times. But the promise and word of the Lord never return empty. The child of promise will come.

Continuing the theme of imminent judgment from last week, Amos opens with a pun not easily translatable in English. The Hebrew words for "basket of summer fruit" and "end" are similar and thus the promise of fruitful harvest stands in sharp juxtaposition to the words of judgment that fall heavily in the following verses. The image is of a people who revel in ritual and worship but do not see how they have become empty because their religiosity has no effect on their lives together. They feast while many go hungry. They worship while many are ground down. God sees right through these worshipful motions and detects a heart unwilling to bend to God's ways.

Psalmody

Psalm 15 (RCL)
Psalm 15:2-3a, 3b-4, 5 (LFM)
Psalm 52 (RCL alt.)

Psalm 15 is a portrait of the faithful life. What does it take to abide in God's shadow? What kind of character exemplifies someone who can live in God's presence? The overriding metaphor of the parable has to do with preparations one must undertake to enter the grounds of the temple. Most striking may be that the credentials outlined are largely ethical. Even more accurately, the requirements are relational. They are fundamentally about how we treat our neighbor, so that Psalm 15 might make an excellent commentary on and a useful reminder of the Gospel reading from last week. The hinge of the psalm may be found in verse 4a, the only place where internal dispositions are markers of faithfulness. However, these internal dispositions are bracketed on both sides (vv. 2-3 and 4b-5) by relational commitments we make to others. We will neither lie nor slander because words—whether evil or deceitful—can shatter our bonds. We will not break promises even if doing so redounds upon us, nor will we allow avarice to determine how we treat others. These are the characteristics of God's people, characteristics still sorely lacking in today's world of broken promises and political spin.

Psalm 52 focuses on but one of the ways we disqualify ourselves from standing in God's holy presence: a lying tongue. Verses 1-4 vividly describe a deceiver so lost in a world of duplicity that words have lost their very meaning. God's judgment falls upon such a person in verses 5-7 while the psalmist lauds a life that relies not on lies but on God's steadfastness as the only true root of a life lived in God's grace.

Second Reading

Colossians 1:15-28 (RCL)
Colossians 1:24-28 (LFM)

Continuing last week's reading in Colossians, the second reading finds a great deal of overlap between the RCL and LFM. Since I wrote about 1:15-20 last week, my focus will be on verses 20-28 this week. The power of Christ's identity and work having been established in verses 15-20, verse 21 makes a sharp turn to the implications for believers and especially for Paul himself.

First, Colossians reminds its readers of their previous state in a life permeated with separation from God and even enmity with God. All this changes through the cross where Christ reconciles us with God. That is, Christ heals the wounds that mark our estrangement from God and bridges the gap our "evil deeds" created. The result is both radical and permanent. Believers are made "holy and blameless and irreproachable before" God (v. 22). The old ways are brought to an absolute end, and new life has begun. Nonetheless, there is a lingering caveat in verse 23: Christ's work is beyond us but also dependent on our persistence in faith.

That faith is precisely the one Paul has been proclaiming from one end of the empire to the other. He suffers for the sake of Christ because of God's call but also because of his commitments to communities of faith whether he has founded them or not. In the case of Colossians, 2:1 suggests that Paul has not actually been in the Colossians' midst. And yet he draws on his suffering as an emblem of the truthfulness of his proclamation. Colossians goes so far as to suggest that Paul's suffering is "completing what is lacking in Christ's afflictions for the sake of his body, that is, the church" (1:24). What might this mean? We could have yet another instance of Paul's insistence that we are "in Christ," that we participate along with Christ in God's work in the world.[5] Here, Paul intercedes for the church in his suffering as Christ interceded for the world in his death. Certainly, Paul is not equating the two but noting the high calling he has received from God and by implication the high calling Paul now exhorts the Colossians to embrace.

Focal Points for Preaching

The essence of hospitality will not be found in a "Dear Abby" column or simply in the practice of good manners. Hospitality is not about social niceties or even right behavior. Instead, the radical hospitality present in both the Luke and Genesis passages are profoundly attitudinal and perspectival. How do we see the world and the many strangers who populate it? Are they potential threats to our well-structured social order or a potential opportunity to host God's messengers? Might radical hospitality invite both possibilities? Hospitality is a deeply relational spiritual practice, one God calls us to practice as often as we encounter people in need. Finally, hospitality is fundamentally about our posture toward the world. Do we reach out to all of God's children with open doors, or will we choose instead to draw in upon ourselves and crowd out the possibility that God might visit us in the guise of the most unexpected guest?

Notes

1. Joel B. Green, *The Gospel of Luke*, The New International Commentary on the New Testament (Grand Rapids: Eerdmans, 1997), 433–34.
2. Loveday C. Alexander, “Sisters in Adversity: Retelling Martha’s Story,” in *A Feminist Companion to Luke*, ed. Amy-Jill Levine (London: Sheffield Academic Press, 2002), 197–213.
3. Ibid., 213.
4. Justo L. González, *Luke*, Belief: A Theological Commentary on the Bible (Louisville: Westminster John Knox, 2010), 141.
5. See Jouette M. Bassler, *Navigating Paul: An Introduction to Key Theological Concepts* (Louisville: Westminster John Knox, 2007), 35–48.

Time after Pentecost / Ordinary Time
Lectionary 17 / Proper 12 through Lectionary 26 / Proper 21

Walter C. Bouzard

The Sundays before us stretch through the dog days of August into September and its first hints of autumn. The pace of life shifts from a meandering season of vacations, gardening, and weekends outdoors to the more rhythmic pace of fall. Schools return to session and, following the last gasp of summer on Labor Day, the faithful will more regularly fill the pews. Besides preparing sermons, most preachers will find themselves planning confirmation classes and the annual stewardship drive, making desperate pleas for someone to teach the sixth-grade Sunday school class, and coloring their calendars with reminders of committee meetings and other appointments.

There is a building urgency in the texts before us that corresponds to the quickening pace of late summer and early fall. In the Gospel readings, Jesus returns again and again to the theme of eschatology and the urgent need of his followers to prepare themselves to live in the dawning kingdom of God. Following the instruction that we should always pray, "Your kingdom come" (Lectionary 10 / Proper 12), Jesus warns us repeatedly about the pitfalls of material wealth, pride, and other obstacles that would prevent us from making our lives of discipleship—and thus, life in the reign of God—our most pressing concern. Many of these teachings are hard to hear because they subvert sacrosanct cultural values that are ubiquitous in North America. Counter to a culture that values rank and position, Jesus urges humility and service. In a context where the poor are blamed for their plight and a growing number of Christians speak of the need for removing public assistance as an expression of "tough love," Jesus talks about Lazarus dying before the front door of a rich man. But, most of all, Jesus insists that cultural norms, including especially those that are propped up with religious-sounding language, are slated for demolition in order to prepare room for the imminent reign of God.

Discipleship that subordinates every other priority and value in life to obedience to God in Christ is demanding work. It is also paradoxically liberating. The good news you get to proclaim throughout these weeks is that our sundry obsessions—whether one party or another runs the government, the economy, our future as a people, the congregation's financial plight, and so on (things about which we generally can do little anyway!)—are important only insofar as they can be brought into service to our Lord. Discipleship, life lived in anticipation of the ever-dawning reign of God, relativizes all other claims on our allegiance, love, and trust, replacing them with a vision of what the world will be when the reign of God is manifest to all.

July 28, 2013
Lectionary 17 / Seventeenth Sunday in Ordinary Time / Proper 12
Tenth Sunday after Pentecost

Revised Common Lectionary (RCL)

Genesis 18:20-32 or Hosea 1:2-10
Psalm 138 or Psalm 85
Colossians 2:6-15 (16-19)
Luke 11:1-13

Lectionary for Mass (LFM)

Genesis 18:20-32
Psalm 138:1-2a, 2b-3, 6-7a, 7b-8
Colossians 2:12-14
Luke 11:1-13

Gospel
Luke 11:1-13 (RCL, LFM)

The example of Jesus' own prayer life and the disciples' request that Jesus might teach them to pray (v. 1) provide the common thread that binds the several units in this Gospel passage. In response to the disciples' request, we have Luke's version of the Lord's Prayer (vv. 2-4) and a parable that emphasizes persistent entreaty (vv. 5-8). The reading concludes with Jesus' encouragement that his disciples should ask for what they need from the heavenly Father (vv. 9-13). Luke has taken care to assemble materials that were not originally together, as the parallels in Matthew indicate. Luke 11:2-4 finds representation in Matthew 6:9-13, while verses 9-13 appear in Matthew 7:7-11. Luke 11:5-8 is not found in Matthew's Sermon on the Mount at all and, indeed, is unique to Luke. We might conclude, therefore, that this evangelist compiled these three sections as a comprehensive response to the request of the disciples—and thus the need of the church—to learn what and how to pray. And, in fact, the five short petitions that appear in verses 2-4 do provide the content of prayer. Taken as a whole, however, this Gospel reading reveals far less about the "how to" of prayer and far more of the character and will of the Lord to whom prayer is addressed.

Verses 2 to 4 comprise a shorter, less liturgical version of the Lord's Prayer than the one recalled by Matthew. The absence of Matthew's possessive pronoun "our" in verse 2 notwithstanding, this is a communal prayer—the prayer of the whole church—as is signaled by the plural forms in verses 3 and 4. The briefer format grounds the prayer in the lived experience of the petitioners, both then and now. The request of verse 2 is that God might act in such a way that God's name would be honored as holy and recognized as sovereign not in heaven, but in the here and now; that God's kingdom might break into this world where other pretending powers claim authority and here, in this world, set things right. Thus the prayer is eschatological in its character and hope. In a world where the scarcity of bread was (and in too many places in our world, still is) a life-threatening reality, the communal petition of verse 3 is for God's reign to come and bring with it "our daily bread." The translational difficulty for "daily" (the rare Greek *epiousion*) need not delay the preacher. Whether the proper understanding is "daily" or "our bread for tomorrow" (see the translation note in the NRSV), the petition seeks the security of God's provision for those things that are necessary for existence, and it implies a confidence that, where God's sovereignty holds sway, there will be sufficiency for all. A reference to Exodus 16 and the daily feeding of Israel in the wilderness likely lingers in the background. Distinct from Matthew's version, verse 4 associates a petition for forgiveness of sins (*hamartias*) with the remission of debt (*opheilonti*). The reign of God brings forgiveness of sin (Jer. 31:34; Ezek. 36:25-32; Isa. 40:2; 55:6-7) but also remission of debt (see the Jubilee laws of Leviticus 25 and 27). In short, the petitions of this prayer are addressed to a Lord for whom salvation is defined by (1) sufficiency of life's necessities, (2) forgiveness of sin, and (3) economic justice. Divine concern for this trilogy of human need and salvation in these terms is constitutive of God's character. The church is enjoined to pray for and work for salvation in all three aspects, neglecting none. The last petition of the prayer (v. 4c) begs the hastening of such salvation: may none be tried in agony before that salvation comes.

Verses 5-8 present the parable of a friend who shows up at midnight begging bread. Indeed, as the parable begins, the subject is us, the listeners: "Suppose one of you has a friend, and you go to him at midnight . . ." (v. 5). Jesus does not flatter us: the character is a loud, annoying, unreasonable version of the petitioner in verse 3. This man comes at midnight wanting not daily bread but loaves for yesterday, today, and tomorrow as well! The focus quickly shifts, however, from the petitioner to the man in bed who must be nagged to leave his warm comfort in order to satisfy his irksome friend. He does so, not for friendship, but simply to get his loud buddy off of his doorstep (v. 8). Whatever the original message this parable may have had, in the present context it is certainly a teaching about prayer. But the point is not to convey the idea that God is some self-absorbed skinflint who must be cajoled and nagged by prayer into action. Rather, we are to comprehend a contrast between the reticent householder's grudging action and God's readiness to respond. If a man abed will get up, however unwillingly, to satisfy his nagging neighbor, how much more will God do for those who ask to experience the reign of God?

The teaching of that parable is carried forward in verses 9-13. Jesus' followers are encouraged to ask, seek, and knock as did the importunate man at his friend's door (v. 9). Such seeking will invariably be rewarded and the proverbial door opened (v. 10).

To drive the point home, the image shifts from a grudging neighbor to parents. Verse 11 begins with the question, "Is there anyone among you who . . . ?" Even before the hypothetical cases are laid out, the question implies a negative answer. Surely no child who asks for a fish will be given a snake or no toddler who requests an egg will be given a scorpion? Surely not! And even if a twenty-four-hour news cycle and our collective awareness of atrocities committed upon children make our response to those questions sadly tentative, the point of Jesus' declaration is not yet lost among us. If people who are not saints have sense enough and love enough to give their children good gifts, how much more will God give "good things" (Matt. 7:11) or the Holy Spirit (Luke 11:13)? Infinitely more, of course, for the character of God's love exceeds that of the best parent (see Isa. 49:15-16). The God to whom all prayers are directed wills to give even the Holy Spirit who creates and directs the church (v. 13; see Luke 24:49; Acts 1:4, 5, 8; 2:38).

First Reading

Genesis 18:20-32 (RCL, LFM)

As with today's Gospel reading, the encounter between Abraham and the Lord serves less as a "how to intercede" or "how to pray" than as a revelation of the character and purposes of God. Contrary to all expectations—and in tension with the "tit-for-tat" notion of retributive justice permeating the Sodom and Gomorrah story in chapter 19—here we find both a God who can be persuaded not to punish the wicked for the sake of the righteous and a God whose gracious forgiveness simply is not based on mathematical formulae for calculating rewards and punishments.

The appointed verses slightly truncate the story. Verses 16-19 reveal an interior monologue in which the Lord ponders whether or not to inform Abraham of what is to take place in Sodom and Gomorrah. The speech emphasizes the gravity of the Lord's partnership with Abraham. Since Abraham is to be the agent of divine blessing on the earth (vv. 18-19; see Gen. 12:1-3), he should know what is at stake in "doing righteousness and justice" (v. 19). Indeed, it is the nature of what is and is not righteous and just that stands at the heart of the conversation between the Lord and Abraham. As the Lord's designated conduit for blessing, Abraham's perspective on justice, judgment, and punishment matters to the Lord. So as the two messengers/angels depart to investigate matters in Sodom, the Lord and Abraham remain to discuss matters, while "Abraham remained standing before the LORD" (v. 22). Or did he? The Masoretes altered and marked the text as a "correction of the scribes," and thus acknowledge another ancient tradition that would leave the Lord standing before Abraham (see the footnote in the NRSV). In this case, posture counts. In the ancient world, the person in authority normally sat while subordinates stood (see Gen. 18:8; 19:27; 43:15; Deut. 4:10; Isa. 6:1; Matt. 5:1). The Masoretic scribes, doubtless offended at the image, simply corrected the text and left Abraham standing before the Lord, there to raise troubling questions: Can God destroy an entire city and remain righteous and just? What if there were fifty righteous persons in the population? Will the Lord annihilate the innocent with the guilty? Given the merits of Abraham's case, the scribes might better have left the text without emendation. Either way, we are given a portrait of a God whose relationship with Abraham is sufficiently intimate that God might be moved by the former's appeals. And appeal Abraham does!

The fascinating part about this text is not the bazaar-like bargaining between the Lord and Abraham (fifty to forty-five to thirty and so on), but the manner of Abraham's supplication. Abraham uses normative, orthodox claims concerning the ways the Lord should act as a rhetorical strategy for persuading the Lord to behave in ways that are consistent with God's true character and purposes. In doing so, Abraham points out the inequity involved should the righteous of Sodom—if any be found there—suffer the fate of the evildoers (vv. 24-25). The twice-repeated "Far be it from you!" in verse 25 obscures the force of the Hebrew's aversive negative, a word that denotes the idea of "profane." The meaning of the exclamation is, therefore, "That is profane of you!"[1] That twice-repeated negative accusation graphically surrounds the proposition that the Lord might slay the righteous with the wicked so that the righteous and the wicked fare the same. For the Lord to do so would be profane.

Abraham clenches his argument in verse 25: "Shall not the Judge of all the earth act justly?"[2] Of course, the Lord shall so act! What choice does the Lord have but to spare the city if even a handful of righteous persons be found there? By acknowledging the Lord's sovereignty as "Judge of all the earth," Abraham limits the range of the Lord's activities. Whatever *else* the Judge might do, the Judge must act justly. That understanding likely explains why the bargaining ceased at the question, "What if" ten righteous might be found? Why stop at ten? Why not one? The lesson does not continue because the Lord comprehends the mathematics. Indeed, the Lord likely had understood already with the hypothetical fifty righteous of verse 25. The point is this: it is counter to God's character and purposes to destroy the righteous for the sake of punishing the wicked. To the contrary, this text shines as an Old Testament light illuminating the New Testament notion that the righteous might be the agents of redemption for the wicked. Indeed, Abraham's intercession and the proposal that the wicked might be saved on account of the righteous point us to Romans 5:12-20. There the apostle Paul argues that just as sin and its deadly consequences came through one person's trespass, "much more surely will those who receive the abundance of grace and the free gift of righteousness exercise dominion in life through the one man, Jesus Christ" (Rom. 5:17). The righteousness of Jesus Christ leads to justification and life for all sinners, and his obedience results in many being made righteous (Rom. 5:18-19).

The story ends with verse 33 (omitted from the lection) and the notice that "the LORD went his way, when he had finished speaking to Abraham; and Abraham returned to his place." Although the words "his way" do not appear in the Hebrew text, the translation suggests what has, in fact, occurred. The Lord is headed on the Lord's way, a new way, which ultimately will lead to the Via Dolorosa.

Hosea 1:2-10 (RCL alt.)

Hosea became prophetically active shortly before the death of Jeroboam II in 743 BCE (1:1). Since his oracles anticipate but do not describe the fall of Samaria (1:11 and passim), most scholars suppose that his ministry ended shortly before the fall of Samaria in 722 BCE. This was a period of political and economic uncertainty as the neo-Assyrian Tiglath-Pilesar III began to apply pressure toward Aram and Israel.

Hosea's call is unusual. The Lord commands him to take as his wife a prostitute (v. 2). Hosea's marriage—the pain he will experience at her infidelity and the love he cannot help but express—will be a prophetic sign that illustrates his message. As is Hosea's relationship to Gomer, so is the Lord's relationship to Israel (see chs. 2, 3).

Throughout the book, oracles of condemnation are offset with words of grace and hope. In this chapter, verses 10 and 11 reflect the latter themes as they point to a time beyond the coming judgment when Israel will be restored. Judgment is signaled in the names of the couple's three children. Jezreel points to the place where Jehu slaughtered King Jehoram (NRSV: Joram) and Jehoram's mother, Jezebel, the last of the Omrides (see 2 Kings 9–10), and to the coming "regime change." The name of Jezreel's sister, Lo-ruhamah ("Not Pitied"), signals a reversal of God's compassionate relationship with Israel (vv. 6-8). Finally, the name of a second son, Lo-ammi ("Not My People"), indicates that the covenant between the Lord and those God called "my people" is shattered (see Exod. 6:7; 19:5). Growing up in Samaria, the three children (as well as Hosea's marriage) provided a constant reminder of the divine judgment of the people's infidelities and of the looming consequences for their sin. Nevertheless, the heart of God is revealed not in judgment but in the promises of verses 10 and 11. Grace, not punishment, is the Lord's aim. Finally, while we recognize that verse 11 refers to a human regent appointed by the people, the oracle points us to consider how the New Testament fulfills—in the sense of "fills with new meaning"—the promise of verse 11 in the person of the Christ (Phil. 2:9-11). May that day dawn!

Psalmody

Psalm 138 (RCL)

Psalm 138:1-2a, 2b-3, 6-7a, 7b-8 (LFM)

Psalm 138 is a psalm of individual thanksgiving in which the psalmist offers his praise and gratitude for some unnamed act of divine deliverance. The psalm divides neatly into three parts, each with its own accent and promise. In the first section, verses 1-3, the psalmist declares his praise before the "gods." The "gods" (the Septuagint has "angels") is best understood as the divine council that was thought to surround the Lord (see Gen. 1:26; 1 Kgs. 22:19-23; Isa. 6:6-8; Pss. 82:1-2; 95:3). The content of this praise well matches the first petition of the Lord's Prayer in Luke 11:2: the psalmist gives thanks for God's name, here explicitly linked to the Lord's steadfast love and faithfulness. The Lord's name, synonymous with God's word, has been exalted over everything (v. 2).

Also reminiscent of the Lord's Prayer is the eschatological character of the hope permeating the second section (vv. 4-6). Here the psalmist anticipates the day when all the kings of the earth will have heard what the psalmist already knows: "Great is the glory of the LORD" (v. 5b). He could have added, "Your kingdom come!" It is especially noteworthy to observe that, from the poet's perspective, the glory of the Lord is bound to the Lord's intimacy with the lowly. This is a Lord who might be expected to be concerned with "daily bread." In contrasts, the Lord holds the haughty and those of high station at a distance.

The third portion, verses 7-8, reassures us that the psalmist—and the Lord he praises—partakes of none of Pollyanna's perception of life. Troubles and enemies persist, but the psalmist remains confident that the Lord has him in God's saving hand (v. 7). The steadfast love he celebrated in verse 2 endures; it will sustain him in his difficulties until the Lord has fulfilled the divine purposes for him (v. 8).

Psalm 85 (RCL alt.)

This lament of the community divides into two parts: the plea (vv. 1-7) and an oracle of salvation, likely uttered by a priest (vv. 8-13). For this psalmist, adversity is associated with sin and divine punishment. Restoration of the land in the past (v. 1) is coupled with God's forgiveness and the cessation of divine anger. While the psalm is multivalent, references to the land (vv. 1, 12) suggest the psalm may have been prompted by a famine. Modern rejection of a consequential link between divine anger over sin and disaster (famines, hurricanes, etc.) should not prevent the consideration of the relationship between greed and unbridled consumerism and environmental degradation.

Second Reading

Colossians 2:6-15 (16-19) (RCL)
Colossians 2:12-14 (LFM)

The writer encourages Christians at Colossae to remember that, contrary to what they heard from some in their community, they were already founded in Christ (vv. 6-7). They should not, therefore, be seduced by those who would rob them of their freedom in Christ by convincing them that full unity with Christ depends upon gaining deeper mysterious knowledge (v. 8) or a life of asceticism (vv. 16-23). To the contrary, verses 9-14 declare that God in Christ put sin to death in their baptisms, with a consequence that all self-justifying schemes such as those pressed upon them by their neighbors already have been "nailed to the cross" of Christ (v. 14). The Colossian Christians had done nothing; God in Christ accomplished all that is necessary for their salvation. Consequently, the Colossian faithful should not sacrifice their evangelical freedom and their salvation to such deceivers. Verses 16-23 rattle off a list of do's and don'ts, many of which sound disturbingly similar to what one hears on Christian media broadcasts today! The author of Colossians urgently proclaims that these are the mere human trappings of piety (vv. 22-23). They do not save and they do not constitute faith!

Notes

1. Walter Brueggemann, *Genesis*, Interpretation: A Bible Commentary for Teaching and Preaching (Atlanta: John Knox, 1982), 171. See Job 34:10 for an assertion similar to the present passage.
2. Author's translation.

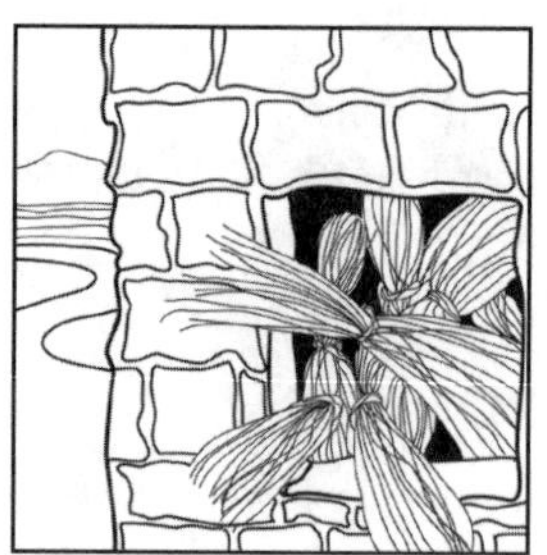

August 4, 2013
Lectionary 18 / Eighteenth Sunday in Ordinary Time / Proper 13
Eleventh Sunday after Pentecost

Revised Common Lectionary (RCL)	**Lectionary for Mass (LFM)**
Ecclesiastes 1:2, 12-14; 2:18-23 or Hosea 11:1-11	Ecclesiastes 1:2; 2:21-23
Psalm 49:1-12 or 107:1-9, 43	Psalm 90:3-4, 5-6, 12-13, 14 + 17
Colossians 3:1-11	Colossians 3:1-5, 9-11
Luke 12:13-21	Luke 12:13-21

Gospel
Luke 12:13-21 (RCL, LFM)

The appointed reading leaps past fifty-one verses of Luke's Gospel from last week's text, including Jesus' general castigation of the crowd that assembled around him (11:29-36) and livid indictments of both the Pharisees (11:37-44) and the lawyers of the Mosaic law (11:45-52). No wonder, then, that we next find words of encouragement and instruction against future persecution, a persecution that doubtless already plagued Luke's audience (vv. 8-11). Jesus tells his followers not to fear (vv. 4, 7) or worry (v. 11), admonitions matched by similar injunctions in verses 22, 25-26, and 32. These instructions surround the parable of the assigned reading and, especially in the latter instances, help interpret it.

Jesus addresses his disciples, but he does so in the full hearing of a throng of followers (12:1, 13, 41), one of which seems not to have been tracking the conversation (v. 13). This individual would cast Jesus in the role of Judge Joe Brown or Judge Judy, arbitrating between the man and his brother over a family inheritance. Jesus, of course, refuses the part, instead exploiting the opportunity to expound on life's priorities by means of the parable of the rich fool. In context, this parable of judgment echoes verse 5 even as it presses toward its application in verses 32-34. Unlike many of Jesus' other parables, however, we are not left to puzzle about this story's meaning. He warns his readers against "all kinds of greed" on grounds that authentic life (*zōē*) does not depend on the abundance of wealth and possessions.

The parable is straightforward. The land of a rich man produced abundantly. Indeed, production was superabundant and the man ran out of storage space in his barns. Captivated by greed, the ancient multimillionaire can think of nothing better to do with his excess wealth than to expand his capacity to store it. Barns would be replaced by larger barns (devices like hedge funds and Caribbean or Swiss bank accounts were not then available!). "Once that is done," he thinks, "I can finally start to live!" But before he can phone the architect and order up blueprints, God tells the rich fool that he will be dead by dawn. Someone else will inherit his fortune. Jesus concludes the parable with the declaration that such is the end of those who hoard treasures but who are not rich toward God (v. 21; see vv. 33-34). Being rich "toward God" is, therefore, that of which one's life (*zōē*, v. 15) ought to consist. Jesus' followers, many of whom were poor and hungry (see Luke 6:20, 21), ought not to worry about their lives or sustenance (vv. 22-32). Nor should they doubt that they will inherit the kingdom of God (v. 32).

Several points about this deceptively simple parable deserve further consideration. First is the source of the rich man's wealth: "The land of a rich man produced abundantly" (v. 16). Whatever effort may or may not have been exerted by the landowner finds no mention. The land produces his wealth. And we can safely assume that the land was itself a gift and came to him as his inheritance (see Num. 27:8-11).[1] This means, of course, that the source of the man's wealth is, ultimately, the gift of a gracious God who made and who continually fructifies the earth. And yet, not a scintilla of awareness that he is the recipient of gifts appears in the rich man's interior monologue. Stunted by greed, his imagination can think of nothing to do with his wealth. Sharing from his superabundance—wealth ultimately given to him by God—is simply not a consideration. Neither God nor neighbor is a factor in his financial calculations or his future plans. He forgets, as many of us do who were born in a society of wealth and power, that none of us is self-made. Anyone reading these words, for example, is the recipient of an education that, whether public or private, was paid for by someone else. We are all recipients of great gifts that leave us, finally, beholden to our neighbors and to our God.

A second point worth pondering is the fact that the text does not intrinsically condemn wealth. To be sure, the parable is a far cry from the so-called prosperity theology, a twisted doctrine which insists that financial prosperity is God's will for all Christians and that the failure to achieve wealth reflects a failure of faith. Indeed, verses 14-34 stand as the antithesis to any such claims. Nevertheless, the parable does not condemn wealth. Instead, God's disapprobation and punishment are invoked because of the idolatrous fixation upon the acquisition and preservation of material wealth and comfort. Wealth will not stave off death and the rich man was a fool to forget that. And he was a fool for postponing life as he ran toward a prize that could never enliven him. The preacher of this parable is likely to face many such fools from the pulpit—or catch a glimpse of one in the sacristy mirror on the way into the sanctuary. In a North American culture where, for example, the U.S. Mint prints the words "In God We Trust" on our *money*, it is difficult to embrace and sustain an alternative vision of life that is "rich toward God."

First Reading

Ecclesiastes 1:2, 12-14; 2:18-23 (RCL)
Ecclesiastes 1:2; 2:21-23 (LFM)

The lesson the rich fool learns too late is one the Teacher sees starkly. In fact, he is dismayed at the futility of discerning meaning not only in his labor, but in *anything* to which a human might put a hand. His opening salvo heralds his dour determination: "Vanity of vanities," he says, "vanity of vanities! All is vanity" (Eccl. 1:2).

The word translated as "vanity" in the NRSV, *hebel*, has no precise English equivalent. Variations of the root show up thirty-eight times in the twelve chapters of Ecclesiastes, nearly half of the total count in the Hebrew Bible. The basic meaning of the Hebrew word *hebel* embraces the concept "vapor" or "breath." For example, the name Abel is derived from *hebel*, a circumstance that implies already that the young man would not last for long—and that well before the reader becomes familiar with his jealous brother, Cain (Gen. 4:2)! The word connotes emptiness, futility, ephemerality, meaninglessness, and worthlessness.[2] And that, says the Teacher, is the sum of all that we can know or experience. The created order is trapped in a repetitive cycle of meaninglessness (1:3-7) and there is nothing worthwhile, novel, or enduring in the whole of human experience (vv. 8-11).

Who is this, then, who makes such a declaration? The "Teacher" is Qoheleth in Hebrew, or "someone who speaks to the assembly." Consequently, Luther presented him as "*der Prediger*," the Preacher. In the narrative world of the book, Qoheleth is "the son of David, king in Jerusalem" (Eccl. 1:1) and "king over Israel in Jerusalem" (v. 12). Those references, coupled with Qoheleth's declaration about his own wisdom and study (vv. 16-18), have led to an identification of Qoheleth with the wise king Solomon (see 1 Kgs. 4:29-34). The attribution is purely traditional, however. Grammatical and historical considerations have led scholars to the conclusion that the book was composed in the third or very early second century BCE. The implication that the author is Solomon purposes to provide credibility to the book even as it embraces the association of that king with the wisdom tradition. That said, Qoheleth wants us to understand his conclusions are not proffered lightly. He has used his powerful intellect and hard-gained wisdom to seek out the answers of existence by investigating "all that is done under heaven" (vv. 13, 16-17). All of this has proven to be a futile effort since the endeavor, like every other human activity, amounts to only a "vanity and a chasing after wind" (v. 14; see v. 17). Nor is there any hope that the sum of human activity ever will add up to more than vanity, for the cosmos God made is static. "There is nothing new under the sun" (v. 9). If something is crooked, it will remain so for so God has established it (v. 15; see 7:13; 3:14).

The assigned reading skips past the first entries in what amounts to Qoheleth's intellectual and spiritual autobiography. His investigative forays into pleasure (2:1-3) and the accumulation of wealth (2:4-8) brought him no satisfaction (2:9-11). Nor was the acquisition of wisdom any more satisfactory. Wisdom is superior to folly, but death and oblivion loom before the wise and the fool alike (2:12-17). Consequently, Qoheleth loathes all of his efforts. He finds it especially galling that the inevitability of his own death means that someone else, be that individual wise or foolish, will inherit all those things for which he labored so hard (2:18-19, 21). The rewards of work and strain lead to a lifetime of days filled with vexatious pain and nights of restless disease (2:22-23). His judgment of the whole is summed up in a single pronouncement: vanity!

Qoheleth's perspective resonates well among young adults and others who live with the mentality of postmodernism (whether or not they are familiar with the term). In an age where absolute truth is often denied, where reality is appropriated in individualistic and relative terms, where existential nihilism prevails, Qoheleth's judgment of "Vanity!" fits. Life's meaning is hidden from us and the purposes of God are unknowable. As a precursor to the theology of the cross, Qoheleth names things as they are lived for him and for us. The "So what?" of life cannot be found in endless, fruitless striving. Death remains the great equalizer. Death will not be denied by pleasure, wisdom, the acquisition of material possessions, or (most especially) ceaseless labor. This may not be an uplifting description of life. It certainly will be a gritty irritant in the oyster bed of any contemporary "praise" worship service that refuses to acknowledge the negativity of human experience including, most especially, death. Nevertheless, Qoheleth's analysis is an authentic description of life as people experience it, at least some of the time. He deserves a hearing.

Nor, finally, is his vision wholly negative. Given that we are unable to discover the meaning of life, given the inevitability of death, and given that the purposes of God remain ultimately hidden from us, we are freed from taking our labors and success as matters of ultimate significance. Instead, he says, we are liberated "to eat and drink, and find enjoyment in [our] toil. This also, I saw, is from the hand of God; for apart from him who can eat or who can have enjoyment?" (2:24-25; see 3:12-13). The preacher may wish to extend the assigned reading by two verses where that gospel declaration appears. Qoheleth would have us understand that by burying ourselves in those things that do not endure and that are ultimately fading, we miss the simple gifts of God that constitute true life.

Hosea 11:1-11 (RCL alt.)

Chapter 11 introduces the memorable metaphor of the parent/child relationship into Hosea's prophetic message. This is a God who bent down to feed the little child, Ephraim. God held Ephraim's hand as he took his first steps and took him up like a parent holding a darling child to her cheeks (vv. 3-4). Nevertheless, the child strayed, betraying its birthright by acts of apostasy (vv. 1-2, 7). Israel is on the cusp of destruction and exile (vv. 5, 8), a circumstance that will signal the sort of servitude experienced long before in Egypt (vv. 1, 5). Although punishment is well earned, the situation agonizes the divine heart (v. 8). Verses 10 and 11 return to the theme of verse 1, "out of Egypt." Punishment is not the last word; the final destiny for God's children is a great homecoming (v. 11; see John 14:2-3). And they will be led there by the fierce leonine love of God (v. 10) where they will see—we will see—Jesus, the Lamb (John 1:29, 36; Rev. 7:17; 21:22-23).

Psalmody

Psalm 49:1-12 (RCL)

Psalm 49 is rooted in the wisdom tradition of Scripture. As far as the assigned reading goes, the sage reinforces themes we have already encountered in Luke and Qoheleth. Wealth is no safeguard against mortality. The wise and foolish perish alike and both leave their wealth to others. Verse 12, repeated in verse 20, asserts that pomp (*yeqar*, preciousness, price, honor) does not endure. People die like animals, like sheep headed to Sheol (v. 14). Unlike Qoheleth, who resents the common end of the rich and poor, this sage rejoices that the wealthy "can't take it with 'em" (v. 17).

Psalm 90:3-4, 5-6, 12-13, 14 + 17 (LFM)

For comments on this psalm, please the psalmody for Lectionary 23 / Proper 18, below.

Psalm 107:1-9, 43 (RCL alt.)

Psalm 107 is a communal thanksgiving. The refrain of verses 8 and 9 is repeated in verses 15-16, 21-22, and 31-32, with the second half of each refrain customized for the content of the section that precedes it. Verse 9 thanks the Lord for preserving the thirsty and hungry as they made their way through the searing desert. When they cried to the Lord, the Lord led them out of the wilderness. The psalm, as do so many stories in the Bible, suggests that the Lord's salvation becomes especially evident in those dry, barren places where we least expect to experience divine care. Verse 43 encourages us to mediate on the Lord's salvation.

Second Reading

Colossians 3:1-11 (RCL)
Colossians 3:1-5, 9-11 (LFM)

Verse 1 begins with the particle *ei*, the marker of a conditional clause, here articulating something assumed already to have happened. It matches and continues the actualized conditional claim of 2:20: "If with Christ you died to the elemental spirits of the universe . . ." The Colossians have so died, presumably through their baptisms, and therefore need not submit to the ascetic regulations—the mere human commands and teachings—that do no more than provide an appearance of piety.

In 3:1, the author employs the same grammatical construction to assert that the Colossians have been raised: "So if you have been raised with Christ," he writes (the particle *ei* asserting "and you have!"), then "seek the things that are above." Thus the Colossians are summoned to recognize their experience of both death and resurrection. On the one hand, the former obviates the need to concern themselves with elemental spirits of the universe (see also 2:8; Gal. 4:3, 9). Being raised with Christ, on the other hand, frees them to celebrate the triumph of Christ who is already "seated at the right hand of God." There is a proleptic character to all of this, of course. The Colossians and we are saved already, but we have yet to see the fulfillment and perfection of that salvation (see 1 Cor. 15:20-28).

Being raised with Christ has implications for our Christian lives. Again, the contrast is between the trappings of piety (2:16, 18, 21; see Gal. 4:9-10) and authentic discipleship, or between the things that are above (*anō*, 3:1, 2) and the things that are on the earth or earthly (*epi tēs gēs*, 3:2, 5). The latter include sexual sins, greed (v. 5), and sundry sins of speech (vv. 8-9). Such sins are characteristic of an old life, of "ways you also once followed" (v. 7), now incompatible with the new being that is "renewed in knowledge according to the image of its creator" (v. 10; see 1 Cor. 15:49; 2 Cor. 3:18). The preacher should, however, avoid using this text as an opportunity to scold the faithful. The imperatives of verses 2, 5, and 8 are predicated upon the indicatives of verses 1, 3, 4, and 10. The Christian life is ever based on a response to the initiative of a gracious God who puts the old being to death in order to make us alive as a new being—and who promises to make us more alive still. As a consequence, human social conventions that divide us are dissolved (v. 11; see Gal. 3:26-28). A discussion of that declaration would be a worthy focus for a sermon. Since we all wear the clothes of the baptized, since we are all renewed in the image of the Creator, since Christ is "all in all," how is it possible to speak of social distinctions (documented/undocumented, gay/straight, conservative/progressive) as matters that should divide?

Notes

1. For a thorough treatment of inheritance laws in the Bible, see Richard H. Hiers, "Transfer of Property by Inheritance and Bequest in Biblical Law and Tradition," *Journal of Law and Religion* 10, no. 1 (1993–1994): 121–55.
2. See the discussion of the meaning of *hebel* in Choon-Leong Seow, *Ecclesiastes*, Anchor Bible 18C (New York: Doubleday, 1997), 101–102, and the bibliography cited there. More recently, see Douglas B. Miller, *Symbol and Rhetoric in Ecclesiastes: The Place of Hebel in Qohelet's Work*, Academia Biblica 2 (Atlanta: Society of Biblical Literature, 2002).

August 11, 2013
Lectionary 19 / Nineteenth Sunday in Ordinary Time / Proper 14
Twelfth Sunday after Pentecost

Revised Common Lectionary (RCL)

Genesis 15:1-6 or Isaiah 1:1, 10-20
Psalm 33:12-22 or 50:1-8, 22-23
Hebrews 11:1-3, 8-16
Luke 12:32-40

Lectionary for Mass (LFM)

Wisdom 18:6-9
Psalm 33:1 + 12, 18-19, 20-22
Hebrews 11:1-2, 8-19 or 11:1-2, 8-12
Luke 12:32-48 or 12:35-40

Gospel
Luke 12:32-40 (RCL)
Luke 12:32-48 or 12:35-40 (LFM)

The Gospel reading is awkwardly apportioned. Verses 32-34 conclude a unit stretching back as far as Luke 12:13 and the parable of the rich fool. Security sought by means of procuring worldly treasure is futile, inappropriate for those who trust God (vv. 22-31), and such treasure is not the proper object of the disciple's quest (v. 31, "strive," *zēteite*). Jesus instructs his followers courageously to liquidate their assets, give the proceeds to charity, and thereby fashion for themselves purses that will be "an unfailing treasure in heaven" (v. 33). "Unfailing," *palaioumena*, denotes something that is declared or treated as obsolete.[1] Handbags constructed of faith and trust will be a treasure that never wears out and is ever "in style" in the dawning kingdom of God.

The balance of the appointed lection consists of the first two of three short parables: the return of the bridegroom (vv. 35-38), the burglar (vv. 39-40), and the two household managers (vv. 42-48). All three parables have to do with the proper conduct of slaves and all three urge diligent watchfulness.

In the first parable, the proper task of slaves is to remain dressed for action, with lamps lit. The act requires diligence, including resupplying the oil and adjusting the wicks. These slaves await the return of the bridegroom and, presumably, his new bride. The reference to the wedding banquet in verse 36 may echo Luke 5:34-35 and its parallels (Matt. 9:15; Mark 2:19-20) where Jesus obliquely refers to himself as the bridegroom.[2] The role of the slaves, therefore, is to remain ever prepared for the arrival of the bridegroom/kingdom. Diligent slaves will be "blessed," an affirmation that begins verse 37 and concludes verse 38 (*makarioi hoi douloi ekeinoi* < *makarioi eisin ekeinoi*). In between the twin blessings we find the bridegroom behaving in ways that are peculiar, to say the least: he prepares a midnight meal and serves the slaves! The master assumes the tasks of the slave while the slaves occupy their master's place and enjoy the prerogatives of their master. The reversal of the master/slave role surely shocked citizens of the Roman Empire for whom social conventions about slaves and their masters were firmly set. In the kingdom of God, such social conventions are voided (Col. 3:11; Gal. 3:28). Masters and slaves, rich and poor alike, are all summoned to wait diligently.

The summons to wait and keep watch continues in verses 39-40. Now, however, the position of the slaves shifts to that of a householder. This, too, is odd since the master of the house (*oikodespotēs*) normally would not be expected to remain on guard through the night. That was a slave's job, an observation that would not have been lost on first-century listeners.[3] Even masters become slaves in the reign of God! The point of this parable is the same as the first: slaves and masters should diligently wait and watch for the signs of the kingdom of God. But one of that reign's signs, evidently, is a challenge about conventional lines of authority. Those who are least powerful are blessed and served by the bridegroom; masters undertake the tasks of slaves. The two parables put a question mark over the authority of those who would lead the household of the Lord. Are they all slaves as in the first parable? Are they householders as in the second parable? And if they are masters of the house, why must they remain awake as though they were not? No wonder Peter utters his nervous question just here. Nodding to the crowd, Peter wants to know, "Is this for them or us?" Are the disciples, Jesus' most intimate companions, not to know the hour? And, more importantly, are they to be no more than slaves to others in spite of their proximity to Jesus?

In answer, Jesus provides a third parable, that of the two household managers (vv. 42-48). Both managers are likely themselves slaves, but they enjoy an elevated role over their fellows. As slaves with intimate access to their master, they are expected to know their absent lord's desires, to anticipate his wishes, and with that knowledge appropriately to manage the master's affairs. The manager whom the absent master discovers diligently working upon his return, the trustee who cares especially for his fellow slaves by "giving them their allowance of food at the proper time" (v. 42), will be rewarded with authority over all of that master's possessions (v. 44). Such a one becomes, in effect, a master. On the other hand, the unfaithful trustee misuses his managerial position. This miscreant abuses the absent lord's trust pointedly by beating his fellow slaves and engorging himself on the food and drink that he knows his fellow slaves need and that he knows he is obliged to give them. Such a one will be killed and his body dismembered upon the master's return (v. 46). The contrast could not be clearer. The good manager tends to the master's concerns by caring for his fellows and, in so doing, by exercising proper stewardship of the master's resources. The wicked manager fails on both counts. The parables conclude with an indication that other rewards or punishments will be meted out on the basis of how well slaves know or do not know the will of their master (vv. 47-48). Thus Jesus answers Peter's question by intimating that, as managers of the household, the disciples' greater authority is matched by an expanded responsibility to see to it that the master's will is enforced. So it is with any who take on the title "Christian." Knowing God's intentions for the world means we are responsible in greater measure for our administration of the master's affairs than if we were ignorant of God's will.[4] It is noteworthy that, in the parabolic world of the wicked manager, signs of his infidelity include the abuse of fellow slaves and a life of unchecked consumption (vv. 45-46). The parable presents an opportunity for reflection on what it is that we modern managers should do in order to be faithful. Do our relationships with our neighbors near and far cast us into the role of a manager the master will commend? Or do we beat our fellows—financially and politically—while we engorge ourselves and get drunk on the bread and wine meant for all?

First Reading
Genesis 15:1-6 (RCL)

Our comprehension of the conversation between Abram (later Abraham, Gen. 17:5) and the Lord depends entirely on the events of Genesis 11 and 12. Abraham, the husband of a childless couple (11:30), is addressed by the Lord and given a promise that contradicts every scintilla of evidence about his circumstances: old, childless, and homeless, Abraham would receive land, blessing, and descendants (12:1-3). He would, in fact, become "a great nation" with many offspring (see also 13:14-17). Abraham and Sarah traveled and lived for untold years of barrenness in the shadow of that promise while their hopes and their bodies withered. In Genesis 15:1, the Lord recalls for Abraham the primal promise, prefacing that with the greeting and command to "fear not." Easier said than done, one suspects, since year after year of childlessness has made holding fast to belief in the promise difficult. Consequently, Abraham protests in two parallel complaints:

A "What will you give me, for I continue *childless*,
B and the heir of my house is Eliezer of Damascus." (v. 2)
A' "You have given me no offspring,
B' and so a slave born in my house is to be my heir." (v. 3)

The Lord's response is a reiteration of the promise of descendants, followed by an illustration based on astronomy. Just as stars cannot be counted, so will Abraham's descendants be innumerable. Note, however, the formula preceding this reassurance: "The word of the LORD came to him" (v. 4). This expression signals, with very few exceptions, an address of the Lord to a prophet (see 1 Sam. 15:10; 2 Sam. 7:4; 1 Kgs. 13:20; 16:1, 7; Isa. 38:4). Indeed, in Jeremiah 1:2 the formula appears as a part of Jeremiah's call narrative, a genre that the present narrative formally resembles: call, prophetic objection, reassurance, prophetic sign, and the commissioning. Ever unbidden, the word of the Lord simply comes to whomever the Lord wills. In this instance, however, the "word of the LORD" comes twice (vv. 1, 4) and thus forms an inclusio around the patriarch's twofold objection of verses 2 and 3. But note that, in so coming, Abraham's fear is surrounded, encompassed, by the word of the Lord. The word of the Lord both precedes Abraham's anxiety and succeeds it. Abraham's past and his unseen future are contained and sustained within the promises of the Lord.

This word of the Lord offers no evidence. The stars in the sky are not *proof* of the declaration, "So shall your descendants be" (v. 5). Nevertheless, the fact that stars serve as the sign reminds us that this word reached Abraham in the dark night. As is so often the case with us, the word comes (Jesus comes!) in the night—in any and every night—when doubt, death, and our own finitude press upon us. The word of promise comes always when we need it the most and expect it least. But everything depends on the promise and trust in the promise! Abraham "believed the LORD," not the stars. The stars the old man viewed were no more numerous that night than they had been the night before. The Lord's declaration did not reverse Abraham or Sarah's age. And yet, encompassed by the word of the Lord, Abraham "believed the LORD; and the LORD reckoned it to him as righteousness" (v. 6). Abraham's faith was based simply on his hope that the Lord would deliver on the promises, notwithstanding common sense and the evidence of his own geriatric body.

Verse 6 is, of course, not simply a pivotal verse in the Abrahamic cycle, but a central declaration of the entire Bible. Righteousness based on faith points us back to Eden and to the relationship that Adam and Eve enjoyed with the Lord in the beginning. Righteousness based on faith defined them; it is who they were before the serpent encouraged them to disbelieve the Lord's intention for them and to "be like God" themselves. And righteousness based on faith points us forward to the heart of the Pauline proclamation of the gospel. The apostle's conclusion that "we are justified by faith, we have peace with God through our Lord Jesus Christ" (Rom. 5:1) is based entirely upon an exegesis of the present Genesis passage in Romans 4. Paul argues that Abraham's righteousness, reckoned to him by God prior to the promulgation of the law, therefore could not be a reflex of any righteousness earned by his adherence to the law. Righteousness came to Abraham in the only way that it can come for any of us: simply by believing that God in Christ has done all that is necessary for our salvation. This is gospel news indeed for people who remain fearful and whose nights are long. We too are embraced by the word of the Lord and with a promise that, however hopeless we feel (or actually may be!), the word of the Lord and the promises of God come to us ever anew.

Wisdom 18:6-9 (LFM)

These verses comprise a snippet from the third section of Wisdom, chapters 11-19, wherein a pseudonymous "Solomon" draws moral lessons from the exodus. Specifically, "Solomon" explains that the divine decision to destroy the Egyptian firstborn children was predicated on the infanticidal program of Pharaoh (see Exod. 1:15-22). Egypt experienced God's retributive justice not only in the tenth plague but also by "a mighty flood," presumably at the Red Sea (v. 5; see Exodus 14). The Israelites were notified in advance (v. 6) so that they might understand and celebrate the divinely wrought destruction of their enemies that simultaneously signaled their own exaltation (vv. 7-8). References to sacrifices and submission to the "divine law" in verse 9 refer to the Lord's commandments concerning the Passover in Exodus 12.

The notion that the followers of the crucified Christ might feel themselves "glorified" by the utter destruction of their enemies and their enemies' children is a difficult one. The text is made more problematic for us by the awareness that much of the world identifies developed nations and North Americans as the Egyptians rather than as the victims turned vindicated Israelites. One homiletical solution would be to allegorize the enemies, treating the ancient Egyptians as symbols of sin, guilt, or temptation that God will utterly annihilate. In any case, the poem celebrates *God's* exercise of justice without countenancing any human precipitation of that justice.

Isaiah 1:1, 10-20 (RCL alt.)

Isaiah's ministry was a lengthy one, stretching from roughly 740 BCE and the reign of Uzziah (Isa. 6:1) until sometime after the death of Hezekiah in 698 BCE. This was a turbulent time in the histories of Judah and Israel; Israel was annexed by the Assyrians in 722 BCE and actually ceased to exist. Assyria threatened Jerusalem itself at least once in 701 BCE. Isaiah was called to prophesy to kings and fellow citizens throughout the changing political and social landscape of his age. The appearance of the relatively rare term "vision" (*chazōn*) in verse 1, coupled with many themes introduced in the first chapter, suggest to most scholars that the chapter is a redacted compilation of Isaiah's sayings, assembled as a sort of overture in order to introduce the entire book.[5]

Verses 10-20 are linked to verse 9 by the catchwords *Sodom* and *Gomorrah*. What was a comparison in verse 9, however, becomes an accusation in verse 10. Perhaps surprisingly to some readers, the sins enumerated in the verses that follow are not sexual; in most biblical references, the two cities become a general symbol of sins of all sorts.[6] In verses 11-14 God's anger is provoked by ritual sacrifices, burnt offerings, the convocation of the assembly on sabbaths and new moons, incense, and prayers—in short, by the entire cult in Jerusalem—not because God despises worship but because of the mendacious foundation upon which that ritual activity was set. "I will not listen; your hands are full of blood" (v. 15; see 29:13). Hearers are commanded to wash and become clean by ceasing to do evil (v. 16). Specifically, they are told to "learn to do good; seek justice, rescue the oppressed, defend the orphan, plead for the widow" (v. 17). Orphans and widows, along with strangers, were the most vulnerable among ancient Israel's citizenry and, consequently, the object of the Lord's particular concern. Maltreatment of these betrayed a misunderstanding of the Lord's word/ teaching (*torah*, v. 10) and exposed the rotten center of liturgical worship. However properly postured, bloodstained hands lifted in prayer revulsed the Lord in Isaiah's day just as twisted worship had earlier in the time of Amos (Amos 5:21-24) and, one can be certain, as it still does today. The good news is that the Lord is willing to wash bloody hands and forgive sins (v. 18). The washing we cannot do for ourselves (v. 16) and the cleansing we need are done for us by other hands, hands that are both bloody and pierced. And we can count on that washing because "the mouth of the LORD has spoken" (v. 20; see Isa. 40:5; 58:14).

Psalmody
Psalm 33:12-22 (RCL)
Psalm 33:1 + 12, 18-19, 20-22 (LFM)

Although not an acrostic, the twenty-two verses of this hymn, equivalent to the total number of letters in the Hebrew alphabet, perhaps intend to convey the praise of God that extends from "A to Z." The imperatives in verses 1-3 summon the congregation to praise while verses 4-19 provide the grounds for that call. Verses 4-11 speak of the Lord's words and pronouncements. "The *word of the Lord* is upright" (v. 4) and the means by which the heavens were made (v. 6a; see, too, the creative power of the "breath [*ruach*] of his mouth" in v. 6b). Verse 9 reports that the Lord *spoke* and the earth came to be, and that he *commanded* and it stood fast. The *counsel* of the Lord (v. 11) upsets that of the nations and their plans.

Verses 12-19 shift attention to the Lord's oversight of God's people and all humankind. The Lord *looks* and *sees* (v. 13); the Lord *watches* from heaven (v. 14) and *observes* (v. 15) human deeds. Whereas a king cannot be delivered (*natsal*) by his army or a war horse (vv. 16-17), the *eye of the Lord*—the consideration of the Lord—on those who fear him (v. 18) is sufficient to deliver (*natsal*, v. 19). The final verses include a statement of trust (vv. 20-21) and an appeal that the Lord's steadfast love (*khesed*) would remain with those who trust in the Lord. Indeed, it is hope in the Lord's steadfast love that is the basis of the psalmist's declaration of trust (v. 20) and the cause of his wonder (v. 5). Whether the preacher focuses on the power of God's word (including, of course, the Word incarnate [John 1:1-18]), the security that comes from the Lord's oversight, or the confidence of those who hope in the Lord's steadfast love, the homily should evoke the praise and joy with which this psalm begins and ends (vv. 1-2, 22).

Psalm 50:1-8, 22-23 (RCL alt.)

The natural three-part division of this psalm is not reflected in the pericope. Verses 1-6 announce the arrival of God from Zion for judgment. Verses 7-15 and 16-21 are two speeches of God (likely offered by a priest) expressing divine dissatisfaction with some aspect of worship. They doubtless reflect the sort of critique offered by Isaiah in today's semi-continuous lesson. Scrupulously made sacrifices and burnt offerings were disconnected to authentic thankfulness and obedience to God's statutes. Both divine statements end with (1) an implied threat or threats (vv. 12-13, 22), followed by (2) imperative verbs that summon the worshipers to offer sacrifices of thanksgiving (vv. 14, 23a), and conclude with (3) a divine promise of rescue (vv. 15, 23b).

Second Reading

Hebrews 11:1-3, 8-16 (RCL)
Hebrews 11:1-2, 8-19 or 11:1-2, 8-12 (LFM)

Chapter 11 contains the roll call of that "great cloud of witnesses" (12:1) who lived and died in faith, that is, who lived and died in "the assurance of things hoped for, the conviction of things not seen" (v. 1). The translation is difficult here. "Assurance" is rendered from *hypostasis*, a word that here denotes something's substantial nature or real essence. The noun appears in Hebrews 1:3 where the Son is declared to be the exact imprint of God's *hypostasis*, there translated as "very being" in the NRSV and "his nature" in the RSV. Both passages are ontological claims. According to Hebrews 11:1, therefore, faith is the genuine substance, the essence of that for which we hope and, moreover, conviction of unseen things (*pragmatōn*) that actually are.[7] Verse 3 clarifies the author's meaning. The truth undergirding the world's existence is the word of God, not the things that can be seen. Our spiritual ancestors found approval because they clung to a vision of reality as it essentially *was* and which *was becoming more fundamentally* itself as they awaited the perfection or completion that came with Christ (vv. 39-40).

Chief among the heroes is the patriarch Abraham (vv. 8-19) who, along with Sarah (v. 11), is praised for having lived and acted in the conviction of the promise of land and descendants. The author cites Genesis 15:5-6 in verse 12 in a way that further expands the first reading appointed in the RCL for this Sunday. If Abraham's righteousness depended upon his sheer belief in God's promises—and it did!—the patriarch also *acted* in the conviction that God's word would come to pass. He set out for an unknown destination (v. 8), "he received the power of procreation" and employed it (v. 11), and he did not flinch at offering the son of the promise (vv. 17-19), all by faith. In short, "the assurance of things hoped for" and "the conviction of things not seen" impel action, for Christ's sake, as we live. Hebrews 12 and 13 provide a blueprint for Christian action.

Notes

1. In Heb. 8:13 another passive participle of this verb appears in reference to the obsolescence of the old covenant. Hebrews 1:11, on the other hand, employs the verb to contrast the permanence of the created order with the eternal presence of God. Earth's foundations and the heavens will perish: "they will all wear out like clothing."

2. For the image of the wedding feast as a metaphor for the kingdom of God, see Matt. 25:1-13 and Rev. 21:2-3, 9.
3. Richard Vinson, *Luke*, Smith & Helwys Bible Commentary (Macon, GA: Smyth & Helwys, 2008), 428.
4. Justo L. González, *Luke*, Belief: A Theological Commentary on the Bible (Louisville: Westminster John Knox, 2010), 164.
5. Patricia K. Tull, *Isaiah 1–39*, Smith & Helwys Bible Commentary (Macon, GA: Smyth & Helwys, 2010), 50–51.
6. In Ezek. 16:56, for example, Sodom is a "byword" (*shemu'ah*) for a people that had "pride, excess of food, and prosperous ease, but did not aid the poor and needy" (Ezek. 16:49).
7. Similarly, in Rom. 8:24-25, Paul describes hope in that which is not seen as the basis of salvation.

August 18, 2013
Lectionary 20 / Twentieth Sunday in Ordinary Time / Proper 15
Thirteenth Sunday after Pentecost

Revised Common Lectionary (RCL)

Jeremiah 23:23-29 or Isaiah 5:1-7
Psalm 82 or 80:1-2, 8-19
Hebrews 11:29—12:2
Luke 12:49-56

Lectionary for Mass (LFM)

Jeremiah 38:4-6, 8-10
Psalm 40:2, 3, 4, 18
Hebrews 12:1-4
Luke 12:49-53

Gospel
Luke 12:49-56 (RCL)
Luke 12:49-53 (LFM)

The Gospel reading picks up where last week's lection left off, when Jesus said, "Everyone to whom much has been given, much will be required" (v. 48). Jesus did not exclude himself from this pronouncement. Verses 49-53, the first of three short passages in today's reading, have to do with eschatological expectation and Jesus' own stress until the end comes. It may seem odd that the Prince of Peace describes himself as someone who has come to toss Molotov cocktails upon the earth (v. 49), but so he has. He has come not to bring peace but fire, not unity but discord and division (vv. 49, 51). It may be that we are to understand that the disruption of intimate relationships was less the *intention* of Jesus' mission than it was a function of his message. As we saw last week, the coming of the reign of God carries with it the reversal of social conventions as well as an expectation of right conduct by those servants who know their master's will. Fidelity to the word of God provides occasion for division and conflict, as painful as that may be for believers and, as we can see, for Jesus. Even within the company of disciples, the church, one sees fire and division over theological differences, social issues, worship practices, and so much more.

The eschatological accent continues in the next two sections. In the first, Jesus charges some in the crowd with hypocrisy. The weather signs in Palestine are easily interpreted. A west wind from the Mediterranean Sea brings rain; a wind blowing from the south or southwest brings air baked by the desert. Knowledge of the impending reign of God is no less obvious, but some in the crowd—and likely a few in the intimate circle of disciples—would rather ignore the summons to live now as though the reign of God were a present reality with Jesus. That reign is a present reality, of course, even if we must acknowledge that God's reign is not yet fully manifest and even if we still pray, "Your kingdom come." Already we can see the clouds. Already we can feel the heat of judgment. "Why do you not know how to interpret the present time?" Jesus demands (v. 56). And yet we continue as though systems of injustice are not scheduled for a regime change—especially those systems that leave some impoverished, others discriminated against, still more marginalized, and all without hope. Racism, for example, is scheduled for demolition, as are financial systems that leave entire nations impoverished and starving. Corporations that wantonly harm our human commonwealth that is the environment are headed for the ash pit. And inasmuch as we benefit from accepting the status quo (as though it were not Jesus' intention that such things be burned [v. 49]), we are liable to judgment. We have heard this already from Mary: "He has filled the hungry with good things, and sent the rich away empty" (Luke 1:53). Jesus assured his listeners of the same in the Sermon on the Plain when he declared that the poor and hungry will be filled while the self-satisfied rich will be sent away hungry and weeping (see Luke 6:20-26). Since changes of this magnitude are already under way, settle your case now! In the short parable of verses 57-59, Jesus indicates that once the hour of judgment has come, it will be too late for us to make amends. And it is *us* to whom Jesus speaks: "Thus, when *you* go with *your* accuser before a magistrate . . ." (v. 58). It is better, therefore, to be reconciled prior to the hour of judgment, whether that judgment comes (at last!) at the promised reign of God or when we are brought before the judgment seat of Christ (Rom. 14:10; 2 Cor. 5:10). The parable pushes us to consider who our accusers might be, both as individuals and as a people, and why they might accuse us. The point, of course, is not that God is anxious to judge and punish. Like the prophets of the Old Testament who said, "Repent or else!" Jesus' pronouncements intend to lead us to live as citizens of the kingdom that is ever approaching and, paradoxically, already here.

First Reading
Jeremiah 23:23-29 (RCL)

Jeremiah 23:9-40 makes up the longest continuous treatment on the subject of false prophecy in the Hebrew Bible. Verses 23-32 comprise the fifth of six units. Although omitted from the lectionary, verses 30-33 summarize many of the themes that precede it.

The passage begins with a series of three rhetorical questions, all aimed to dispel the erroneous notion that the Lord is too far removed from the affairs of people to be concerned with the shenanigans of the false prophets. The question of verse 23, "Am I a God when near, Yahweh demands, and not a God when far away?" (NJB), can only be answered in the affirmative. Consequently, no one "can hide in secret places" so as to remain unseen by the Lord. "Do I not fill heaven and earth?" asks the Lord (v. 24). Absolutely! As a consequence, the Lord is fully present when the false prophets claim to have received a divine word through a dream, when they speak, and when they lead others astray. The issue was not that a prophetic word was incompatible with dreams[1] but, rather, that these dreamers prophesied lies. They proclaimed the "deceit of their own hearts" (v. 26), a phrase we should understand as "their own thoughts," since, in Hebrew anthropology, the heart was the locus of reason and thought. Worse, they conspired to make people forget the Lord's name, and that in direct violation of the law (Deut. 13:1-5). In verses 28 and 29 the Lord challenges such dreamers to a contest. Let them utter their dreams while an authentic prophet like Jeremiah faithfully speaks the word of the Lord. The results will be like comparing combustible but useless chaff with the nourishment that comes from wheat. No ephemeral dream, the Lord's word achieves its own end (see Isa. 55:10-11). The word of the Lord burns like fire and smashes rocks.

Although the images of verse 29 are often understood as signs of judgment, fire is more often associated with the divine presence (e.g., Exod. 3:2; 19:18; 40:38; Deut. 1:33; 1 Kgs. 18:24). The "hammer that breaks a rock in pieces" is harder to interpret since the word *hammer* occurs elsewhere only in Isaiah 41:7, referring to a tool of artisans, and Jeremiah 50:23, where Babylon is likened to a hammer of the whole earth, now broken. The equally rare verb "breaks" (*yefotsets*) occurs beyond the present context only in Job 16:12 and Habakkuk 3:6. In both of these instances, however, the subject is the Lord and, in Habakkuk, the context describes God's advent. It seems likely, therefore, that we are to understand that God is present *in and through* God's word. The God who is both far off and near, the Lord who fills the earth, is the one who fills God's word with power as well. Such a claim ought to embolden the preacher and her listeners. Since the Lord is present in God's word, the claims of false prophets must collapse before it. While few today would claim to be prophets (there are a few!), there remain many who weave dreams and speak with self-proclaimed authority about the economy, national prosperity, social conventions, and more with such force that they, too, would make people forget the Lord (v. 27). Not only does the Lord oppose any and all who would lead God's people to fear, love, and trust other powers or gods, but we have been given a word—and a Word—that defeats them.

Jeremiah 38:4-6, 8-10 (LFM)

Jeremiah once again reaps the reward of a prophet who speaks an unpopular word. In consequence of his announcement urging surrender to the Babylonians (vv. 2-3; see 21:8-9; 38:17-23), powerful men complained to King Zedekiah that Jeremiah ought to be put to death (vv. 1, 4). His message, they said, undermined the war effort. In their minds, Jeremiah sought not the welfare (*shalom*) of the people, but their harm. Zedekiah, likely helpless to act independently under the thumb of Egyptian hegemony (v. 5), surrenders the prophet to the pro-Egyptian officials. Rather than kill him outright, however, these officials lower Jeremiah into the muddy bottom of Prince Malchiah's nearly dry water cistern, where he will surely starve to death (v. 9).

The mention of the owner of the cistern in verse 6 may not be incidental. Malchiah means "My King is Yah(weh)." The prince himself is not an actor in the drama, but another individual, an Ethiopian royal servant named Ebed-melech, straightaway comes on the scene. Ebed-melech means "Servant of the King" and, although he serves Zedekiah, the juxtaposition of his name in verse 7 with that of the royal prince in verse 6 hints that he is actually in the service of King Yahweh, the Lord. Certainly Ebed-melech's behavior is exemplary of a servant of the Lord, appearances notwithstanding. He is, after all, (1) an Ethiopian, and therefore a foreigner; (2) a servant; and (3) a eunuch, and therefore excluded from full participation in the religious life of the temple (see Deut 23:1; Lev. 21:18-21). He makes Zedekiah aware of Jeremiah's plight and secures permission to rescue Jeremiah from the cistern. Ebed-melech finds mention but once more in Jeremiah: in 39:15-18 Jeremiah is commanded to go and tell Ebed-melech that he shall neither become a prisoner of war nor die as a consequence of the Babylonian siege. Instead, "you shall have your life as a prize of war, because you have trusted in me, says the LORD" (v. 18).

Without Ebed-melech, Jeremiah's prophetic ministry—and his life—would have been considerably shorter. Ebed-melech serves as a model for a life of service. Moreover, his negative status as a foreigner, as a person who is apparently neither rich nor wealthy, and as someone whose genitalia (or lack thereof!) is a problem for the community of faith, ought to cause a reconsideration of who God might choose to use as a servant.

Isaiah 5:1-7 (RCL alt.)

There is little scholarly consensus on the genre of this poem, although the designation "juridical parable" suits.[2] A juridical parable invites its hearers to convict themselves by reaching a judgment about a situation in the parable before recognizing themselves. In this instance, the prophet tells of his beloved who carefully constructs a vineyard. Isaiah's hearers would have no problem recognizing the trope as a reference to Israel (see Hos. 10:1; Jer. 2:2; Ezek. 19:10-14; Ps. 80:8-13), although they might not have anticipated the twist at the end of verse 2. Though every effort was taken to perfect the vineyard with the expectation that it would yield grapes, it produced "wild grapes" (*be'ushim*, v. 2).[3] A description of that frustrated expectation is repeated in verse 4b, but now the speaker is the prophet's "beloved." The indictment surrounds the summons to judgment in verses 3 and 4a. The only possible answer to the beloved's charges, of course, is a verdict of guilt. Without waiting for an answer, the speaker pronounces judgment. The vineyard will be utterly destroyed and made a waste. If any lingering doubts about the identity of the beloved remain, they are resolved by the declaration that the speaker would command the clouds (v. 6). The pronouncement of verse 7 discloses the meaning of the poem. The case against the people of Judah is ironclad. The disappointed expectation for fine fruit in verses 2 and 4 is matched by the play on words in 7b. The Lord "expected justice [*mishpat*], but saw bloodshed [*mishpakh*]; righteousness [*tsedaqah*], but heard a cry [*tse'qah*]!" Specific accusations occupy the balance of Isaiah 5, significantly beginning with the charge of avaricious acquisition so that "there is room for no one but you." Once again we see that a constitutive characteristic of the God of Israel is a concern for justice and righteousness. Where that is absent, the Lord remains prepared to act.

Psalmody

Psalm 82 (RCL)

This brief psalm has us peering into the divine council. God is seated upon a throne before the assembled ranks of "the gods," the pagan deities that were presumed to help rule the world (see Pss. 89:5-7; 95:3; Deut. 32:8). God tries and convicts these deities on grounds they have judged unjustly and have shown partiality to the wicked (v. 2). "Wicked" (*resha'im*) could legitimately be translated "criminals" here and in verse 4. The standards of justice are the same for the entire human family, namely justice for those who are otherwise defenseless. The four verbs of verses 3 and 4 are all imperatives: give justice, maintain the right, rescue, deliver! Failure to do this has threatened to topple the earth from its foundations (v. 5). The psalm concludes with the pronouncement of a death penalty for the gods (v. 7) and an appeal from the worshiping congregation that God might bring justice to all the nations (v. 8).

While we no longer subscribe to the henotheistic presuppositions of this psalm, it takes little imagination to picture other powers (corporate, political) that fail the test of justice by favoring the wicked/criminal and denying justice to the powerless. Judgment for them is assured, even as we pray, "Rise up, O God, judge the earth!"

Psalm 40:2, 3, 4, 18 (LFM)

The few verses appointed for this lovely psalm by the LFM employ the versification of the Vulgate, reproduced in the New American Bible (NAB), in which the superscription is counted as verse 1. Verses 2-4 constitute an individual prayer of thanksgiving. The psalmist recalls a time of distress from which the Lord delivered him. The images are multivocal: the pit and miry bog can be incorporated into the lived experience of anyone praying this psalm, as can the salvific images of feet set on a rock and secure steps. The psalmist avers that, because of his song of salvation, others will see and fear (*yir'u*; the NAB's "look on in awe" well captures the meaning) and trust the Lord. Verse 18 in the NAB reflects a turn in the circumstances of the psalmist recorded in verse 12 (v. 11 in the NRSV) where the psalmist once again perceives his need for rescue. At the end, the psalmist expresses his confidence in the Lord's concern and prays for a speedy deliverance.

In a modern culture that largely privatizes faith, the psalm is an important reminder of the strength that comes from sharing our faith stories. Whether we sing a song of deliverance or one that confesses "I am poor and needy," honest testimony allows the body of Christ, the church, to experience the comfort of God through the mutual conversation and consolation of believers.

Psalm 80:1-2, 8-19 (RCL alt.)

This communal lament begins with a summons for God to deliver the people. The images in the opening verses are royal ones. God, the king, is a shepherd for his people (2 Sam. 5:2; 1 Chron. 11:2; Ezek. 37:24; Ps. 23:1) seated above the cherubim (1 Sam. 4:4; 2 Sam. 6:2; Ps. 99:1; Isa. 37:16). God the king should stir power up, come (v. 2), restore, and look with favor (v. 3). The refrain of verse 3 is repeated in verses 7 and 19 and thus frames the bulk of the assigned reading from this psalm. In verses 8-13 the psalmist recalls the deliverance of Israel from Egypt and settlement in the land. Viticulture images predominate. Israel was the vine carried from Egypt (v. 8, the exodus) and transplanted in ground cleared for it (v. 9, the conquest). The vine grew enormous (vv. 10, 11) as, the psalmist presumed, was God's purpose. And yet, unaccountably, disaster struck. The psalmist does not flinch at laying the responsibility for the nation's plight at the feet of God: "Why then have *you* broken down its walls? (v. 12; see vv. 4-6). God is by implication also responsible for the ravaging of the fruit and the ravages of the boar (v. 13).

The exact historical circumstances to which the psalm refers cannot be known. The reference to the Assyrians in the superscription of the Septuagint reveals that the translators responsible for that version believed that the psalm found its inspiration in the destruction of the northern kingdom of Israel in 722 BCE. Certainly the psalmist had in mind a horrific destruction of the entire vine/population (vv. 15-16). As a whole, verses 14-19 are a prayer for deliverance, accompanied by the promise of future faithfulness (v. 18).

The psalm is an appropriate selection for reading with Isaiah 5. Unlike in that poem, however, any hint that sin or rebellion precipitated the national crisis is muted to near silence in verse 4. Rather than focus on the cause, the psalmist concentrates on the solution. God who is both king and able to save (vv. 1-2) should restore and turn with favor once again toward the nation. Only when God's face shines upon God's people, that is, when God is favorably inclined toward them, is there hope of salvation. In the canonical order of the book of Psalms, the call for collective praise that is Psalm 81 signals that the prayer for rescue was answered.

Second Reading

Hebrews 11:29—12:2 (RCL)
Hebrews 12:1-4 (LFM)

Remarks on this continue from those appearing in Lectionary 19 / Proper 14, above. The recitation of heroes in Genesis 11 leads to the conclusion that those paragons of faith died before attaining perfection (*teleiōthōsin*). The verb is an important one for the author of Hebrews (Heb. 2:10; 5:9; 7:19, 28; 9:9; 10:1, 14; 12:23; cf. John 19:28). For something to be perfected means that it is "complete" and that it has come to its goal. The author asserts that these faith heroes had reached that end for which they hoped and believed. That hope has been perfected for them and for us in the Christ event. Consequently, and supported by "so great a cloud of witnesses," we should imitate Christ, the "pioneer and perfecter" of our faith (see Heb. 2:10) who endured the cross for the sake of the state of joy set before him (see Matt. 25:21, 23; Phil. 2:5-11). The author implies that his readers endure hostility from sinners (v. 3; see also the text-critical note in the NRSV). Christ had likewise endured before them. Therefore, they also should struggle against sin and against those who might draw blood (v. 4), regarding their sufferings as divine discipline (vv. 5-11). While North American Christians rarely suffer the sort of bloody trials experienced by the readers of Hebrews, the text does warn us that we can expect difficulties and hardships. This is a helpful word in a culture where the Christian's success, happiness, well-being, and prosperity are too often proclaimed as an assured benefit of faith. Lack of success in those areas does not signal faith's failure, and we do well to consider Christ's endurance so that we might not grow weary or lose heart (v. 3).

Notes

1. To the contrary, see Num. 12:6; Joel 2:28. Examples of the divine word coming in dreams occur in Gen. 20:3, 6; 28:12; 31:24; Dan. 1:17; 2:2ff. Presumably, God spoke to Balaam in a dream (Num. 22:8-9).
2. Patricia K. Tull, *Isaiah 1–39*, Smyth & Helwys Bible Commentary (Macon, GA: Smyth & Helwys, 2010), 119. Tull draws from the work of Uriel Simon, "The Poor Man's Ewe-Lamb: An Example of a Juridical Parable," *Biblica* 48 (1967): 207–42; and Gale Yee, "A Form-Critical Study of Isaiah 5:1-7 as a Song and a Juridical Parable," *Catholic Biblical Quarterly* 43 (1981): 30–40.
3. The form occurs only here and in v. 4, so the translation "wild grapes" is derived on the presumption of antithetical parallelism. The stem upon which the noun is based, *ba'ush*, means to have a bad smell and is often associated with the smell of rotting flesh. See Isa. 34:3; 50:2; Joel 2:20; Amos 4:10.

August 25, 2013
Lectionary 21 / Twenty-First Sunday in Ordinary Time / Proper 16
Fourteenth Sunday after Pentecost

Revised Common Lectionary (RCL)
Isaiah 58:9b-14 or Jeremiah 1:4-10
Psalm 103:1-8 or 71:1-6
Hebrews 12:18-29
Luke 13:10-17

Lectionary for Mass (LFM)
Isaiah 66:18-21
Psalm 117:1, 2
Hebrews 12:5-7, 11-13
Luke 13:22-30

Gospel
Luke 13:10-17 (RCL)

The text tells us that Jesus taught at "one of the synagogues on the sabbath" as was his custom (Luke 4:15-16). We know, moreover, that Jesus was acclaimed because he "routinely" healed people afflicted with diseases (Luke 4:40; 5:15; 6:18; 7:21; 9:11; Matt. 4:23; 9:35). The problem came, as it sometimes did with Jesus, when he healed on the sabbath (Luke 6:7-11; 14:1-6). Jesus knew full well that curing people on the sabbath was not an approved holy-day activity. Nevertheless, when a woman suffering from some malevolent spirit that crippled and bent her body came to the synagogue, Jesus did not hesitate to cure her. Nor did he wait for her to ask him for healing; to the contrary, when he saw her Jesus summoned her.

There are tantalizing details in this text. Jesus knew that the woman suffered from "a spirit that crippled her" for eighteen years (vv. 11, 16). Luke does not tell us how Jesus came by information pertaining to the length of her affliction, but as it is mentioned twice, he does intend for us to notice it. The only other time that number appears in Luke is earlier in this chapter, in verse 4. Evidently, eighteen workers were killed in an otherwise unknown construction accident when the tower of Siloam fell on them. Jesus noted that these eighteen did not die because they were worse sinners than the rest of Jerusalem's citizenry, but used the example to encourage all to repent. Jesus said this notwithstanding an association of accidents and affliction with sin, common in antiquity (John 9:2) and still lingering in our culture. Thus, while the reference to eighteen years in verses 11 and 16 certainly is a rhetorical device connecting the two pericopes,[1] it seems likely also to drive home the idea that her eighteen years of contention with a crippling spirit were not an indictment of the unfortunate woman. She was no more or less sinful than the victims of verse 4. She was simply a suffering victim. In any case, Jesus summoned her, announced her release from her "ailment" (*astheneias*, v. 12, translated as "infirmity" in v. 11), and touched her. She was immediately able to stand erect.

Appropriately enough, the now cured woman began praising God. Praise is the invariable response to Jesus' healing touch. The leader of the synagogue, however, saw matters differently. This healing was a violation of sabbath and thus a violation of Torah and the will of God. Six other days were available for healing; those who had come for healing (the verbs are plural) should "come back tomorrow" or any other day.

It is hard to be sympathetic to the synagogue leader. Looking at the incident from his perspective, however, one can see his point. He wished to maintain his faith community's core religious principles. The sabbath should be preserved for religious activities appropriate to it. The hallowing of the sabbath was, after all, commanded by God. Healing, like business transactions and other labors, was properly conducted on other days of the week. He had, moreover, the Holy Scripture to back him up. In his mind, the sacrosanct character of the principles sufficiently justified a delay in the delivery of this afflicted woman's health and *shalom* for another day. Someone who suffers neither from disease nor from the binding powers of evil and so who does not know the urgent need of the sufferer for relief can afford such luxurious sentiments. That certainly was not Jesus' position. Once he saw her, Jesus delayed not a minute, let alone a day, before healing the woman.

The leader was completely wrong, of course, as Jesus' successful argument demonstrates. Animals are loosened and led to water on the sabbath. The sabbath law should not be grounds for any postponement in loosing this "daughter of Abraham" whom Satan had bound. Even so, while Jesus' adversaries were temporarily put to shame, subsequent events (14:3-6) illustrate that not all who held this synagogue leader's view were convinced. The latter's speech does, however, demonstrate the lurking danger that religious principles and traditions—and the church leaders who espouse them—may be found aligned with the forces of evil.[2] Anyone preparing to proclaim this text would do well to inventory those high religious principles that bind brothers and sisters in Christ and cause them needless pain. Jesus' acts of salvation, of healing, and of loosening come on Sunday, whether or not congregational leaders are prepared to have Jesus trump those tenderly held principles that nevertheless ensnare others and prolong their grief and suffering. And the preacher must announce Jesus' loosening, lest she be in the unhappy role of the synagogue leader, urging both Jesus and the congregation to come back at a more suitable time.

Luke 13:22-30 (LFM)

The passage finds Jesus wandering through the wilderness, making his slow but inevitable way toward Jerusalem (Luke 9:51). Someone—the text does not say who—poses a question about salvation. Will there only be a few? Rather than answer directly, Jesus begins to speak of a narrow door and of those who will be left outside, denied admittance. "Strive to enter," Jesus says. The verb, *agōnizesthe*, provides us with the English word *agonize* and suggests an intense struggle or fight. The stakes are enormous: admission or expulsion, joy in the kingdom or weeping, inclusion or exclusion from the company of the Lord and master of the house. Jesus' response to the nameless inquirer, therefore, is a prophetic warning, couched in an extended metaphor. Nevertheless, Jesus does not speak hypothetically or abstractly. Addressing his audience directly, he warns of a circumstance where "*you* begin to stand outside and to knock" (v. 25). Jesus presumes his hearers will see the inaugural events of the kingdom of God and entertains that possibility that "*you yourselves* [will be] thrown out" (v. 28).

Those left on the outside of the locked door begin familiarly ("Lord, open to us," v. 25) but are surprised to hear the owner—who we are to understand is the Messiah—claims not to know from whence they come. The petitioners are shocked by this since, as they point out, they ate and drank in the presence of (*enōpion*, "in front of, before") this Lord. For the readers of Luke's Gospel, eating and drinking in the presence of the Lord signaled the central feature of Christian worship, Holy Communion. Those left on the outside had participated in the weekly meal in the presence of Jesus but were nevertheless excluded at the end as evildoers (*ergatai adikias*, workers of injustice or unrighteousness). The owner of the house repeats his claim not to know from whence they come (vv. 25, 27). Clearly, simple participation in the worshiping community was no guarantee that the door would be opened. Their seats at table consequently will be given to the crowds who stream into the kingdom and to the banquet table from all directions.

Jesus does not prescribe how one struggles to get through the narrow door before it is locked altogether. Nevertheless, the fact that the narrow door will, at some point, be a closed option leaves us with a pressing need to discern how we might struggle to enter. The condemnation of the excluded as *ergatai adikias* suggests, however, that we ought to become their opposites, namely workers of justice. For those in a North American context, that may mean a reduction in our consumption of food and in our ceaseless accumulation of possessions.[3] Otherwise, we may well find we cannot fit through that narrow door!

First Reading

Isaiah 58:9b-14 (RCL)

The oracles delivered by the sixth-century prophet speaking in Isaiah's name seek to instill an understanding that proper fasting and proper piety have to do with acts of justice. If the postexilic community struggled (and it did), the problem was prayers and fasts that ignored the social and economic inequity that persisted among them (vv. 1-9a). In the present passage, the Lord offers God's people guidance and renewal (vv. 11-12). They are to "remove the yoke from among you" (v. 9b). A description of the yoke began already in verse 6, where the "thongs of the yoke" are parallel to the "bonds of injustice" from which the oppressed should be set free. Such cords are braided by hunger (v. 7a), homelessness (v. 7b), and material need (v. 7c), all signs of injustice that find reference again in verse 10. The people who remove that sort of yoke from the necks of their brothers and his sisters will be called a "repairer of the breach, and the restorer of streets to live in" (v. 12). The people who do not put "business first" over devotion to God shall be exalted (vv. 13-14).

The will of God for the community of God's people could not be clearer. What remains unclear is how we who claim Jesus as Lord, on the one hand, and who live in a representative democracy, on the other, can remain quiescent (or, worse, vote selfishly) when 1.6 million children in North America are homeless, when in 2010 17.2 million households, 14.5 percent of households (approximately one in seven), were food insecure (the highest number ever recorded in the United States), or when the poor die on our proverbial doorsteps for lack of equitable medical care.[4]

Jeremiah 1:4-10 (RCL alt.)

After a historical introduction locating the prophet Jeremiah's ministry within the particular circumstances leading up to and slightly beyond the fall of Jerusalem (vv. 1-3), we are presented with Jeremiah's prophetic call. Prophetic call narratives formally consist of the following parts:[5]

1. God confronts and calls the prophet (vv. 4-5).
2. The prophet forwards some objection to this summons (v. 6).
3. God overcomes the prophet's objection with words of assurance and often the promise of God's own presence (vv. 7-8).
4. Often there follows a sign that confirms the commission (v. 9).

Typically, these parts are followed by a sort of summary of the major themes of the prophet's message, here a commission "to pluck up and to pull down, to destroy and to overthrow, to build and to plant" (v. 10). In the main, Jeremiah's oracles would consist of unrelenting messages of judgment and impending disaster, although words of consolation ("to build and to plant," v. 10) also appear in the course of his long ministry.

Much mischief has come about from isolating aspects of this passage and pressing them into service as proof texts of modern issues that are completely alien to both the historical context of Jeremiah and the plain meaning of the passage. Verse 5 is not a commentary on the issue of abortion, for example, but rather serves to describe the inevitability of Jeremiah's summons to prophetic ministry. He was "made for it" and has no real choice in the matter. But it is an equally egregious mistake to conclude from this passage that the Lord has some predetermined, detailed plan for Jeremiah's life and from that to suppose that God has in view our vocations, life partners—or, for that matter, our cancers, automobile accidents, or house fires—as a part of a similarly predestined plan by God. First of all, the possibility of failure presented in verse 17 undermines any notion of an immutable series of planned events. If there is a plan at all, it is the Lord's predetermined decision to be present and gracious to Jeremiah (and the rest of us!). Paul's language about predestination in Romans 8:28 (however that verse is best translated) is helpful. God's promise to be with us and for us come what may is God's plan. That "plan" finds clear expression in verse 8: "And I am with you to deliver you." And, because of Christ, we can be bold to claim that promise of Immanuel, "God is with us." Indeed, the God who abides with us bids us, like Jeremiah, to speak the word of the Lord forthrightly, whether that word condemns or quickens the hearer.

Isaiah 66:18-21 (LFM)

In the closing verses of Isaiah, the prophet returns to and expands upon the theme of God's glorious revelation to the nations. Verse 18 is corrupted in the Masoretic Text but is plain in the Septuagint and in other versions (see the note in the NRSV). The Lord comes to gather all nations and tongues to himself in Jerusalem where they will behold the divine glory (v. 18). The exact identity of the "sign" (*'oth*) is not clear. Christopher Seitz proposes it is the sign of Isaiah 11:12, a sign of covenantal kindness toward all nations, here promised for the exiles among the nations.[6] This is surely possible, albeit 11:2 speaks of a signal or ensign (*nês*) rather than of a sign (*'oth*). In any event, some will be sent to the far-flung corners of the earth, there to proclaim the glory of the Lord to those who have not previously heard it. It is noteworthy that emissaries are sent to the non-Semitic sons of Noah, whose lands and nations appear in Genesis 10. These people, too, will bring offerings to Jerusalem and there offer ritually clean grain offerings in the house of the Lord (v. 20).

The theme of the nations streaming to Jerusalem is a frequent one in so-called Trito- (or Third) Isaiah (the author of chapters 56–66). Isaiah 56:1-8 reports that foreigners as well as eunuchs, all of whom were previously excluded from Jewish fellowship, will be welcomed provided they keep the sabbath. Isaiah 60 describes a universal processional to Jerusalem from around the world. Nations and their kings will come bringing the wealth of the world with them. So in Isaiah 66: the non-Semitic world will come, bringing exiles and rich offerings with them. And from these, the Lord declares, some will be made priests and Levites (v. 21). This last is a remarkable assertion. Not only are foreigners and Gentiles welcomed to worship, but some will even become divinely appointed faith leaders. The future toward which Isaiah points stands as a reminder that kindness and hospitality to the foreigner and stranger are a mark of God's redeemed people. Moreover, even those we might disqualify from leadership and service in the faith community may be the very persons whom the Lord will take as priests.

Psalmody

Psalm 103:1-8 (RCL)

Subsequent to her healing at the touch of Jesus, the woman afflicted by a debilitating spirit in Luke 10:10-17 might well have used Psalm 103 as the means to voice her praise to God. Verses 3 and 4, at any rate, appear to be a response of thanksgiving for a recovery from some illness. The whole being of the psalmist praises the Lord. His "soul" (*nafeshi* < *nefesh*, that which breathes, the *anima* that makes one alive) and all that comprises his interior self are summoned to bless God, that is, to adore the Lord on bended knees. The Lord acts as a kinsman redeemer (Lev. 25:25), rescuing him from death (Lam. 3:58; Hos. 13:14), here described as the Pit.[7] The Lord, moreover, satisfies him with lifelong goodness so that he believes his youthful vigor to be renewed as heartily as was the proverbial strength of an eagle (Isa. 40:31). Verses 6-18 continue to praise the Lord, but the contrast is between human transience (vv. 14-16) and the everlasting, steadfast love of the Lord. As is so often noted in the psalms, a mark of the Lord's character is the work of vindication and justice for the oppressed (v. 6). This character was revealed to Moses and Israel (v. 7) and is summarized by the doxological formula that appears in verse 8.

The psalm ends as it began, with a summons to "bless the Lord, O my soul" (*nafeshi*, v. 22). By the end, however, the psalmist's praise is accompanied by the whole company of heaven (vv. 19-22).

Psalm 71:1-6 (RCL alt.)

Psalm 71 is the prayer of an aged person who pleads for the Lord's deliverance from personal enemies. The psalmist attests to the Lord's support from the moment of birth (v. 6) to his present old age (vv. 9, 17-18). The reference to "you who took me from my mother's womb" brings to mind Jeremiah's call (Jer. 1:5), appointed as the alternative first reading for the RCL for this day. The psalmist assumes that God is able to deliver him and, moreover, that it has been the Lord's will to do so since the psalmist's nativity. Verse 3 serves as a summary of the admixture of cries for help and expressions of trust that comprises verses 1-8: "Be my rock of refuge, to which I can always go; give the command to save me, for you are my rock and my fortress" (TNIV). Affirmations about the Lord who is the rock and fortress surround the plea "give the command to save me." Followers of the Christ, whether young or old, have even more reason for confidence in the mighty fortress who is our God.

Psalm 117:1, 2 (LFM)

Psalms 113–118 are recited annually by Jews in connection with the Passover celebration. Psalm 117, the shortest psalm in the book, is a summons for all people of the world to "praise the LORD!" In fact, the summons to praise in verses 1 and 2c surrounds the actual praise in verse 2ab. The world should praise the Lord because of God's steadfast love (*khasedo* < *khesed*) and the Lord's eternal faithfulness (*'emeth*). Within the context of the canon, Psalm 117 follows a thanksgiving for personal deliverance, Psalm 116. The gratitude of the ransomed psalmist there concludes with the summons to "praise the LORD" (Ps. 116:19), a summons answered with Psalm 117's declaration of praise.

The preacher might pause to consider what it means that the invitation to praise the Lord includes "you nations" and "all you peoples" (v. 1). Echoes of the LFM Gospel lesson and Isaiah 66 can be heard. Who is in and who is out in this vision? In the Gospel lesson, those who expect to be included are locked out. On the other hand, people who are not of the children of Abraham are included in the eschatological vision of Isaiah. In Psalm 117 we hear that "all you peoples" will extol the Lord and "all you nations" will praise God. In other words, "*every knee should bend*, in heaven and on earth and under the earth, *and every tongue should confess* that Jesus Christ is Lord, to the glory of God the Father" (Phil. 2:10-11). The universal scope of the Lord's salvation leaves us breathless—and possibly nervous! The scope of the Lord's steadfast love and faithfulness (v. 2ab) exceeds our expectations and leaves us open to consider whether or not those of whom we might not approve are just God's proverbial cup of tea.

Second Reading

Hebrews 12:18-29 (RCL)

For commentary on this text, please see the second reading for Lectionary 22 / Proper 17, below.

Hebrews 12:5-7, 11-13 (LFM)

Hebrews 12:3-13 reminds us that the book was addressed to Christians under persecution and who, because of that, were tempted to turn back to their Jewish roots. The possibility of martyrdom existed (v. 4). The author declares that such trials as were presented by their persecutors should be considered as the discipline of a loving Lord. Citing the Septuagint of Proverbs 3:11-12, the author proposes that *trials* (*paideian*, training, discipline) are proof of an intimate, parent-child relationship with God (v. 7). Indeed, without that *discipline* (*paideias*), "then you would be not sons but bastards" (v. 8 NJB). God so disciplines us so that we may partake in divine holiness (v. 10). The writer grants that no one likes discipline (*paideia*) at the time but that those trained in it receive the reward of righteousness (v. 11). Therefore, his readers ought to renew their efforts to be disciplined in order that they might run with perseverance the race set before them (v. 1). Lift drooping hands and weak knees; straighten the paths so that even the lame (those weak in faith? apostates?) might not be injured! Verses 12 and 13 allude to Isaiah 35:3-4 and Proverbs 4:26, respectively.[8] If the readers of Hebrew knew their Scriptures—and we may assume they did—the allusion to Isaiah would also remind them that God would soon come with vengeance, ready to recompense those who suffered. Proverbs 4 is a series of hortatory remarks from a father to his child, recalling the parent-child analogy of the previous verses.

The notion that violence and bloodshed might represent the discipline of a divine parent is not a compelling argument for enduring pain. Moreover, and inasmuch as passages such as the present one have been used to condone domestic abuse of women and children, a sermon on this text ought carefully to distinguish between suffering on behalf of others as did Christ (vv. 2-3) and suffering that comes by the hand of sinful and sick people. A situation of domestic abuse, for example, should never be brought under the rubric of divine training, and a preacher will do more good than he likely can imagine by saying just that. Yet the summons to renewed strength and resolve may help communities of faith that struggle to achieve justice and peace for themselves and their neighbors.

Notes

1. Frederick W. Danker, *Jesus and the New Age: A Commentary on St. Luke's Gospel*, rev. ed. (Philadelphia: Fortress Press, 1988), 261. Danker also notes that Judges 13:14 and 10:8 both refer to eighteen years as a means to describe a long period of oppression.
2. Justo L. González, *Luke*, Belief: A Theological Commentary on the Bible (Louisville: Westminster John Knox, 2010), 174.
3. Richard Vinson, *Luke*, Smyth & Helwys Bible Commentary (Macon, GA: Smyth & Helwys, 2008), 464.
4. For these statistics and more information, please see the websites http://www.familyhomelessness.org/children.php?p=ts; http://www.worldhunger.org/articles/Learn/us_hunger_facts.htm; and http://www.answers.com/topic/poverty-and-health.
5. On the form-critical shape of the prophetic call narrative, see Norman C. Habel, "The Form and Significance of the Call Narrative," *Zeitschrift für die Alttestamentliche Wissenschaft* 77, no. 3 (1965): 297–323. Habel treats Jeremiah's call on pp. 305–309.
6. Christopher R. Seitz, *The Book of Isaiah 40–66*, in *The New Interpreter's Bible*, ed. Leander E. Keck et al. (Nashville: Abingdon, 2001), 6:548.
7. The Pit is a synonym for Sheol. See Pss. 16:10; 30:3; Prov. 1:12; Isa. 14:15; 38:18; Ezek. 31:16.
8. Edgar McKnight and Christopher Church, *Hebrews-James*, Smyth & Helwys Bible Commentary (Macon, GA: Smyth & Helwys, 2004), 293.

September 1, 2013
Lectionary 22 / Twenty-Second Sunday in Ordinary Time / Proper 17
Fifteenth Sunday after Pentecost

Revised Common Lectionary (RCL)	**Lectionary for Mass (LFM)**
Proverbs 25:6-7 or Sirach 10:12-18 or Jeremiah 2:4-13	Sirach 3:17-18, 20, 28-29
Psalm 112 or 81:1, 10-16	Psalm 68:4-5, 6-7, 10-11
Hebrews 13:1-8, 15-16	Hebrews 12:18-19, 22-24a
Luke 14:1, 7-14	Luke 14:1, 7-14

Gospel
Luke 14:1, 7-14 (RCL, LFM)

It is hard to imagine Jesus ever getting a second invitation to a dinner party. As the NJB alternatively translates the Greek, he seems already to have been at dinner when, again (!), he heals on the sabbath. Jesus then proceeds to offend both his fellow guests by offering unsolicited advice on seating etiquette (14:7-11) and his host by critiquing the guest list (vv. 12-14). Before he is done eating, Jesus shares a parable that implies his fellow diners might be in for a nasty shock at the eschaton (vv. 15-24). All of this parallels 13:10-35.

At dinner, Jesus notes the fellow guests jockeying for seats of honor. This prompts a parable that is nominally about their behavior in the dining room but, as the reference to a wedding banquet indicates, really has to do with the eschaton (Luke 12:35-38; Matt. 22:2-14; 25:1-13; Rev. 19:9). Those who exalt themselves before others and before God will have their comeuppance, while those who humble themselves (*ho tapeinōn heauton*) will be exalted (Luke 18:14). The ultimate exaltation of those of low degree has been a motif of Jesus' teaching throughout Luke and was heralded already in the Magnificat (Luke 1:52).

Jesus' critique of his host's guest list leads to the same conclusion. Rather than invite friends, brothers, relatives, or rich neighbors with the expectation of a return invitation or some other favor, Jesus enjoins his host to invite those who could never repay him. The four types Jesus encourages his host to put on his "A list" correspond to the four groups he recommends crossing off the list in verse 12: the poor, the crippled, the lame, and the blind. Since these could do no more than thank the host or pray God's blessing upon him, the host could look forward to repayment at the eschaton and his participation in the resurrection of the righteous.

We are not told what the Pharisaic host thought about Jesus' proposal; someone tried politely to point the conversation in a different direction (v. 15). Chances are, however, that the Pharisee embraced the proposition with about as much enthusiasm as does the church today. Those who are most welcome are the ones who can repay the invitation, or at least pay a tithe. The homeless, the drug addicted, the HIV-positive patient, the mentally ill or mentally challenged, and the poor—to name but a few—are rarely invited and too often made to feel uncomfortable should they somehow find their way into Sunday worship. And yet such people are precisely those who will be exalted at the wedding feast of the Lamb.

First Reading

Proverbs 25:6-7 (RCL)

Proverbs aims to provide practical advice for all aspects of life. Here we have instruction on conduct in the royal court. This advice is much the same as that which Jesus speaks to his fellow dinner guests: do not assume an honored place in the presence of the king, for it is better to be elevated from a humbler place than to be humiliated. Jesus, however, applies the insight to the eschatological reign of God.

Sirach 10:12-18 (RCL alt.)

Sirach offers his readers reflections on pride and arrogance and, in particular, the pride of kings and rulers. "The king of today will die tomorrow" (10:10) and, like the rest of humanity, will inherit rot and decay. Verse 12 declares that the beginning of human pride (*huperephania*, an arrogance bordering on insolence) is to forsake the Lord. The verb translated as "forsake" in the NRSV, *anastato*, connotes rebellion (Acts 21:38; 17:6; Gal. 5:12). The human rebels against the Lord and the heart rebels (another form of *anastato*) from its Maker. The message, therefore, is not simply that "pride goes before a fall." It does, of course, but this pride confuses and distorts the proper place of human beings in relationship to the Lord who made them and who rules the world. Once again, the temptation to "be like God" meets with disaster. The consequence of hubris is calamity and regime change. The lowly will replace the rulers. Sin and pride are inexorably linked, but pride, like sin, was not created for human beings (v. 18).

Jeremiah 2:4-13 (RCL alt.)

If, as many scholars propose, this unit comes from an early point in Jeremiah's career, it is also a word addressed to and heard by the exilic community (v. 9). The latter speak in 2:35 and 3:4b-5 where Israel's claims of innocence find divine refutation.

The Lord's relationship to Israel is described in verse 2 as a bride beloved by her husband and, in verse 3, as the first fruits of a harvest reserved as holy to the Lord (Exod. 23:16-19; Lev. 23:10ff.). Verse 4 begins a divine lament. The accusations against the ancestors of Jacob and Israel gush forth. The Lord wonders what "wrong" (*'avel*, injustice, unrighteousness; see Lev. 19:15, 35) the Lord might have done that they would pursue "worthless things" and become "worthless" themselves. The NRSV suggests "worthless" for the enigmatic *hebel*, a word signifying something base, meaningless, worthless, or empty. *Hebel* is vanity. The ancestors did not seek the Lord when they ought to have done so, especially in light of the history of the exodus (v. 6). They defiled "my land" and they made "my heritage" an abomination. That defilement (*watteamme'u* < *tame'*, to be ritually impure), it turns out, was a violation of the first commandment (vv. 8, 11). Priests did not seek the Lord and skilled handlers of the law (*torah*) did not know him. The shepherds, a common metaphor for kings (see the footnote in the NRSV), transgressed and prophets prophesied by means of Baal (v. 8). The authorities who should have been able to guide the people to the Lord were ignorant and useless.

Nor is the condemnation for the ancestors alone. Verse 9 indicates that the "children's children," the exiles, are accused. They are invited to look west to Cyprus and east to Kedar to see if any nation has dared even to trade their nondeities for other gods. In Deuteronomy 30:19, the heavens and earth are called to bear witness of the covenant treaty. In verse 12, the heavens are summoned to witness the shocking behavior of the people who protest their innocence (v. 35) but who are guilty of two evils. First, they abandoned the Lord and, second, they forsook the "fountain of living water" (a synonym for the Lord; see Jer. 17:13) for a cistern (gods) of their own devising that cannot hold water by comparison (v. 13)!

The hope in this passage is signaled by the fact that the Lord continues to speak to the people. The ancestors, the exilic generation, and the twenty-first-century listeners have botched every aspect of our relationship with the Lord. Who could argue with the charge that we are a nation that has changed its gods, substituting endless acquisition and self-gratification—things that do not profit and gods that are not gods!—for the glorious inheritance God wills for us still. The grief this has caused God is incalculable and its expression continues well past this appointed reading. And yet God finally will not leave the people to suffer the consequences of their own betrayal. The "fountain of living water" will come again—to a woman at a Samaritan well (John 4:10-15), to us in the living waters of baptism—so that we may never thirst again.

Sirach 3:17-18, 20, 28-29 (LFM)

Here again Sirach takes up the subject of humility, a favorite topic of his and of sapiental literature in general (Sir. 4:8; 10:28; Prov. 11:2; 15:33; 22:4). Verse 17 implies that those whom God accepts are the humble (*prautēti*, gentle in attitude and behavior) who love others like themselves. Greatness demands humbling oneself (*tapeinoō*, 4:7; 11:1; 35:17), but the reward is the Lord's favor (*charin*, grace). Indeed, the Lord's great might is glorified by the humble person (*tapeinōn*). This last is a remarkable claim: the humble, by their conduct, cause the Lord to be glorified in ways that augment God's already considerable might. God is praised not just for the exercise of power, but for the right conduct of God's humble people. In contrast, calamity fells the prideful person who cannot endure adversity since pride grows within like "an evil plant" or a malignant tumor.

Psalmody

Psalm 112 (RCL)

Psalm 112, an acrostic psalm rooted in Israel's wisdom tradition, considers what it is that constitutes an abundant life. The psalm begins where Psalm 111 ends. "The fear of the Lord is the beginning of wisdom; all who practice it have a good understanding" (111:10). Psalm 112 paints a picture of just such an individual.

According to the psalmist, a person who reverences the Lord and who is delightedly steeped in the Lord's commandments is happy (*'ashre-'ish*, v. 1; see Pss. 1:1-2; 128:1; 119:2). Biblical authors generally considered God's activity in the world to be constituted either by saving or by blessing. This psalm testifies to the latter. A person who delights in the Lord's commandments experiences wealth and riches (v. 3a) but, more importantly, "his righteousness will endure forever" (vv. 3b, 9b). In Psalm 111:3 it is the Lord's righteousness that is eternally enduring. Here, that divine characteristic is extended to the one rooted in the commandments and those who share their blessings with the poor (v. 9). Indeed, generosity is a constitutive characteristic of the righteous person and it is part of what comprises "affairs conducted with justice" (v. 5).

The psalmist includes a sober appraisal of the difficulties and challenges that a righteous person must face. There is darkness in the world against which they serve as light (v. 4; Matt. 5:14). They encounter evil tidings (v. 7) and wicked foes (vv. 8, 10). Nevertheless, no foes shall prevail (vv. 8, 10). Moreover, as persons summoned to share the blessings that have been extended to them (vv. 5, 9), they become the means by which the Lord's enduring righteousness becomes a reality for all of God's people. Through the person who is "gracious, merciful, and righteous" (v. 4b), people will come to know the Lord who is likewise "gracious and merciful" (Ps. 111:4b).

Psalm 81:1, 10-16 (RCL alt.)

The psalm begins, quite literally, with a shout. Indeed, the summons that is verse 1 uses two synonyms for shouting: *ranan*, to cause to ring out for joy (Job 29:13; Pss. 65:8; 32:11; Deut. 32:43) and *rua'*, to raise a shout (Pss. 47:1; 66:1; 95:1, 2; 98:4, 100:1). Ancient Israel's worship was a noisy affair, including shouts, instruments, and the blast of the ram's horn or *shofar.* There is power in such worship, as the story of the collapse of Jericho's walls in Judges 6 attests.

But sometimes there can be too much shouting, too much noise. In the second part of this psalm, someone—it was likely a priest or a professional prophet—announces,

"I hear a voice I had not known" (v. 5c). Verses 5-10 record the words of that voice. God speaks and, in so doing, alludes to the history of the people's rescue from the exodus to the giving of the law. In the midst of that recitation, God summons the people to *hear* God's admonition and to *listen* to God (v. 8). The implication may be that the shouting and other noises of public worship actually prohibited them from hearing the voice of God. Verse 10 concludes with a recitation of a portion of Exodus 20:2, the prologue to the Ten Commandments, again conclusively claiming the congregation's obligation to the Lord. The last portion of verse 10 is puzzling. It may report the priest's or prophet's report of the Lord's instruction to him. That is, the priest was instructed to open his mouth that it might be filled, presumably with the words of the Lord.

The admonition heralded in verse 8 is delivered in verses 11-13. Because the people did not *listen* to God's voice, they "would not submit [*'abah*, yield] to me" (v. 11). As a consequence, God gave them up to their own counsels (v. 12). Even now, however, if they would but *listen* and obey (v. 13), God would rescue them from their enemies (v. 14). In verses 15 and 16 the priest or prophet speaks again in what appears to be an executive summary. Those who hate the Lord are doomed (v. 15). The text of verse 16 is doubtless corrupt. The NRSV simply emends the text by substituting the pronominal suffix "him" with a second masculine singular suffix, thus correcting the parallelism between the two halves of the verse. Perhaps the verse is directed to the priest or prophet, completing a promise of verse 10. On the other hand, the pronoun may be used as a collective. In that event, the promise of rich foods, including honey secreted in rough cliff faces (Deut. 32:13-14), will be for all who stop making religious noises long enough to listen to the Lord and walk in God's ways. In any case, the psalm serves as a reminder that worship is not simply a celebration but an opportunity to listen for the word of God.

Psalm 68:4-5, 6-7, 10-11 (LFM)

The interpretation of Psalm 68 has long and famously eluded psalm scholars. Some points are clear, however. Verse 4 summons us to worship the Lord who is sometimes depicted as riding upon the clouds (Pss. 104:3; 18:9-12). The psalm returns to that image in Psalm 68:32-34. Verses 5 and 6 supply a cause for the faithful to sing to God: God protects society's most defenseless and vulnerable people, including orphans, widows, the homeless, and the imprisoned. That theme is echoed in verse 10. The accent is on the power of the Lord before which Israel and, indeed, all nations must submit.

Second Reading

Hebrews 12:18-19, 22-24a (LFM)

The author continues to contrast the old covenant with the new, urging his hearers not to forsake their birthright (vv. 16-17). Sinai is not mentioned by name, but the references to the theophany there are unmistakable (see Deut. 4:11; Exod. 19:16, 19). The contrast is between two mountains, Sinai and Zion, one physical and the other spiritual. They had not *come* to a physical spot of terror, but they have *come* to the heavenly city of Jerusalem (compare Heb. 11:15-16). There angels gather with the assembly of the "firstborn who are enrolled in heaven" (v. 23) who share in the inheritance (v. 16) of the "firstborn," Christ, referred to in Hebrews 1:6.[1]

Hebrews 13:1-8, 15-16 (RCL)

Chapter 13 contains concluding admonitions to the community. First and foremost is the enjoinder to let brotherly love (*philadelphia*) abide. Beyond that, the author encourages his readers to *remember* the imprisoned (*mimnēskesthe*, v. 3) and to (*strongly*) *remember* their faith leaders (*mnēmoneuete*, v. 7) in order to imitate their example. The author also admonishes his readers not to forget (*epilanthanesthe*) in verses 2 and 16. While the NRSV translates "do not neglect" in both instances, the verb often appears in the Septuagint for the Hebrew *shākach*, "to forget." Readers are not to forget to show hospitality to strangers (*philoxenias*, literally "love for strangers"). Likewise, they are not to forget to do good deeds and to make a contribution (*koinōnias*, v. 16; see 2 Cor. 8:4; 9:13; Rom. 15:26). It is remarkable that the church continues to struggle with collective amnesia in precisely these areas.

Note

1. Edgar McKnight and Christopher Church, *Hebrews–James*, Smyth & Helwys Bible Commentary (Macon, GA: Smyth & Helwys, 2004), 299.

September 8, 2013
Lectionary 23 / Twenty-Third Sunday in Ordinary Time / Proper 18
Sixteenth Sunday after Pentecost

Revised Common Lectionary (RCL)

Deuteronomy 30:15-20 or Jeremiah 18:1-11
Psalm 1 or 139:1-6, 13-18
Philemon 1-21
Luke 14:25-33

Lectionary for Mass (LFM)

Wisdom 9:13-18b
Psalm 90:3-4, 5-6, 12-13, 14 + 17
Philemon 9-10, 12-17
Luke 14:25-33

Gospel
Luke 14:25-33 (RCL, LFM)

With verse 25, we are jolted out of the dinner party and put back on the road with Jesus. Jesus quickly makes it clear that traipsing along behind him, even cheering him on, does not constitute discipleship. For the balance of this chapter, he instructs the crowds about discipleship and its cost.

First, anyone coming to him who does not "hate" his father and mother, wife and children, brothers and sisters, yes, and even life itself (*psyche heautou*) cannot become his disciple (v. 26). Unfortunately, the word *hate* in English has affective connotations that the Greek *misei* (< *mise*) does not necessarily carry. The Septuagint often renders a form of *mise* for the Hebrew *sane'* in contexts that inform us that "hate" here means to "hold in disfavor, to be disinclined to, have relatively little regard for" (see Deut. 21:15-17).[1] The meaning is clear: no familial relationship nor even a regard for one's own being can have a priority over discipleship. Moreover, the disciple must be willing to bear his or her cross (v. 27). For Jesus' first-century listeners, references to the cross and crucifixion would not have been abstract. Romans rather routinely crucified criminals. For example, during the reign of the incompetent Herod Archelaus (4 BCE to 6 CE), the Roman governor of Syria, Publius Quinctilius Varus, suppressed a Judean insurrection and crucified two thousand individuals. Incidents like this provide the historical context of Jesus' claim, "Whoever does not carry the cross and follow me cannot be my disciple" (v. 27). The trivialization that this statement has undergone among us (e.g., cross bearing as tolerating an obnoxious boss or a demanding Aunt Minerva) simply won't do. In the context of first-century Palestine, Jesus' statement signals that his followers must put the claims of the reign of God over that of civil authorities, daring to bear even the punishment of law for the sake of fidelity and obedience to the Lord who stands over all Caesars, presidents, and tyrants.

Jesus follows that bombshell with three short parables, all having to do with assessing the cost of discipleship. A tower's construction price, if not accurately projected, leads to ridicule. A king must assay the cost of aggression before committing troops and risking the loss of all. Slipped in before the parable about salt losing its saltiness (vv. 34-35) is what perhaps stands as the most difficult demand of discipleship for us. Jesus says, "None of you can become my disciple if you do not give up all your possessions" (v. 33). In a society wherein people assay education, vocation, compassion, individual self-worth, and virtually all of life's meaning in pecuniary terms, the demand that disciples surrender their possessions and the value system that accompanies them is a profoundly subversive message. Christians who live under the authority of Christ are not bound to the value system of the old regime, however powerful and seductive its allure. Trusting in the generosity and reliability of a providing Lord *frees* Jesus' followers to be as generous as their Lord who did not stint to hand over his very life. Failure to trust and adherence to the securities of the old regime disqualify us as disciples.

So does the preacher enjoin her listeners to give away all their possessions? Only if she has done so by way of example! She can, however, urge the followers of Jesus to strike a blow for evangelical freedom and faithful discipleship by incremental sacrifices of time, talent, and money. But mostly Christ followers ought to give money, for devotion to that god most patently threatens our ability to follow Jesus.

First Reading

Deuteronomy 30:15-20 (RCL)

Deuteronomy 30:15-20 concludes a unit that begins in 29:1 [Heb. 28:69]. In the narrative world of Deuteronomy, the larger passage purports to be a new covenant made in Moab, before the Israelites crossed the Jordan into the promised land. Nevertheless, the material is literarily dependent upon the Covenant Code (Deuteronomy 12–26) and the section of blessings and curses (chs. 26–27). Moreover, Deuteronomy 30:1-10 describes an exilic context from which the author hopes his people will be redeemed.

In verses 15-20 Moses sets before the people what is literally a life-or-death decision. Either the people will choose life/good, defined in verse 16 as obedience to the commandments and love of the Lord, or they will choose death/evil, understood in verse 17 as disobedience and apostasy. On the one hand, a decision for life/good produces progeny, blessing, and land (v. 16), the three elements of the ancient covenantal promise of the Lord to Abraham (see v. 20; Gen. 12:1-3). On the other hand, a choice of death/evil leads to a quick extinction in the land beyond to Jordan (v. 18; see Deut. 4:26). Heaven and earth are summoned as witnesses that Moses has explicated Israel's choice between life and death (see Deut. 4:26; 31:28; 32:1; Isa. 1:2). An appropriate decision will lead to life for this and future generations. Verse 20 echoes verse 16 both in the offer of life and in the means by which that life might be attained: by loving, obeying, and holding fast to the Lord. The last verb, an infinitival form of *dābaq*, denotes the idea of cleaving or clinging and here signals loyalty (Deut. 4:4; 10:20; 11:22; 13:4; Josh. 22:5; see Gen. 2:24).

Verses 16 and 20 also have in common the infinitival phrase "to love the Lord your God" (*le'ahabah 'et yehvah 'eloheyka*). A sermon on this passage might do well to start with that phrase since it contains within it an indicative claim that the Lord is actually Israel's God. Prior to the summons for Israel to choose life by walking in the Lord's ways, keeping the divine statutes, clinging to the Lord, and so on, is the graceful saving work of God who restores exiles to their homeland (Deut. 30:4-5) and who "will circumcise your heart and the heart of your descendants, so that you will love the Lord your God" (*le'ahabah 'et yehvah 'eloheyka*, Deut. 30:6). A circumcised heart signifies a person who is responsive to God's will (Deut. 10:16; Jer. 4:4; Lev. 26:41). As God ever does, God gives what God demands. God's people can live as is appropriate to their calling, but that is because the God who saves is the God who first gives new hearts (Ps. 51:10; Ezek. 11:19; 36:26). When God makes new hearts, new wills, the result is that "you will love the Lord your God with all your heart and with all your soul" (Deut. 30:6).

Jeremiah 18:1-11 (RCL alt.)

The pericope divides into two segments, each introduced with the announcement that the word of the Lord reached Jeremiah (vv. 1, 5). In the first instance, the prophet is instructed to observe a potter working wet clay on a spinning wheel. Jeremiah notes that, from time to time, the vessel is not shaped as the potter intended. It is "spoiled" (NRSV) or "marred" (TNIV, KJV),[2] a circumstance that prompts the potter to rework the clay as he sees fit.

The second "word of the Lord" transforms the potter's behavior into an allegory of the Lord's relationship with the house of Israel. As with the potter, God's divine sovereignty is such that God is free to press down and rework the people of Judah as seems good to God. Verses 7-10 apply the allegory to the Lord's relationship with nations in general. A decision to preserve or destroy depends on whether a nation repents from evil or stubbornly refuses to listen to the voice of the Lord. This principle is applied to the inhabitants of Jerusalem in verse 11, although the inconsistent translation of the NRSV disguises that. The Lord is shaping "evil" (*ra'ah*) against Judah (v. 11), but this is just the sort of disaster (*ra'ah*) about which the Lord says he would rather "change my mind" should that nation turn (v. 8). Consequently, in verse 11b, the potter/Lord urges Judah to follow the example of the repentant nation that turns "from [its] *evil* way" (*middarko hara'ah*).

The summons to repent in verse 22 invites contemplation about the exercise of God's power. On the one hand, the analogy of the potter asserts the sovereignty of God to shape nations "as seemed good to him" (v. 4), be that by means of breaking/destroying (v. 7) or building/planting (v. 9). On the other hand, the analogy doesn't quite work. Centrifugal forces of the potter's wheel, forces ever imbedded in the nature of a decision to create, are factors not completely within divine control. Moreover, and unlike inanimate clay, nations (and Judah) enjoy autonomy; they are capable of responding to God in ways that influence God's behavior, moving God to respond differently to the "facts on the ground." God's will, rooted in the character and purposes of God, does not change, but the passage makes it clear that the means by which God achieves God's ends are worked out in response to a creation that, for the sake of an authentic relationship with that creation, God wins by wooing.

Wisdom 9:13-18b (LFM)

Taken as a whole, the pseudepigraphal Wisdom 9:1-18 deliberately echoes the scene in 1 Kings 3:6-9 (par. 2 Chron. 1:8-10) and the young king Solomon's prayer for wisdom. Verses 9-11 assume the existence of an independent entity, Lady Wisdom. Wisdom is here celebrated as intimate with God and God's works (v. 9). Present with God at the dawn of creation (see 8:3-4; compare Prov. 8:27-30), she is enigmatically everywhere present in creation and yet not discernible in any one location (Job 28). God eventually provided a home for her in Jerusalem (Sir. 24:3-12) and in "the law that Moses commanded" (Sir. 24:23). Thus, when the king asks that Wisdom be sent forth from God's presence (see Sir. 24:2) to labor at his side and guide his actions as king and judge of God's people (vv. 10-12), there is an implicit appeal to be guided by the Torah. The king knows he cannot succeed on his own (v. 13) since, he avers, the human ability to discern the counsel and will of God is hampered by the failures of human reason (v. 14) and by the constraints on human knowledge that stem from human corporeality and finitude (vv. 15-16). Consequently, knowledge of God's counsel comes only by gracious revelation as God sends an illuminating holy spirit from on high (v. 17). People who are so taught are consequently saved (*esōthēsan*) by wisdom (v. 18). Verse 18 marks a turning point in the book as the chapters that follow focus on the link between wisdom and salvation.[3]

The hidden wisdom about which our author speaks and for which he asks God to send him (v. 10) is echoed in Paul's understanding of the wisdom of God that reveals the cross (1 Corinthians 2). The mystery of God, God's hidden, secret wisdom, is Jesus Christ, and him crucified (1 Cor. 2:2, 7). God's wisdom is revealed by God to us through the Spirit "for the Spirit searches everything, even the depths of God" (v. 10). Since we have been given that Spirit, Paul concludes, "we have the mind of Christ" (v. 16). What Solomon prayed for, the wisdom that saves, has been conclusively given to the followers of Jesus.

Psalmody

Psalm 1 (RCL)

This wisdom-type psalm introduces the Psalter with a meditation on the delight of those who are rooted in the law of the Lord (v. 2; see Ps. 119:1). As is usual in the wisdom tradition, the psalmist understands the way one lives to be an "either/or" choice. On the one hand, "happy" (or "blessed" < *'shre-*, v. 1) is the one who eschews the council of the wicked and instead delights in the law (*torah*) of the Lord (v. 2). They are like verdant trees, watered by a stream. In contrast, the wicked are like chaff, dried up and blown away (v. 4). "The LORD knows the way of the righteous,"[4] but the sinners will not survive the judgment (v. 5) and, consequently, will perish.

The lovely metaphor of the righteous prospering perpetually like a tree beside a stream of water provides an opportunity to consider the starting point of all our happiness. Rooted in the waters of baptism, we will not wither and fade (even if our bodies do!); we shall bear fruit of the Spirit in season (see Gal. 5:22-23).

Psalm 139:1-6, 13-18 (RCL alt.)

The prayer for deliverance from the poet's personal enemies (vv. 19-22) is predicated upon the psalmist's conviction of God's deep knowledge of him (vv. 1-18, 23-24). Verses 1-6 praise the Lord who knows (*yada'*). Word pairs abound. He says the Lord "has searched/known" (v. 1), "knows/discerns" (v. 2), "searches out/is acquainted" (v. 3). The Lord knows what the psalmist will say before he says it (v. 4), and the Lord completely encompasses the psalmist. The Lord's *knowledge* (*da'at* < *yada'*) of him is too wonderful for him to comprehend (v. 6).

Verses 7-12 are dominated with praise because God *sees* the psalmist in all circumstances and wherever he may roam. In verses 13-18 the psalmist affirms that God's deep knowledge of him is a consequence of God's creative activity (Ps. 33:15; 94:9-11). Note, however, that the accent is on the Lord, beginning with the redundant pronoun in verse 13: "For *you*, you formed my inner self . . ."[5] The poet marvels in wonder at his own created being: "I am fearfully and wonderfully made." Indeed, that his existence is a consequence of God's work is the one thing that the *psalmist* knows in this psalm (v. 14); all other assertions of knowledge are credited to God (vv. 1-2, 4, 6, 23).

In the present author's considered view, the tension in the metaphors in verses 13 and 15-16 ("form/knit" versus "not hidden/beheld") makes it problematic to employ this passage as a proof text about present social controversies. Nevertheless, the psalmist certainly affirms both that his life is a consequence of God's complex creativity and that his entire life is within the scope of divine concern. In the face of that, the psalmist can but stand in worshipful awe (vv. 17-18).

Psalm 90:3-4, 5-6, 12-13, 14 + 17 (LFM)

The superscription notwithstanding, Psalm 90 is a modified communal lament, likely composed in the time of the exile. In that anxious world, the psalmist recalls that the Lord had been their "dwelling place" in all generations (v. 1). In contrast to God's eternal constancy, verses 3-12 focus on human finitude. God returns "mortals" to dust (v. 3). The translation "mortals," however, disguises the Hebrew's evocative "children of Adam" and the curse of Adam in Genesis 3:19. In the face of God's eternity, a thousand years are a mere moment and human beings as ephemeral as a dream (vv. 4-5a). Indeed, human life is like the grass that comes and goes in a day (vv. 5b-6). Even should we last seventy or more years (vv. 9-10), those years are surrounded by God's ire (vv. 7, 11).

Verse 12 is the heart of the psalmist's prayer. Given our finitude, we should treasure our days and so gain wisdom. The petitions of verses 13-17 are directed by that conception. A wise heart petitions that the God who calls *us* to "turn back" (*shuvu*, v. 3) might likewise himself turn (*shuvah*) to God's servants (v. 13). If God will but satisfy us with steadfast love (*khesed*, v. 14) there can be satisfaction and gladness (vv. 14-15). Even the fleeting work of our hands, made new by the Lord's favor, will prosper (v. 17).

Second Reading
Philemon 1-21 (RCL)
Philemon 9-10, 12-17 (LFM)

The shortest of Paul's epistles, the letter is addressed to Philemon, the leader of a house church in Colossae, as well as to the congregation that gathered there (compare vv. 2, 10 with Col. 4:9, 17). The issue is the return of Onesimus, a runaway slave who had become a believer and the spiritual child of Paul (v. 10). Paul would have Philemon receive the formerly useless slave as someone who is newly useful ("Onesimus" means "useful"!). More importantly, Paul hopes and expects that Philemon would, for Paul's sake, receive Onesimus as a beloved brother in Christ.

Paul's request demonstrates how the gospel began to reconstitute the social and economic distinctions that operated in the ancient world. Onesimus would return as a slave, sure enough, but a slave who, like Philemon, answered to a different Lord. Consequently, Paul hopes Philemon will welcome Onesimus as he would the apostle himself (v. 17), since in Christ "there is no longer slave nor free" (Gal. 3:28). While the institution of slavery has been banished from among us, discrimination based on class, race, economic status, and even political persuasion still divides in ways that it should not and would not were we to take the claims of the gospel upon us more seriously. We might then be useful ourselves!

Notes

1. Frederick W. Danker, *A Greek-English Lexicon of the New Testament and Other Early Christian Literature*, 3rd ed. (Chicago: University of Chicago Press, 2000), 652.
2. The Hebrew *niščhat* (< *šāchat*, compare Jer. 13:7) appears in other contexts where it means "ruined" (Exod. 8:24) or "corrupted" (Gen. 6:11-12; Ezek. 20:44).
3. Ernest G. Clarke, *Wisdom of Solomon*, Cambridge Bible Commentary (Cambridge: Cambridge University Press, 1973), 65.
4. Author trans. The Hebrew word is a masculine singular participial form of *yāda'*, a verb that denotes intimate and profound knowledge. The same construction appears in Ps. 37:8.
5. Author trans.

September 15, 2013
Lectionary 24 / Twenty-Fourth Sunday in Ordinary Time / Proper 19
Seventeenth Sunday after Pentecost

Revised Common Lectionary (RCL)	**Lectionary for Mass (LFM)**
Exodus 32:7-14 or Jeremiah 4:11-12, 22-28	Exodus 32:7-11, 13-14
Psalm 51:1-10 or Psalm 14	Psalm 51:3-4, 12-13, 17 + 19
1 Timothy 1:12-17	1 Timothy 1:12-17
Luke 15:1-10	Luke 15:1-32 or 15:1-10

Gospel
Luke 15:1-10 (RCL, LFM alt.)
Luke 15:1-32 (LFM)

Jesus' habit of welcoming sinners and even breaking bread with them offended the Pharisees and scribes. Pointedly, they "grumbled" (*diegongyzon*), a verb almost exclusively reserved in the Septuagint to describe the Israelites' complaining about their leaders (Exod. 15:24; 16:2, 7, 8; Num. 14:2, 36; 16:11; Deut. 1:27.).[1] Appended to Jesus' parabolic response about a lost sheep and the shepherd, Luke has gathered two more parables about the lost and the found.

In the first parable, Jesus asks, "Which one of you, having a hundred sheep and losing one of them, does not leave the ninety-nine in the wilderness and go after the one that is lost until he finds it?" (v. 4). In spite of what this shepherd does, the proper answer is "none." This shepherd's behavior is abnormal. Losing one sheep is unfortunate, but a shepherd would be a fool to abandon the ninety-nine remaining sheep to be attacked by predators or scattered by aimless wandering. But this shepherd does just that! Moreover, when he finds the solitary lost sheep, he does not return it to the flock. Instead, he goes out of the shepherding business. Leaving the other sheep in the wilderness, he puts the found sheep upon his shoulders, goes home, and summons his neighbors to a party. The joy of that celebration reflects the heavenly joy over one sinner's repentance. The implication, of course, is that God is like that good shepherd.

In the second parable (vv. 8-10), a woman searches frantically for a lost silver coin. The Greek specifies the coin as a *drachma*, worth about a day's wage for a laborer. We are ignorant of the woman's circumstances, but since she lives in a home large enough for a lost coin to require some diligent searching, we can safely suppose that the loss of a single coin of this value was not a financial catastrophe. Nevertheless, she searches persistently, urgently, until she discovers the lost coin. Like the shepherd, she summons her neighbors to rejoice with her, another reflection of heavenly joy over a sinner who repents. The point is the same as the first parable, but the accent here is on bringing the lost back together with the rest.

A third parable, that of the so-called prodigal son (vv. 11-32), appears only in the longer LFM pericope and should really be titled "The Waiting Father" or "The Seeking Father." The traditional title inappropriately sets the focus of the parable on the prodigality of the younger son. But the parable is about neither the younger son nor his resentful older brother. It is, instead, about the father who, while his son was still far off, "saw him and was filled with compassion; he ran and put his arms around him and kissed him" (15:20). He could only have seen the son while he was still far off if he was looking for him. We have to imagine this father straining his eyes, peering down the roadway, hoping to see his long-lost child once more. And when the young man finally does return, the celebration is extravagant.

All three parables reveal a God who relentlessly searches for the lost and who celebrates lavishly when the lost is found. The preacher therefore would do well to focus on the searching God who stops at nothing—not even the blood of the Son—to recover the lost. On the other hand, the parables were aimed at the grumbling scribes and Pharisees (the "church" people), cast as the abandoned sheep, the never-lost coins, and the grumpy older brother. "Church" people then and now have a difficult time understanding that God's love ever encompasses a larger circle than they can imagine or than their understanding of the Scriptures and tradition allows.

First Reading

Exodus 32:7-14 (RCL)
Exodus 32:7-11, 13-14 (LFM)

The background for this reading is the apostasy of Aaron and the people recorded in Exodus 32:1-6. Even atop Mount Sinai, the Lord is aware of what the people have done. The Lord mocks the language of the Israelites, referring to them as "your [Moses'!] people" whom *Moses* had delivered from Egypt (v. 7). This is a painful break from the Lord's repeated identification of Israel as "my people" when the Lord first spoke to Moses (Exod. 3:7-10). Israel had forsaken the God who claimed her. They offered sacrifices and burnt offerings as part of a "festival to the LORD" (v. 5). It was those behaviors, quite apart from any "reveling" (v. 6), that constituted the people's perversion and defined how they turned aside from the way they were commanded. Consequently, the Lord intends to destroy Israel (v. 10). But we are not told how the

Lord will execute vengeance. God commands Moses to leave the divine presence, seemingly that the Lord might consider Israel's destruction. Perhaps, however, God sends Moses away because God knows that Moses will not let the wrath of God be the final word, even if it is tempered with an echo of the ancient promise to Abraham (v. 10).

Verses 11-13 report Moses' intercession before the Lord on behalf of the people. Moses appeals to the Lord on the basis of the Lord's reputation, noting that the Egyptians will read the wrong message (v. 12; see Num. 14:13-19). The closing argument, however, is a reminder of the Lord's unconditional promises to Abraham, Isaac, and Israel, recalling Genesis 15:7 and 18.

The NRSV translates the Hebrew verb *vayyinnakhem* as "changed his mind."[2] While correct, the translation does not provide the nuance of sorrow and regret that the verb connotes. Based on the appearance of the precise expression in Genesis 6:6, the verse might also be translated: "And the LORD was sorry about the disaster that he intended to do to his people." In any case, the idea of God changing God's course of action on the basis of Moses' intercession astonishes. The statement reminds us, first, that divine vengeance purposes to bring about the Lord's larger will of salvation. Second, the statement reminds us of the efficacy of intercessory prayer and the urgent need for it. Finally, the fact that the Lord so responds to Moses points us to Christ "who entered into heaven itself, now to appear in the presence of God on our behalf" (Heb. 9:24).

Jeremiah 4:11-12, 22-28 (RCL alt.)

Jeremiah prophesies of national disaster and destruction that will come from the north (v. 6). Verses 11 and 12 conclude an extended call to arms begun in verse 5. The poet describes the foe as a desiccating sirocco, sent as a judgment by the Lord, which is a consequence of Judah's rebellion (vv. 17-18). Verse 22 concludes a cry of anguish begun in verse 19. The cry is usually interpreted as an expression of Jeremiah's pain, although the references to "my tents" and "my curtains" in verse 20 and to "my people" in verse 22 leave open the possibility that we have here to do with the anguish that the Lord experiences in meting out God's own punishment. Verses 23-28 report a vision of the land subsequent to the apocalyptic destruction. The consequences of sin and rebellion revert the earth to the sort of formlessness and emptiness it had been before the creation (*tohu vabohu*, v. 23; see Gen. 1:2 where the same phrase is rendered "a formless void"). The celestial luminaries disappear (v. 23) and the mountains that support the firmament shake (v. 24). Indeed, the description is one of a horrific reversal of the creation in Genesis 1. The whole land will become "a desolation" (really, "a sinister wilderness"; *shemamah*, v. 27). Even so, the Lord's mercy is such that God declares, "I will not make a full end."

The link between human sin and environmental degradation has received a new and less metaphorical meaning in recent decades. Whatever one thinks about the scientific causes of global warming, the fact remains that unchecked consumption has filled our seas with plastic and our rain with acids. This is not the direct judgment of God, of course, but it does seem that God has created the world in such a way that sin's consequences are felt in our environment. What might Christians do?

Psalmody

Psalm 51:1-10 (RCL)

Psalm 51:3-4, 12-13, 17 + 19 (LFM)

The superscription associates this psalm with David's abuse of power in his affair with Bathsheba in 2 Samuel 11. While that tradition is late and artificial, the sentiments expressed in the psalm reflect what David surely ought to have said after forcing himself on Bathsheba and orchestrating the murder of Uriah. Verse 4 is a glaring exception, of course.

Formally, the psalm is an individual lament. The address (v. 1) is mixed with an appeal for mercy and forgiveness (vv. 1-2). Verses 3-5 represent a confession; the psalmist declares that he was a sinner *in utero*. More petitions for cleansing and forgiveness follow in verses 6-12. The petition for a clean heart (v. 10) is a petition for an ethically clean mind since, in Hebrew anthropology, the heart was considered the organ of reflection and reason. The vow typical of laments begins in verse 13: the psalmist will instruct transgressors (v. 13) and he will sing of God's salvation (v. 14). The psalmist recognizes that a contrite heart is the sacrifice God seeks (v. 17). Verses 18 and 19 are exilic or postexilic additions to the psalm.

The existence of online confession sites—and especially those that are simply public postings with no word of absolution—serve as a reminder that all of us have need of God's forgiveness, even if some of our neighbors are not sure how they might achieve that peace. The psalmist knew, of course, that his heart would be troubled until it was cleansed and his spirit renewed by God.

Psalm 14 (RCL alt.)

Psalm 14 is virtually identical to Psalm 53, but there are a few notable differences. Besides the name for God, in Psalm 14 the end of verse 5 differs from its counterpart in Psalm 53:

> There they shall be in great terror, *for God is with the company of the righteous.* (Ps. 14:5)
>
> There they shall be in great terror, in terror such as has not been. For God will scatter the bones of the ungodly; they will be put to shame, for God has rejected them. (Ps. 53:5)

In addition, verse 6 of Psalm 14 is missing in Psalm 53: "You would confound the plans of the poor, but the Lord is their refuge." For Psalm 14, therefore, the contrast is between the fool and the company of the righteous. The fool (*naval*) is not an atheist; Hebrew has no word for that concept. But the fool denies that God holds him accountable for his abominable deeds and his failure to do good (v. 1). In his view, there is "no God" in that sense. In addition, this fool turns aside (*sar* < *sur*, here "apostatizes"; see Deut. 9:12, 16) and becomes "perverse,"[3] unable to do any good. These evildoers consume the Lord's people like bread[4] and refuse to call upon the Lord (v. 4).

Such fools are promised terror for "God is with the company of the righteous" (v. 5), which includes the poor for whom the Lord is their refuge (v. 6). The psalm ends with an expression of hope that the Lord will soon restore the people.

Fools such as are described in this psalm abound still. The clear message of this psalm, however, is that the Lord keeps company with the righteous, including especially the righteous poor. The Lord is their refuge; their fortunes will be restored.

Second Reading

1 Timothy 1:12-17 (RCL, LFM)

The center of this section of praise is verse 15 and the christological claim there. "The saying is sure" is a formulaic saying restricted to the Pastoral Letters (also 1 Tim. 3:1; 4:9; 2 Tim. 2:11; Titus 3:8). Specifically, the sure saying is that "Christ Jesus came into the world to save sinners," of which group Paul regards himself as the foremost. That Christ Jesus came into the world to save sinners is, of course, a central tenant of the Christian faith. In this thanksgiving, Paul offers himself as an example of the quintessential saved sinner. He is "foremost" of sinners (v. 15), by which description we should understand that he regarded himself as the "greatest of them" (NJB) or the "worst" among them (TNIV).

Working from the extreme ends of the pericope back toward verse 15, we see a concentric pattern emerge. A passage that begins with thanksgiving (v. 12) ends with doxology (v. 17). Why is Paul thankful? Why does he praise? Paul is thankful because Christ strengthened him, judged him faithful, and appointed him to Christ's service (v. 12). "Service" (*diakonian*) is the apostle's favorite word for ministry and for the role of a leader in the community of faith.[5] Paul wonders at his appointment because at that juncture in his life he was "a blasphemer, a persecutor, and a man of violence" (v. 13). In contrast, Christ made him an example (*hypotypōsin*, a prototype, an example) for those who would come to believe in Jesus Christ (v. 16).

Paul's transformation is twice marked by the claim that he "received mercy" (*alla ēleēthēn*, vv. 13, 16). In the former instance, mercy came because he acted ignorantly in his unbelief (*apistia*). In the latter instance, Christ's mercy served to demonstrate Christ's unfathomable patience (*makrothymian*, patience, forbearance, to bear up under provocation).

One might wish to quibble with Paul about his status as "foremost" of sinners. His point, however, was how God in Christ was able to take the most improbable of people and make them into a prototype for those who would come to believe in him for eternal life. And for that he was filled with thankful praise.

Notes

1. Jesus will hear grumbling in Jericho (Luke 19:7) when he dines with Zacchaeus.
2. Other translations offer "repented" (KJV, RSV, JPS), "relented" (NJB), or "renounced" (Tanakh).
3. Based on an Arabic cognate meaning "to turn (milk) sour," the NJB translates "all alike turned sour." See Job 15:16.
4. A similar image appears in Mic. 3:1-3; Ps. 27:2; and Prov. 30:14.
5. W. Hulitt Gloer, *1 and 2 Timothy, Titus*, Smyth & Helwys Bible Commentary (Macon, GA: Smyth & Helwys, 2010), 122.

September 22, 2013
Lectionary 25 / Twenty-Fifth Sunday in Ordinary Time / Proper 20
Eighteenth Sunday after Pentecost

Revised Common Lectionary (RCL)

Amos 8:4-7 or Jeremiah 8:18—9:1
Psalm 113 or 79:1-9
1 Timothy 2:1-7
Luke 16:1-13

Lectionary for Mass (LFM)

Amos 8:4-7
Psalm 113:1-2, 4-6, 7-8
1 Timothy 2:1-8
Luke 16:1-13 or 16:10-13

Gospel
Luke 16:1-13 (RCL, LFM)
Luke 16:10-13 (LFM alt.)

The meaning of the parable of the unjust steward is maddeningly elusive. The steward "cooks" his master's books, but how does that help him? And why is the steward commended by his master? Are Jesus' listeners encouraged to emulate the steward? If so, how? By being dishonest? And what does Jesus mean when he says, "Make friends for yourselves by means of dishonest wealth so that when it is gone, they may welcome you into the eternal homes" (v. 9)?

In spite of the questions that the parable evokes, some points are clear. First, the parable is eschatological in character. Both the steward's behavior and the master's judgment nudge us to consider a final reckoning for which we ought to prepare. Second, whatever the steward is up to, he is commended by the master in the parable (and, we suppose, by Jesus) because "he had acted shrewdly" (v. 8). We are to learn from that, but what is the lesson?

Much depends on what the steward actually does when he deals with his master's debtors. The steward knows he will be sacked and that his termination is a consequence of his "squandering" of his master's property. The text actually says that he "spread around his possessions" (*diaskorpizōn ta hyparchonta autou*). The profligate son did likewise (*dieskorpisen*) in the parable of the waiting father (Luke 15:13). As the steward is, by his own confession, too puny for manual labor and too proud to beg, he hits upon a strategy to save himself before he has to pack up his personal items and leave the office forever. As keeper of his master's books, he forgives a portion of the debt owed to his master's accounts by those debtors.

The crux is what the price reduction might signify, other than a relief for the debtors. The text is silent, of course. If, however, we suppose that the discount offered (50 percent for oil, 20 percent for grain) represents the steward's "commission," then aspects of the text become clear.[1] The debtors, on the one hand, rejoice because their debt is greatly relieved. If they understand that this has come about because the steward has sacrificed his own immediate interests in the transaction, they are quite likely to welcome him as a generous fellow and a friend after the steward is officially handed his pink slip. The steward, on the other hand, calculates that the short-term loss will be worth the longer-term reward. He will live off the gratitude and the largess of his master's debtors long after he has lost his place. And the master, who has lost nothing in the transaction, applauds the cunning of the steward who planned for his future by sacrificing all of the resources at his disposal.

If the parable is viewed as an eschatological cautionary tale, Jesus' listeners might understand that the impending reign of God will bring judgment for which they should be prepared. And, in Luke's view, that judgment will be especially harsh on the wealthy (1:53; 6:24; 12:13-21; 16:13). In this case, however, the unjust steward has divested himself of his resources in order to save himself. So should the "children of light" do with their planning and resources as they prepare for their eternal homes (v. 9).

Verses 10-13 are parabolic-like sayings gathered about the subject of money and the need for wisdom in its use. Verse 13 serves as a summary of these sayings and of the parable that precedes them. Money, and the pseudo security that it brings, is the wrong master to which to pledge our allegiance. That said, our social values make serving God rather than mammon quite difficult. Just ask any congregational treasurer about that!

First Reading
Amos 8:4-7 (RCL, LFM)

Amos 8:1-3 comprises the fourth of five prophetic visions (see 7:1-3, 4-6, 7-9; 9:1-4), for which verses 4-14 provide an interpretation. In the vision, the prophet is shown a basket of pleasant summer fruit. But, by a play of words, the Lord announces that the summer fruit (*qayits*) points to Israel's end (*qets*). Divine abandonment ("I will never again pass them by") precedes mourning and slaughter (v. 3).

Why will this come to pass? The Lord explains through Amos by repeating earlier charges and employing language used elsewhere in the book.[2] The summons "Hear this!" (3:1; 4:1; 5:1) is followed by accusations against the rich for their pitiless assault on the poor. They trample (*sha'af*; see 2:7) the needy (*'evyon*). Their abuse of the holy days in verse 5 echoes Amos 5:21-23 and the Lord's disapprobation of the pseudo piety disclosed in that earlier chapter. In this instance, the wealthy pine for the holy days to pass so that they might resume their dishonest business practices (see Isa. 1:12-17;

Lev. 19:35; Deut. 25:13-16). The wealthy buy the needy (*'evyon*) for the price of a pair of sandals (in Amos 2:6 they sell the *'evyon* for that price). They even sell the refuse or sweepings of the grain as if it were actual grain (v. 6). Swearing by the pride of Jacob (see 6:8), the Lord avers that none of their deeds will be forgotten. In this instance, the Lord's memory is not good news for Israel!

It takes precious little imagination for Amos's indictment to be translated into our contemporary circumstances. The temptation is to pillory persons in our own day whose fantastic wealth and comfort have come by "trampling the needy and bringing ruin to the land." Some of those rascals surely deserve public "outing." But the problem is that, from the perspective of the developing world, most of North America's citizenry look like the wealthy Israelites of Amos's day. Will the Lord forget our deeds? Is our incessant drive for "more" appropriate for the followers of Jesus?

Jeremiah 8:18—9:1 (RCL alt.)

It is difficult to determine who the speakers might be in the anguished lament of Jeremiah 8:18—9:1. Is this the Lord speaking? Or is the grief expressed that of the prophet? Terence E. Fretheim is doubtless correct when he suggests that we need not distinguish sharply between the voice of the prophet and the voice of the Lord in this and other lamenting texts: "The voice of God is primary; if Jeremiah speaks these words, it is because God first speaks them. The lamenting prophet embodies the words of a lamenting God."[3]

What is it, then, that makes the Lord heartsick (v. 18)? The answer is the cry of "my poor people,"[4] whose confidence is imperfectly placed in a belief in the Royal Zion tradition. That tradition held, in part, that the Lord would never let Jerusalem and the temple fall. Jeremiah's contemporaries mouthed slogans to that effect: "Is the Lord not in Zion? Is her King not in her?" (v. 19b; see 7:4). The prophet's contemporaries comprehended neither that people who lived in God's presence should conduct themselves accordingly nor that they could not violate the commandments and then come to the Lord's house proclaiming, "We are safe!" (Jer. 7:10). Jeremiah's contemporaries violated the first and most basic commandment, the prohibition against worshiping other gods (v. 19c; see Jer. 7:18; 44:17-19, 25). Consequently, their complaint (quoted by the Lord/Jeremiah) to the end that the season has passed for their salvation (v. 20) is just pathetic. The Lord is hurt and mourns in verse 21 (and, probably, in v. 22).

The assumed answer to the question in verse 22a is, "Yes, there is." The Gilead styrax tree produces a resin that then was widely thought to be medicinally efficacious. So why are the Israelites not healed? There *is* a balm in Gilead! The fact that the people are not healed causes profound pain to the Lord/prophet since healing and reconciliation are at hand. Jeremiah 9:1 concludes the lament and points the reader back to the God whose joy is gone and who laments for the sake of God's people. It also points us forward to the heartsick Father who witnesses the crucifixion of the Son.

Jeremiah's oracle illuminates the passion of the Lord. The ultimate expression of that passion, however, and the embodiment of the God who suffers in anguish and who would bring an erring people home, is Jesus. Jesus wept over Jerusalem and invited his auditors to a sure refuge comprised of the wings of God (Matt. 23:37 // Luke 13:34). This Lord asks only that we believe that he has already purchased us, "not with silver and gold, but with his holy and precious blood and his innocent sufferings and death."[5] Such is our true balm.

Psalmody
Psalm 113 (RCL)
Psalm 113:1-2, 4-6, 7-8 (LFM)

Appropriately, this praise psalm begins and ends with the summons for the servants of the Lord to praise the Lord, *Halleluia!* The comprehensive nature of this praise is expressed in terms of time (v. 2) and space (vv. 3-4). From the exalted place of God in the heavens, the Lord looks down (vv. 4-6). The description of the Lord sitting in the heavens, holding sway over the nations, calls to mind the ascension of Jesus Christ (Acts 1:4-12) where Christ rules with God, exercises God's authority, and, as the Apostles' Creed confesses, "from whence he will come to judge the living and the dead." A preview of that judgment and of God's will for the kingdom appears in verses 7-9: the poor will be raised from the dust and the needy from the *ash heap*[6] and set in places among the royalty (v. 8; see 1 Sam. 2:8). The childless woman will be stigmatized no longer; she will have a home and children (v. 9). The psalm insists that this vision of reality will replace the present injustices. This is good news for the poor, the outcasts, and all who would see the Lord's dominion hold sway from east to west. Praise the Lord!

Psalm 79:1-9 (RCL alt.)

Psalm 79 is a communal lament bewailing the destruction of the temple and Jerusalem. While this psalm was long thought to be a reflection of the destruction wrought by the Babylonians in 586 BCE, recent research has pointed to the similarity between this psalm and Babylonian ritual laments that were unattached to any historical event.[7] As it is, the images of this psalm depict a scene of horrific destruction, the likes of which were largely unknown in North America before September 11, 2001. The psalmist summons God to put away divine anger (v. 5) and, instead, to direct God's wrath toward kingdoms that do not acknowledge God (v. 6). The psalmist asks that the iniquities of their ancestors not be held against them (v. 8; see Exod. 20:5 // Deut. 5:9; Lam. 5:7), and urges God to act for the following reasons: (1) for the sake of God's reputation (v. 10a); (2) for the sake of the blood of the Lord's people, shed by their enemies (v. 10b); and (3) because God's people have become prisoners (v. 11). In contrast to the enemy taunt in verse 10, the psalmist pledges the eternal praise of the Lord's people.

Although North Americans rarely suffer homeland assaults from a national enemy, communities of faith around the world do. This psalm helps us to be compassionate and pray for our suffering brothers and sisters. It is noteworthy that here, as in the lament psalms generally, the psalmist prays that God would execute God's justice and *not* that the psalmist himself might become the agent of vengeance.

Second Reading
1 Timothy 2:1-7 (RCL)
1 Timothy 2:1-8 (LFM)

The instructions that the author introduces in 1 Timothy 1:18 begin to unfold in 2:1 and continue to 3:15. These are the instructions to the "church of the living God" (3:15).

Timothy is informed that the highest priority ("first of all") is supplications, prayers, intercessions, and thanksgivings. Each noun has its own nuance. "Supplications" (*deēseis*) is an urgent request to God to meet a need. "Prayers" (*proseuchas*) signifies a conversation with God or a request to God. *Enteuxeis* occurs in the New Testament only here and in 1 Timothy 4:5. The word refers to intercessory prayer, or speaking to God on behalf of others. The church's prayer life should also include thanksgivings (*eucharistias*; see 1 Tim. 4:3-4; Phil. 4:6). Again, prayer in all of these forms is "first of all"—the preeminent task that is to occupy the household of God. More than that, such prayers are to be offered "for everyone" (*hyper pantōn anthrōpōn*). Intercessions and thanksgivings are to be offered even for kings and others in high positions—including some who doubtless were hostile to the household of God. The benefit of prayers for such authorities is that believers might live peaceable lives that are characterized by godliness (*eusebeia*) and dignity (v. 2). Verse 4 reveals why prayers should be offered "for everyone," since God desires that "everyone" (*pantas anthrōpous*) might be saved and come to understand the truth, namely that "there is one God; there is also one mediator between God and humankind [*anthrōpōn*], Christ Jesus, himself human [*anthrōpos*]." For this reason, the writer avers, he was appointed a "herald and apostle" to the Gentiles.

It is striking that these "instructions"[8] accent the universality of God's work in Christ. God desires that "everyone" should be saved and that all might know that Jesus is the sole mediator between God and human beings—*all* human beings. The passage instructs us to pray and to evangelize. It is not just the writer of 1 Timothy, but *all* of the baptized who are called to herald the good news. And we dare not be discriminating about who it is to whom we speak and for whom the household of God prays! God desires that everyone should be saved and come to the truth (v. 4), even those—perhaps especially those—we do not much like or love.

Notes

1. Joseph A. Fitzmyer, *The Gospel According to Luke (X–XXIV)*, Anchor Bible 28A (Garden City, NJ: Doubleday, 1985), 675–981.

2. James D. Nogaski, *Hosea–Jonah*, Smyth & Helwys Bible Commentary (Macon, GA: Smyth & Helwys, 2011), 344.
3. Terence E. Fretheim, *Jeremiah*, Smyth & Helwys Bible Commentary (Macon, GA: Smyth & Helwys, 2002), 148.
4. Literally, "the daughter of my people" (*bat 'ammî*). The expression is a personification of Jerusalem. See Isa. 22:4; Jer. 4:11; 6:26; 8:11, 19, 21ff.; 9:1 [Heb. 9:6]; 14:17; Lam. 2:11; 3:48; 4:3, 6, 10.
5. Martin Luther, "The Small Catechism," in *The Book of Concord*, trans. and ed. Theodore G. Tappert (Philadelphia: Fortress Press, 1959), 345.
6. *Me'ashpot*, "ash heap," refers to piles of garbage and manure.
7. Walter C. Bouzard, *We Have Heard with Our Ears, O God: Sources of the Communal Laments in the Psalms*, Society of Biblical Literature Dissertation Series 159 (Atlanta: Scholars Press, 1997).
8. The noun is *parangelian* (1 Tim. 1:18), and it refers to an announcement of something that must be done.

September 29, 2013
Lectionary 26 / Twenty-Sixth Sunday in Ordinary Time / Proper 21
Nineteenth Sunday after Pentecost

Revised Common Lectionary (RCL)

Amos 6:1a, 4-7 or Jeremiah 32:1-3a, 6-15
Psalm 146 or 91:1-6, 14-16
1 Timothy 6:6-19
Luke 16:19-31

Lectionary for Mass (LFM)

Amos 6:1a, 4-7
Psalm 146:6c-7, 8-9a, 9b-10
1 Timothy 6:11-16
Luke 16:19-31

Gospel
Luke 16:19-31 (RCL, LFM)

If you thought you finally had heard the last word on the dangers of money in last week's reading with Jesus' declaration, "You cannot serve God and wealth" (Luke 16:13), it turns out that the subject is important enough to bring it back in the parable of the rich man and Lazarus. Between verse 13 and the parable are an odd collection of sayings, mostly dropped into a mysterious relationship to what comes before and after them. With verse 19, however, we return to the subject of the dangers of mammon or of being a money lover.[1]

Jesus tells the parable far better than I could; the reader is encouraged thoughtfully to reread the parable. Several points do, however, merit special attention. First of all, the income disparity between the nameless rich man and the starving, sore-encrusted Lazarus could not be more evident. Lazarus lay at the rich man's gate, longing to satisfy his hunger (*chortasthēnai*) with what fell from the rich man's table. The verb translated "to satisfy his hunger" (here an infinitive) appears elsewhere in Luke at 6:21, the beatitude about how the hungry will be filled. That beatitude's promise is previewed in 9:17 when the hungry crowd is satisfied with the loaves and fishes Jesus provides. Finally, the prodigal son longs to have his hunger satisfied in his father's home (Luke 15:17). Satiation, the satisfaction of hunger, is clearly a mark of God's reign. Moreover, in this parable, that aspect of God's reign and will is just as plainly something the rich man might have advanced from the things that, in his opulence, he simply wasted.

Second, it is not just the narrator (or Jesus) who knows Lazarus's name. When the rich man sees Lazarus resting comfortably at Abraham's side, he begs, "Father Abraham, have mercy on me, and send Lazarus, that he may dip the tip of his finger in water . . ." (v. 24). The request is a self-indictment: he knew Lazarus's name! That means, however, that he knew of Lazarus's suffering, of Lazarus's hunger, and of Lazarus's illness. He saw the very face of the most abject poverty and misery. He stepped past it every day as he headed to his richly laden table. He could give that despair a name, Lazarus (!), but he did not bother to lift the tip of his finger to provide a thing that Lazarus needed physically to survive, let alone what Lazarus needed to live with human dignity (see 1 Tim. 6:19 in today's second reading). Day after day, for who knows how long, he simply ignored the man who lay dying at his doorstep.

Third, and most obviously, the parable teaches that there are consequences for willful neglect of our neighbor. The wealthy are held particularly responsible (see Luke 6:25). If many of our neighborhoods are too pristine to see Lazarus literally lying at the gate (most neighborhoods are so sanitized, although many are not!), we are not let off the hook. The need of our neighbor and the faces and names of Lazarus appear in virtually every evening news broadcast and on our denominational websites.

Fourth, the rich man reaps his reward precisely as a member of the household of faith. Familial terms abound: "Father Abraham" (vv. 24, 27, 30), "son" (v. 25), his "father's house" (v. 27), and his five "brothers" (v. 28). The rich man knows that his father's household—sons of Abraham all—are headed for his same wretched end. These people knew what he should have done with respect to Lazarus and others like him. They had the Torah but did not heed it. Abraham ruefully tells this son of Abraham that not even a postmortem message from Lazarus will persuade them.

The parable doubtless was as much of a punch in the gut for the money-loving Pharisees as it is for us. The rich man doesn't seem to be particularly evil. He does, after all, intercede for his brothers. But neither does he connect the dots between his identity as a child of Abraham and the summons to be a conduit of God's blessings to the world ("and in you all the families of the earth shall be blessed," Gen. 12:3).

There is a lot of that selective disconnect going around the Christian household of faith as well. We hear the increasingly loud voices of apparently heartless people blame the poor and distressed in the world for their own plight. Card-carrying Christians side with political ideologies and policies that keep Lazarus away from the scraps on the basis that relief should come to the poor through personal acts of noncompulsory kindness, or that the poor should become more personally responsible and improve themselves, or that families should take care of their own. No doubt the rich man thought the same. But that sort of thinking—and the point of the parable—is to keep us on the proper side of the chasm standing between Hades and Father Abraham, together with his prominent Son. And that happens, in part, when we take our eyes off the dinner table and look around to see and care for Lazarus.

First Reading

Amos 6:1a, 4-7 (RCL, LFM)

Amos 6:1-7 comprises a unit that begins (v. 1) with a woe oracle addressed to Judah (Zion) and Israel (Mount Samaria). Charges of gross self-indulgence (vv. 3[?], 4-6) and the promise of appropriate punishment (v. 7) conclude the unit. Verse 2 and possibly verse 3 may be later insertions since the cities mentioned fell to the Assyrians between 738 and 734 BCE. Verse 3, however, seems more likely to be a part of the condemnation of Amos's contemporaries. First, there is no reason to suppose that verse 3 completes the thought expressed in verse 2. Moreover, the crimes of those charged by Amos appear as masculine plural participles with a definite article, placed at the first word of verses 4, 5, and 6. This pattern is matched exactly by verse 3. Finally, the "alas" inserted by the translators of the NRSV in verse 4, doubtless to link it to the woe oracle of verse 1, could just as defensibly have been inserted at the beginning of verse 3. If this reading is correct, the "evil day" may refer back to the misplaced hopes in the "day of the LORD" in Amos 5:18-20.

Through the Lord, the prophet condemns those who live lives of selfish luxury, who lie upon their ivory overlaid beds while stuffing themselves with lamb and veal. Moreover, they "sing idle songs" (*happoretim*, v. 5). The exact meaning of *happoretim* remains a mystery, although the present context suggests the NRSV is close to the mark. The point is not the Lord's antipathy to music, but the sort of purposeless, indolent lounging about that the context implies. Images of self-indulgence follow. James D. Nogaski proposes that wine consumption was so exaggerated, ordinary goblets would not do; the Samaritans were obliged to drink from the mixing bowls in which the spices and wine were combined in order to keep up. Likewise, rather than anoint honored guests at a special festival as was the custom, the wealthy in Samaria anointed themselves.[2] Self-indulgence such as this would not be long tolerated; the revelry of the loungers would soon end as the nation was taken captive (v. 7).

These words from Amos provide yet another opportunity to reflect on our own lifestyles and the priorities of faith communities. Personal and congregational budgets are a good place to begin. Do our expenditures reflect self-service or service to others?

Jeremiah 32:1-3a, 6-15 (RCL alt.)

The time frame of this oracle can be established with some certainty. Nebuchadrezzar II, the king of Babylon, was besieging the city while Jeremiah was imprisoned in the palace (32:2; 33:1). It was King Zedekiah's tenth year of rule. Since Nebuchadrezzar placed Zedekiah on the seat of royal power in 597, the present scene comes from near the end of 587 BCE. Once again, Jerusalem was besieged by Nebuchadrezzar, and this time Judah teetered on the cusp of utter destruction. Against any who still upheld the old Royal Zion tradition of Zion's inviolability, Jeremiah consistently pronounced impending doom. In fact, King Zedekiah upbraided Jeremiah for his treasonous message, which included word of the king's own dismal future as a captive in Babylon (vv. 3b-5).

Contrary to all expectations, and in the face of the immanent chaos from the military conquest of Judah, the word of the Lord comes to the prophet with instructions for him to redeem a piece of family property near his hometown of Anathoth, which would soon be offered by his cousin Hanamel (vv. 6-7). When Hanamel subsequently appears before Jeremiah with the sales proposal, the prophet perceives that—as the word came to pass—he had heard an authentic word of the Lord (see Deut. 18:21-22).

Jeremiah takes no small amount of effort to make sure that the transaction is duly and legally executed, with witnesses procured to testify to the price, the exchange of deed, and the terms and conditions of the sale. The deed itself is given to Jeremiah's scribe Baruch with a strict charge that two copies of the deed—one sealed and the other opened—might be secured in a clay jar and thus preserved.

All of this, of course, must have mystified Hanamel and the rest. Land purchase under such conditions was counterintuitive at best since all the land was quite soon to belong to Nebuchadrezzar. Verse 15, of course, clarifies the prophet's motives. As a part of his larger message of consolation (chs. 30–33), the prophet asserts that, on the other side of doom, "Houses and fields and vineyards shall again be bought in this land." Jeremiah must, of course, accept that outcome by faith since nothing in the historical situation pointed toward any such end. Nor did the prophet live to see the promise fulfilled; the waning of Babylon was four decades later. Still, he acted in faith and, one can suppose, lived in hope that God's purposes would be worked out in the course of time. The writer of Hebrews hints that he might have done just that since the prophets are listed among those who, "though they were commended for their faith, did not receive what was promised, since God had provided something better so that they would not, apart from us, be made perfect" (Heb. 11:39-40). The promises of restoration all find their completion in Christ in whom we live and hope.

Psalmody

Psalm 146 (RCL)

Psalm 146:6c-7, 8-9a, 9b-10 (LFM)

This hymn of praise extols the Lord's work in nature (v. 6) but also the Lord's just rule in society. In contrast to the power of princes who perish (vv. 3-4), the Lord "keeps faith forever" (v. 6). The eternal faith (*'emeth*) signifies God's trustworthiness and constancy. That divine faithfulness expresses itself in concrete acts of salvation directed toward those whom society has marginalized. Indeed, verses 7-9 list those people who are of special divine concern. Yes, the righteous are included (v. 8), but mostly we hear the Lord's treatment of prisoners, alien sojourners, and the poor. The verbs associated with the Lord's actions in verses 7-9 provide a blueprint for the activities of God's people and the means by which the Lord's reign (v. 10) is manifested among us.

Psalm 91:1-6, 14-16 (RCL alt.)

Psalm 91 is a temple liturgy that praises the Lord's power and will to care for and to protect those who abide near the Lord. First, we hear from someone who urges people who enter the sanctuary to profess their confidence in the Lord, and who continues by describing the benefits that surround those for whom the Lord is their refuge and fortress (vv. 3-13). The speaker is likely a priest or some temple minister who seemingly speaks from his own experiences that the Lord is reliable in all of life's circumstances. In verses 14-16 we hear the Lord confirm the claims of what has come before.

Verses 1 and 2 are a response to the petitions of Psalm 90 that urge the Lord to save. Here images of safety and protection are preeminent, all calculated to affirm the claim made explicit in verse 2: God is a reliable *refuge* and a *fortress.*

Any who trust God to be their refuge will escape the fowler and will instead be sheltered under the wings of the Almighty (see Deut. 32:11; Exod. 19:4). Protected by such wings, the faithful need not fear assault. The images in verses 5 and 6 alternate between dangers of the night and day and so connote God's constant vigilant care (see Ps. 121:6-7).

The Lord speaks, likely through a liturgical actor, in verse 14. A deluge of seven verbs (a complete or whole number?) promising the Lord's salvation all surround the verbless clause "I [will be] with them" that is found in verse 15 and in the dead center of the divine speech in verses 14-16. The fact that these verbs of promise surround the declaration of the Lord's presence is interpretively important. The protection of God does not befall the psalmist because he has made a decision about the Lord. To the contrary, he simply confesses what he experienced: the Lord simply is his "refuge" and "fortress," the trustworthy God (v. 2). The promises of God now radiate out from the center of these verses and from the promised presence of God with God's people. When disaster strikes, as it does for all of us, we can also look to the angel ("messenger," v. 11) whom God has sent to remind people, through words and deeds, of God's sheltering presence. Indeed, from time to time we are summoned to be just such an angel for others.

Second Reading

1 Timothy 6:6-19 (RCL)

1 Timothy 6:11-16 (LFM)

In these closing verses of 1 Timothy, the writer turns to the subject of godliness or piety toward God (*eusebeia*), suggesting that this characteristic, combined with contentment, is a benefit (v. 6). Having sufficient food and clothing is enough (v. 8), especially considering we came into the world with nothing and will take nothing with us. On the other hand, much of verses 9-19, like other lessons appointed for this day, have to do with the dangers of seeking wealth since that leads to temptations and foolish desires "that plunge people into ruin and destruction" (v. 9). Although few believe it, the author asserts that the love of money is a root of all kinds of evil (v. 10a); and the desire to be rich has led many away from the faith. To the contrary, Timothy is to pursue six higher virtues (v. 11) and thereby fight the good fight of faith (v. 12). The first three of the virtues are addressed to God—righteousness (*dikaiosynēn*, living in right relationship with God), godliness (*eusebeian*, a way of life acceptable to God; see v. 6), and faith (*pistin*, trust to the point of obedience)—while the latter three have to do with conduct toward the neighbor—love (*agapēn*, self-giving love to others), endurance (*hypomonēn*, the ability to hold on in faith), and gentleness (*praupathian*, either humility or gentleness toward others).[3]

Some ambiguity exists about the "commandment" Timothy is to keep (v. 14). Certainly, he is to cling fast to the one who is the quickening God (*zōogonountos*) and to Jesus Christ who testified (about himself?) before Pilate.

In verse 17, Timothy is instructed once again on the handling of the rich who tend to bank on mammon rather than on the Almighty. The proper use of resources is to do good works and to share (v. 18), an investment strategy that allows the wealthy (and the rest of us) to "take hold of the life that really is life" (*hina epilabōntai tēs ontōs zōēs*, v. 19). That lovely last expression, distinguishing as it does between the futile search for substance in our ceaseless acquisition on the one hand, and authentic being on the other, is a word much needed in an age where life is no deeper nor more substantial than whatever screen we happen to be viewing.

Notes

1. Verses 14 and 15 do continue the theme of money and wealth in that the Pharisees, charged as *philargyroi*, "lovers of money" (lit. "lovers of silver"), scoff at Jesus (*exemyktērizon*; see 23:35, the only other appearance of this verb in the New Testament).
2. James D. Nogaski, *Hosea–Jonah*, Smyth & Helwys Bible Commentary (Macon, GA: Smyth & Helwys, 2011), 329.
3. W. Hulitt Gloer, *1 and 2 Timothy, Titus*, Smyth & Helwys Bible Commentary (Macon, GA: Smyth & Helwys, 2010), 202.

Time after Pentecost / Ordinary Time
Lectionary 27 / Proper 22 through Christ the King / Reign of Christ

Lance Pape

The designation "Ordinary Time" is not a judgment about the lack of excitement on offer in the final weeks of the Christian year. Rather, it refers to the numbers or "ordinals" that mark and distinguish these Sundays. At the same time, it is true that the reason they are simply numbered is that these weeks do not fall within one of the special liturgical seasons by which the church marks time. Yet these concluding weeks of the church's calendar do include three special festivals: All Saints Day is celebrated on November 1, or on the following Sunday; Reign of Christ crowns the year by crowning Christ as King; and readings are provided for Thanksgiving Day, which is celebrated on the following Thursday, just a few days before the beginning of Advent and a new year.[1]

During these weeks, the Revised Common Lectionary offers an optional series of semicontinuous readings from the Hebrew Bible. In addition to readings selected to complement the Gospel, these weeks afford the opportunity to explore readings from the Prophets including brief ventures into seldom-explored territory like Habakkuk and Haggai. The Gospel readings from Luke include passages from the end of Jesus' journey toward Jerusalem (9:51—19:27). As Jesus draws near the city where he will suffer and die, discipleship is a recurring theme. Once he enters Jerusalem, we encounter texts about the promise and nature of the resurrection life (20:27-38), and an extended discourse on how disciples should dispose themselves toward upheaval, persecution, and last things (21:5-19). The epistle readings during these weeks encourage the church to engage passages that tend to fall outside the functional canon of many congregations. Readings from the Pastoral Epistles and even the disturbingly confrontational 2 Thessalonians present a challenge for preaching that should occasionally be embraced.

One feature that surfaces with surprising regularity in Year C Ordinary Time is apocalyptic discourse. Between pop-culture obsession with zombies and other end-of-the-world-as-we-know-it scenarios, and the preoccupation of some conserving traditions with elaborate timetables and triumphalistic raptures, many progressive Christians are too willing to cede these important parts of the Bible over to those who understand them least. In *Preaching from Memory to Hope*,[2] homiletician Tom Long argues that the mainline churches are suffering from an inability to be articulate about our Christian hope in the face of apathy and despair. During these weeks, readings from Joel, Daniel, Revelation, Luke, and 2 Thessalonians provide an opportunity to think through these issues and explore the outlines of an eschatology that takes seriously both our late modern context and the Bible's unshakable insistence that the future belongs to God and God alone. These passages include strange imagery intended to shake us out of our normal patterns of thinking and open our eyes to the ways God's will and creation's ultimate destiny are being "uncovered" ("apocalypse" means "uncovering") in the midst of a world that is often hostile to the purposes and people of God.

During "Ordinary" Time, and all the time, the church goes about its extraordinary work of attending carefully to the testimony of Scripture, displaying its surprising world through liturgy and preaching, and reimagining life's possibilities anew in its light.

Notes

1. Lutheran churches and some other Protestant denominations celebrate Reformation Day/Sunday on October 31 or the previous Sunday (on October 13 in 2013). Commentary on the texts for this festival is not provided here but may be found in *New Proclamation Commentary on Feasts, Holy Days, and Other Celebrations*, ed. David B. Lott (Minneapolis: Fortress Press, 2007), 208–13, along with commentary on other minor festivals of the church year.
2. Thomas G. Long, *Preaching from Memory to Hope* (Louisville: Westminster John Knox, 2009).

October 6, 2013
Lectionary 27 / Twenty-Seventh Sunday in Ordinary Time / Proper 22
Twentieth Sunday after Pentecost

Revised Common Lectionary (RCL)	**Lectionary for Mass (LFM)**
Habakkuk 1:1-4; 2:1-4 or Lamentations 1:1-6	Habakkuk 1:2-3; 2:2-4
Psalm 37:1-9 or Lamentations 3:19-26 or Psalm 137	Psalm 95:1-2, 6-7b, 7c-9
2 Timothy 1:1-14	2 Timothy 1:6-8, 13-14
Luke 17:5-10	Luke 17:5-10

First Reading
Habakkuk 1:1-4; 2:1-4 (RCL)
Habakkuk 1:2-3; 2:2-4 (LFM)

Habakkuk is identified as a prophetic oracle in 1:1, but the genre of the opening verses is actually closer to an individual psalm of lament. Rather than speaking a word from the Lord, this first-person passage is a record of the prophet being articulate with God in the face of a growing threat to Judah from the Chaldeans. The cry of "How long?" (1:2) is a raw insistence that intolerable circumstances demand a divine response. This is a cry of faith, not doubt: to complain that God is deaf to our cries of "Violence!" (disruption, chaos) is to cling to the conviction that God is real and could respond if willing.

In the second part of the lection (2:1-4), the prophet stakes out a position at the watchpost, high on the city wall, to wait for an answer to his complaint. He is determined to wait for as long as necessary—wait in the place where he will be the first to know if and when news comes at last. Exposed on the rampart, he places himself in full view of God and all creation. However this ends, there will be witnesses. When God's answer comes at last, there is an assurance that all this complaining and waiting is not in vain. Although it is late, it is not too late. From God's perspective the outcome was never in doubt, "for there is still a vision for the appointed time" (2:3). The promise is as certain as ever: "You can write it down," God promises; "make it plain on tablets" (2:2) for all to see. The imagery of this passage is one of the church's great resources for responding faithfully to experiences of God's absence.

Lamentations 1:1-6 (RCL alt.)

Because Lamentations is traditionally associated with the prophet, the opening verses of this book are included as part of the semicontinuous readings from Jeremiah. Written in the aftermath of the brutal siege and capture of Jerusalem by the Babylonians in 586 BCE, the poem is an anguished lament for all that is lost, and a daring bid to make theological sense of a national catastrophe. In this lection, the city is compared to a grieving and lonely widow; in her youth she was a princess, but now a subservient vassal (v. 1). She is awake all night crying because the other nations she once took as "lovers" have abandoned and betrayed her to Babylon (v. 2). The poet is clear about the cause: "The LORD has made her suffer for the multitude of her transgressions; her children have gone away, captives before the foe" (v. 5). This brutally honest expression of sorrow and searching admission of guilt is without analog in our culture, making the preacher's task all the more strange and difficult. The power of Lamentations is its refusal to blink in the face of bewildering experience. The preacher who embraces the challenge of this text should honor this courage by weaving connections to the congregation's own experiences of the absence of God, and resisting the temptation to move too quickly or easily toward resolution and reorientation. See the psalmic response from Lamentations 3:19-26 (below) for a word of hope in the midst of such anguish.

Psalmody

Psalm 37:1-9 (RCL)

Psalm 95:1-2, 6-7b, 7c-9 (LFM)

Psalm 37 is the response to Habakkuk, the first portion of which (1:1-4) is itself a psalm of lament. The obvious connection between these poems is the theme of waiting: "Be still before the LORD, and wait patiently for him" (v. 7). Unlike the poem in Habakkuk, the genre here is wisdom. Psalm 37 is chock-full of advice about what to do while you wait. Three times in the span of these nine verses we are told not to "fret" (vv. 1, 7, 8). Positively, the reader is encouraged to "trust," "take delight," and "commit" (vv. 3-5). Somehow all this activity is not in conflict with the admonition to "be still" in the presence of God (v. 7). Not only is this psalm boldly imperative, but it does not hesitate to predict the outcome of such confident and productive waiting: "He will make your vindication shine like the light, and the justice of your cause like the noonday" (v. 6). With a similarly confident tone, Psalm 95 resolves the waiting of Habakkuk with a description of the people entering God's presence to worship with great joy (vv. 1-2). Bowing before God, we acknowledge that we are kept safe in God's hand (vv. 6-7).

Lamentations 3:19-26 or Psalm 137 (RCL alt.)

Lamentations 3:19-26 is the response to the first reading from Lamentations 1:1-6. Verses 21-26 fall like a beam of dazzling light piercing the gloom of five chapters of despair. The preacher should remember that this brilliant effect depends upon context and contrast—the word of hope expressed in these verses shines all the brighter because it comes so unexpectedly in the midst of lament. Given the unmitigated disaster of the present, what resources can be summoned to articulate hope? The poet draws upon deep wells of memory (v. 21) to fuel anticipation of deliverance (v. 26), and so, despite all appearances to the contrary, confesses that God's steadfast care is as sure as each morning's new light (v. 23).

The alternative response to Lamentations 1:1-6 is Psalm 137. In striking contrast to Lamentations 3, this poem explores a different use of memory, and the liturgy that follows its cues will test the limits of honesty with God by descending still further into grief and even anger. For this psalmist, memories of Zion's former glory are not a comfort and a source of hope, but a bitter reminder of the heights from which Israel has fallen (vv. 1-3). As if through clenched teeth, the poet vows allegiance to the memory of Jerusalem (vv. 4-6) and lashes out with shocking rhetorical violence against the Babylonian captors (vv. 7-9). This poem is not a guide for ethics, but it does model honesty over decorum in prayer.

Second Reading

2 Timothy 1:1-14 (RCL)
2 Timothy 1:6-8, 13-14 (LFM)

In the opening verses of 2 Timothy, Paul (or, more likely, one of Paul's loyal followers writing in his name after his death) highlights the importance of familial ties to the life of faith. In contrast to sayings of Jesus that assume the hostility of families of origin and emphasize the need to forsake all such loyalties in order to fully embrace the new community (e.g., Luke 14:26), this text speaks to believers of later generations and celebrates the way extended family can fortify faith, shoring up our crumbling defenses in the face of shame and persecution (v. 8). Not only the "sincere faith" of his biological grandmother, Lois, and mother, Eunice (v. 5), but also the courage and conviction imparted by his spiritual father, Paul (1:2, 6-7), are imagined as constitutive of young Timothy's own faith. But there is a sense in which these potencies lie dormant within us until embraced; these powers are not genetic traits that can be passively inherited, but gifts that must be intentionally "rekindled" (v. 6). The spiritual gifts mediated to us by those who come before us in faith are stirred up in us when we imagine our own lives caught up into a larger story that began long before us—a grand narrative that gathers up our small projects into God's larger purposes (vv. 9-10).

One consideration for many mainline preachers is how to proclaim this text as good news to aging congregations that have an abundance of "Loises" and still a fair number of "Eunices," but precious few "Timothys" to go around. For many of our churches, ties to the past seem all too secure—it's the future that is in question. Does this text simply stand in judgment of the church's older generation and its apparent failure to kindle the faith of its young, or is there another way to read it? Perhaps it would be possible to creatively and winsomely address a sermon to the (mostly) absent Timothys and Tracys of the church—a sermon to be overheard by their worried elders. This would afford the preacher an opportunity to model ways of talking about this urgent problem that go beyond hand wringing. Such talk might include repentance for the ways the church has failed its young, even as it dares to celebrate the very real gifts of faith that *have* been faithfully transmitted, though in forms that are often difficult for the institutional church to recognize. At the same time, a word to the departed Timothys in the hearing of their worried mothers and grandmothers should give voice to the fears and hopes of a people who know that the challenges that await their adult children will demand a robust faith buttressed by all manner of ties: familial, communal, and, yes, even institutional.

Gospel

Luke 17:5-10 (RCL, LFM)

Discipleship is an important theme in Luke's telling of Jesus' journey toward Jerusalem (9:51—19:27). This lection includes two of the four sayings Jesus addresses to his disciples in 17:1-10. On first reading, this cluster of sayings appears only loosely connected. Aside from the mention of the "sea" in 17:2 and 17:6, it is difficult to find thematic links between the four units that Luke has assembled. One way to take them as a literary unit is to read the exchange as a plotted conversation between Jesus and his closest followers. The first two sayings about the danger of causing others to stumble (vv. 1-2) and the call to first rebuke and then repeatedly forgive sinners (vv. 3-4) paint such a demanding portrait of community life that the dismayed disciples respond with an appeal for the increased faith they think they will need to live up to such high standards (vv. 5-6). On this reading, the parable (vv. 7-10) counters that these practices should not be regarded as the meritorious behavior of the few graced with exceptionally "large" faith, but are assumed and expected in the new community.

Taking a closer look at the brief exchange that begins with the apostles' plea for Jesus to "increase" their faith (vv. 5-6), the preacher should note the unusual grammatical construction of Jesus' response. The first part of the conditional sentence ("If you had faith the size of a mustard seed") explores what would happen if they did, in fact, have the faith Jesus is talking about. But the second half of the sentence is constructed grammatically as if the whole statement were contrary to fact. The effect is a striking reversal of expectation: "Suppose you have faith the size of a mustard seed—if only you did you would be able to say to the mulberry tree, 'Be uprooted . . ." They ask for an increase of faith, and this seems like a worthy request. But as is so often the case, the answer Jesus gives challenges the assumptions of those who ask. Faith, it turns out, is not like mashed potatoes. You cannot simply ask for a larger helping of the stuff. A "little" faith is plenty to transform completely the landscape because genuine faith points beyond what is "large" or "small" in the believer toward the hidden power of God, which is always enough. What they need is not "increased" faith—as if the efficacy of faith depends on some quality in the believer—but mustard-seed faith that looks expectantly beyond the self's apparently large or small resources.

Continuing on this same trajectory of thought, the brief parable (vv. 7-10) challenges the implication that the apostles' role in the new community, or the virtues that empower that role, should be regarded as worthy of special consideration. Rather, they should think of themselves as slaves. No matter how hard a slave works plowing or tending sheep outside all day, the master is not in his or her debt when evening comes. Indeed, everyone understands that the slave's duties continue inside at suppertime as he or she dons an apron, proceeds to cook, and serves the master at table. The demands of duty are so pervasive, and the status difference between slave and master so absolute, that there is no way for the slave to get ahead by going above and beyond the call of duty.

In our context, "slave" is a hurtful word that evokes a tragic and shameful past, but translating "servant" instead does little to remedy or even obscure the injustice of the relationship depicted in this parable. This text does not stop to ponder or critique the evil of slavery, but takes it for granted as something about the world that every reader will immediately recognize and understand. Sadly, after all these centuries we still do. The question for the preacher is: Can a relationship that we now condemn as evil when it obtains between people nevertheless play a constructive role in helping us rightly imagine the mystery of our relationship with God? If we accept the challenge to think along with this way of imagining God, we soon realize that this parable is focused like a laser on the very aspect of slavery that is most offensive to us. In this telling, there is no attempt to romanticize the relationship between master and slave as one of mutual regard, nor is there any talk of a job well done (compare 19:17). It is precisely the cold, hard reality of an absolute difference in status that is evoked to help us understand how things are between us and God. Lest we forget, God is not our buddy or our business partner; God never "owes us one."

This may be a difficult lesson for people so well practiced at calculating obligation based on the long list of credits and debits we meticulously log in our invisible mental ledgers. Not just in our work lives, but in our personal lives, and surely also in our church relationships, we are always doing the math—figuring out who owes whom, and how much. Even so small a calculation of privilege and responsibility as who should clear the dinner table can turn on a staggeringly complex formula that may include variables as straightforward as who did it last time, and factors as subtle as who has been hinting that they have had an especially hard day. No wonder we have disagreements about these things—the math can get extremely complicated!

But, thanks be to God, there is one relationship in our lives that is not so complicated. With God there is no mental ledger, no subtle calculus of obligation, no way to "get ahead." We can always know exactly where we stand with God. As the sun sets and our work in the fields comes to an end, there is no need to worry about tallying up our hours to see if we deserve a break or overtime pay. It's time to put on the apron and set the table. God is no slave driver, but there is some truth in imagining our status before God in this way. At the end of the day, those who freely take the slave's admission on their lips are not suffering from resentment or low self-esteem, but enjoying the uncomplicated grace of knowing exactly where they stand with the one to whom they belong: "We are worthless slaves; we have done only what we ought to have done!" (v. 10).

October 13, 2013
Lectionary 28 / Twenty-Eighth Sunday in Ordinary Time / Proper 23
Twenty-First Sunday after Pentecost

Revised Common Lectionary (RCL)

2 Kings 5:1-3, 7-15c or Jeremiah 29:1, 4-7
Psalm 111 or 66:1-12
2 Timothy 2:8-15
Luke 17:11-19

Lectionary for Mass (LFM)

2 Kings 5:14-17
Psalm 98:1, 2-3a, 3b-4
2 Timothy 2:8-13
Luke 17:11-19

First Reading
2 Kings 5:1-3, 7-15c (RCL)
2 Kings 5:14-17 (LFM)

Although both lectionaries abridge the story of the healing of Naaman the leper (2 Kings 5:1-19), a sermon on this text should carefully retell this subtle, humorous, and subversive story from beginning to end. Naaman is a great general who has earned favor with his king by defeating the enemies of Syria ("Aram," v. 1). That these defeated rivals to Syrian power include Israel is a plot point disclosed with skill and restraint when we learn that the general's wife is served by a young Israelite girl captured in a raid (v. 2). But even as the story admits Syrian mastery embodied in its successful general, the careful reader will note that the details of the telling conspire to subvert Syrian national pride. To human eyes, Naaman's armies have conquered all enemies, but the narrator assures us that on a deeper level Naaman is merely a tool deployed by YHWH to serve a hidden purpose (v. 1). Furthermore, and in plain view of all, right down to the lowly servants, Naaman is a flawed symbol of national strength because his body is stricken with the most visible stigma imaginable; he is a leper (v. 1b). Ironically, the great general's only hope for wholeness turns on the serendipity of the slave girl, who remembers that back in her home country there is a man who can do something about the general's malady (v. 3).

On hearing this, Naaman turns to the channels of power he knows best. If you want something done right and done fast, and if you have the proper connections, get the kings involved. But, funnily enough, the kings make a mess of it. When Naaman arrives before the king of Israel with an official correspondence from the king of Aram demanding a cure for the letter's bearer (v. 6), the result is not a healing, but an escalation in international tensions. "When the king of Israel read the letter, he tore his clothes and said, 'Am I God, to give death or life, that this man sends word to me to cure a man of his leprosy? Just look and see how he is trying to pick a quarrel with me'" (v. 7). The kings are not much help. This is a story that knows how to poke fun at the nationalistic pretensions of both Syria and Israel.

Fortunately for Naaman, word somehow reaches "Elisha the man of God" (v. 8), and soon the general, with all his horses and chariots and valuables, is parked in the prophet's driveway awaiting his ministrations (v. 9). Picture the prophet inside, peeking out the window at the trappings of the entourage and pondering what form the cure should take. In a moment, the door opens, and much to the great general's consternation, a mere messenger appears to tell him to go wash in the Jordan seven times (v. 10). Naaman is enraged. This whole affair is not unfolding with the proper decorum. He has already come at the behest of a servant girl, and now he must take orders from a messenger? This is not the way he had pictured it when he daydreamed about the Israelite prophet standing beneath his chariot and dramatically "waving his hand" over the spot to effect a cure (v. 11). And now he must go and wash in the Jordan, that filthy puddle these Israelites call a river (v. 12)? But once again the lowly servants save the day with wise counsel. If the prophet had demanded something difficult of him, surely Naaman would have embraced the challenge. If the healing would be worth great effort on his part, surely it must also be worth little effort (v. 13). To his credit, the general is persuaded by this seamless logic. He washes seven times in the Jordan "according to the word of the man of God," and his flesh is made clean like that of a young boy (v. 14). The end of the matter is that Naaman learns that "there is no God in all the earth except in Israel" (v. 15), and that the favor of this one true God cannot be bought by kings or generals at any price (v. 16).

Since this story features a foreigner cured from leprosy and confessing faith in Israel's God, it is clear why it has been chosen as a complement to today's Gospel story about the healing of the Samaritan leper (Luke 17:11-19). Another fascinating and preachable connection between this text and Luke is the way Jesus uses this story in his inaugural sermon at Nazareth (Luke 4:20-30). While the telling in 2 Kings 5 is clearly subversive of Syrian nationalism, Jesus' surprising reading shows that this story can also serve to poke holes in Israelite national pride. "There were . . . many lepers in Israel in the time of the prophet Elisha," Luke's Jesus observes, "and none of them was cleansed except Naaman the Syrian" (Luke 4:27). If it is necessary for the Syrian general to learn that "there is no God in all the earth except in Israel," Jesus insists that it is equally necessary for his hometown church to learn that there is no God in Israel except the one in all the earth. This is an important and challenging realization for any people of God who may be tempted to assume that God's ways and purposes are so transparent and available to us that we can safely name God's favor and blessing among our national assets.

Jeremiah 29:1, 4-7 (RCL alt.)

The semicontinuous reading from Jeremiah is from a letter the prophet sent to the first wave of exiles carried away to Babylon (29:1). In contrast to the optimistic word of the false prophet Hananiah who predicted doom for Babylon and the return of the exiles within two years (28:1-4), Jeremiah's oracle foretells a long captivity measured not in years, but in generations (29:6). For this reason, the Israelites in Babylon are encouraged to accept their situation as the will of sovereign God (v. 4), put down roots in the new place (vv. 5-6), work for the long-term good of the city where they find themselves, and even pray for its well-being (v. 7). This lection has implications for the mainline church's relationship to the wider culture. The notion of the church as a people in exile is surely more seriously imaginable today than it was a generation ago. If we are, in some sense, a people displaced from the cultural mainstream, the surprising implication of this oracle is that we must not give in to the temptation to circle the wagons and think only of our own well-being. This text may also speak to the question of raising false hopes in the midst of a crisis, such as our current economic downturn. Whether in the name of God or in the name of the god of the market, there are many who are eager to announce that with the right policies everything will be back to normal shortly. After all, no one wins an election by predicting that we are in this for the long haul, or that this is the new normal. Jeremiah's sober vision of the future invites us to pause and consider the deeper causes of our new situation, and to ask what we need to do to live faithfully into the future that is actually before us, not the one we once imagined for ourselves.

Psalmody

Psalm 111 (RCL)

Psalm 98:1, 2-3a, 3b-4 (LFM)

Psalm 111 is an appropriate response to the healing of the foreigner Naaman, and so also resonates well with the Gospel reading. The great works of the Lord are worthy of thanks and praise (v. 1), and by such "gracious and merciful" demonstrations God "has gained renown by his wonderful deeds" (v. 4). In a similar vein, Psalm 98 boasts that God "has made known his victory; he has revealed his vindication in the sight of the nations" (v. 2).

Psalm 66:1-12 (RCL alt.)

Psalm 66 responds to the sober oracle of the Jeremiah lection by acknowledging that life with God is troubled with "tests" (v. 10), detours "into the net" (v. 11), and even journeys "through fire and through water" (v. 12). But, as with the Israelites before us (vv. 5-7), God ultimately leads us through danger into "a spacious place" (v. 12b).

Second Reading
2 Timothy 2:8-15 (RCL)
2 Timothy 2:8-13 (LFM)

Second Timothy reads like a final testament to Paul's life of ministry—last words shared from prison with a young protégé attempting to carry on the difficult work of the gospel. In this passage, the apostle's chains (v. 9) are a reminder that he has suffered for the sake of this work; Timothy, therefore, should not be surprised at hardships in his own ministry (1:8; 2:1-3). Ultimately, both Paul and Timothy stand in the shadow of Jesus, whose memory (v. 8) is the hermeneutical key to the minister's own experiences (vv. 11-13). Caught up into the story of Jesus, the suffering of the Christian leads not only to life (v. 11) but, ultimately, to life in the presence of Christ who reigns (v. 12a). The threat of apostasy is real (v. 12b) but, finally, even our faithlessness will not frustrate Christ's purposes (v. 13). This is the story that the aging apostle calls "my gospel" (v. 8): not just that Christ suffered, died, and was raised to reign, but that the Christian's own life recapitulates this astounding plot. The final verses of the RCL lection speak of the need to "avoid wrangling over words" (v. 14) and the challenge to "rightly explain the word of truth" (v. 15). A good measure of whether our religious talk (including our preaching) conforms to these high standards is how far it strays from this core narrative about Jesus—a story that is also, mysteriously, our own.

Gospel
Luke 17:11-19 (RCL, LFM)

The lection begins with another reminder that Jesus is still on his way to Jerusalem (v. 11), a journey that is nearing its momentous conclusion. This story takes place in "the region between Samaria and Galilee" (17:11). This setting is well suited to the logic of the narrative, if not the finer points of Palestinian geography. Upon entering an unnamed village, Jesus is approached by ten lepers. The events that follow correspond closely to descriptions of leprosy in the Hebrew Bible. Since they meet Jesus as he enters the village, the suggestion is that the lepers are isolated at the outskirts of the community (Num. 5:2). (For a description of lepers gathering at the entrance to a city, see 2 Kgs. 7:3-5.) They are said to "approach" but are also described as "keeping their distance" and calling out (vv. 12-13; cf. Lev. 13:45-46). What they know of Jesus gives them reason to hope, for their cries are not "Unclean!" as the law demands, but "Jesus, Master, have mercy on us!" (v. 13). This vocative, "Master," is frequently on the lips of the disciples in Luke. Jesus' command for them to go and show themselves to the priests assumes the protocol described in Leviticus 13:2-8. It is a strange demand, since they are not yet healed, but they all obey—apparently all ten believe that Jesus is able to do this for them. The healing itself is described without fanfare: "And as they went, they were made clean" (v. 14).

This would be a fitting conclusion to a healing story, but the narrative continues and takes an unexpected turn. One of the ten (at this point we are told no more about him) decides to break ranks and, indeed, to disobey. Upon seeing that he is healed, he disregards the instruction to go to the priests and instead turns back, "praising God with a loud voice" (v. 15). Only after he has returned and fallen at the feet of Jesus to thank him are we told what the story's setting foreshadows: this one is a Samaritan (v. 16). Before, he was simply a leper like the other nine. Now, healed of his leprosy, we see that he was doubly despised as one who inhabits the disturbingly ambiguous no-space between Jew and Gentile. Ironically, the companions he kept in sickness when leprosy trumped all other measures of status will not find him suitable company in his and their newfound health.

The disciples are not explicitly mentioned as present, which makes it unclear whom Jesus is talking to when he asks, "Was none of them found to return and give praise to God except this foreigner?" (v. 18). But the point seems clear enough. All ten show a measure of faith by obeying before any sign of healing, but only this outcast follows faith to its proper end in gratitude and praise. Like the Samaritan in another passage unique to Luke (10:33), he is a surprising exemplar. He also calls to mind the foreign leper Naaman (see the first reading, above), the story of whose healing incited the synagogue assembly at Nazareth (4:27). Is it possible that it is precisely the Samaritan leper's status as a double outsider that has prepared him to see more in his healing than a fortunate turn of events? All ten find health, but only one allows himself to be caught up in praise and thanks—to fall prostrate in that humble posture of worship that sets the stage for Jesus to invite him to get up and be not only "healed," but "saved" by faith (*sozo* in v. 19 carries both meanings). It is those who first humble themselves by acknowledging their need and low station who can be lifted up (14:11; 18:14).

This story makes an interesting companion to last week's lection. In 17:7-10 the disciples learn that they are due no special thanks for obediently upholding the community's standards of conduct. With God, all obedience is rightly understood as duty. Unlike all our other relationships, there is never a sense in which God is in our debt. The other side of that coin is that we should always be looking for opportunities to acknowledge our unending debt of gratitude and praise. This grateful way of being grows out of a particular way of seeing. Like Jesus (v. 14), and unlike the other nine, we are specifically told that the Samaritan "saw" what was happening to him (v. 15).[1] The habit of seeing well, of perceiving our lives in proper relation to God and God's world, is the beginning of gratitude.

Another striking feature of this story is the contrast between dutiful obedience and grateful praise.[2] Praise and thanks are not merely another dimension of obedience. Indeed, the other nine were perfectly obedient. Doing as they were told, they went directly to the priest and then got on with their lives. If they had been around later to hear Jesus wonder at their ingratitude, they might well have complained that he did not say that they should come back and fall at his feet, or they would have happily done so. They might win that argument, but what would it benefit them? There are some things necessary to human flourishing before God that cannot be encapsulated in a command. In fact, to insist that someone break out in a spontaneous act of praise and thanks is to preclude the possibility of it actually happening. For this reason, dutifully obedient church folk like us would do well to pay close attention to the Samaritan leper. Our duties are ever before us, and, of course, we must not neglect them, but there is another and deeper register in which our most profound responses to God must be worked out. The winsome thing about this Samaritan is that even in the sparse language of this text, it is fairly clear that he simply cannot help himself. He would liked to obey—he had every intention of doing so—but then he saw, he turned, he praised loudly, prostrated, and thanked. He just does not seem to be able to restrain himself. Is there a danger in letting ourselves get so caught up in what God has done for us that we forget to keep all the rules just right? Or might there be a more profound danger in the sober-minded, dutiful obedience that never risks losing itself in spontaneous outpourings of heartfelt thanks and praise?

Notes

1. Alan R. Culpepper, "The Gospel of Luke," in *The New Interpreter's Bible*, ed. Leander E. Keck et al. (Nashville: Abingdon, 1995), 9:326.
2. Barbara Brown Taylor, "The Tenth Leper," in *The Preaching Life* (Boston: Cowley, 1993), 107–13.

October 20, 2013
Lectionary 29 / Twenty-Ninth Sunday in Ordinary Time / Proper 24
Twenty-Second Sunday after Pentecost

Revised Common Lectionary (RCL)

Genesis 32:22-31 or Jeremiah 31:27-34
Psalm 121 or 119:97-104
2 Timothy 3:14—4:5
Luke 18:1-8

Lectionary for Mass (LFM)

Exodus 17:8-13
Psalm 121:1-2, 3-4, 5-6, 7-8
2 Timothy 3:14—4:2
Luke 18:1-8

First Reading
Genesis 32:22-31 (RCL)

The fascinating account of Jacob wrestling with God at Peniel has an important backstory that should be told. It can no longer be assumed that listeners know all about Jacob's history as a trickster, his betrayal of Esau, or his twenty-year sojourn with his uncle Laban in Haran. Even those who have read the entire cycle many times will appreciate a refresher. Fred Craddock, who once built a homiletic around the assumption that people already know these stories, has in recent years set aside time in the sermon for laying out the relevant plot points, albeit with his usual light touch: "You will remember that . . ." In this case, the verses immediately preceding the lection are especially important. When news comes that Esau is approaching with "four hundred men" (32:6), Jacob, who has good reason to fear this reunion, is unclear about his brother's intentions. Always thinking on his feet and searching for an angle, Jacob takes several measures against an uncertain future, including (1) dividing his people and possessions into two separate companies in the hope that one might escape an attack (vv. 7-8); (2) offering an eloquent prayer asking for God's care (vv. 9-12); and (3) sending generous gifts of livestock ahead of him on the road (vv. 13-21).

With every humanly possible precaution thus taken, Jacob finds himself alone on the banks of the Jabbok as night falls (vv. 22-24a). The encounter that follows does not take place in the daylight realm of plain sight and practical measures, but in the twilight world of theophany. Without explanation "a man" appears seemingly from nowhere and wrestles with him "until daybreak" (v. 24). The identity of this figure is cloaked in mystery, but there are enough clues along the way that by the time Jacob ("the Supplanter") receives the new name Israel, we are not surprised to learn that it is because he has "striven with God and with humans" and prevailed (v. 28). We have already seen that Jacob can be quite formidable in conflicts with people, but what could it possibly mean to win a fight with God? The answer seems to be more about Israel's tenacity and willingness to stay engaged with God through thick and thin than any physical prowess. Wrestling is the right image—you don't trick God or beat God back with your fists, but you may be able to hang on for dear life until a blessing is given (v. 29). As the sun rises, the carefully executed strategies of the day before must seem inconsequential compared to the realization that he has survived a face-to-face skirmish with God (vv. 30-31). The encounter proves transformative. Indeed, limping out to meet his brother by morning's first light (33:1), he will say that to look on the face of Esau "is like seeing the face of God" (33:10). Not surprisingly, a reconciliation follows. When we wrestle honestly with God, all other relationships have a way of falling into place.

Jeremiah 31:27-34 (RCL alt.)

Jeremiah 31:27-34 is an oracle of restoration pronounced in the midst of the destruction, suffering, and exile suffered at the hand of the Babylonians. The promise is that "the days are surely coming" when both Israel and Judah will be repopulated (v. 27) as God's close attention to them turns from punishment to renewal (v. 28). The future imagined in this text is not free of all judgment, but consequences will fall only upon those who give offense (vv. 29-30). The promise of a new covenant (vv. 31-34) is a passage various New Testament authors echo (Luke 22:20; 2 Cor. 3:1-6; Heb. 8:6-13). Christian sermons on this text can celebrate the way these words anticipate the good news we have received in Jesus without constructing such new meanings at the expense of Judaism. This passage is not a license for the preacher to dismiss Israel's covenant as obsolete, for it speaks of the enduring and ever-renewing covenant faithfulness of YHWH, not the fickle, reneging god some Christians insist on worshiping. The new and more direct relationship promised in this text is, in the first place, neither a revocation of Jewish law nor a vision of a distant future beyond the horizons of the historical Judah and Israel to which it is explicitly addressed (v. 31). Nevertheless, Christians cannot help seeing in the prophet's powerful words an intimation of that life-giving word of forgiveness that Israel's God has spoken to us in Jesus, poured out for us in the new covenant of his blood, and indeed written on our very hearts by a life-giving Spirit.

Exodus 17:8-13 (LFM)

Exodus 17:8-13 recounts a skirmish in which the Amalekites (Gen. 36:12) attack the wandering Israelites at Rephidim. The image of Moses, weary-armed and seated upon a rock, his arms (and thus the "staff of God," v. 9) literally supported by Aaron and

Hur (v. 12), is a reminder that Israel's success against opponents depends upon God's power, not military prowess. The lection ends before the troubling declaration of unending war against the Amalekites (vv. 14-16). For a more expansive account of this skirmish, perhaps motivated by the Deuteronimist's desire to justify the harshness of the call for the extermination of Amalek, see Deuteronomy 25:17-19.

Psalmody
Psalm 121 (RCL)
Psalm 121:1-2, 3-4, 5-6, 7-8 (LFM)

As a "Song of Ascents," Psalm 121 was likely a poem sung by travelers on pilgrimage to Jerusalem. The imagery evokes a strong sense of life on the road: menacing hills rising in the distance (v. 1),[1] the question of stable footing (v. 3), and the constant problem of exposure to the elements (vv. 5-6). In the face of these trials of the journey, the poem's best-known line asks, "From where will my help come?" (v. 1), and then answers with the same breath, "My help comes from the LORD, who made heaven and earth" (v. 2).

Psalm 119:97-104 (RCL alt.)

Every one of the 172 verses in Psalm 119 celebrates the beauty and perfection of God's Torah. The lection (vv. 97-104) is a fitting companion to the promise of the new covenant in Jeremiah, and attention to it will help the preacher avoid the pitfall of supersessionism described above. There is a thematic connection between the psalmist's sense of being directly under God's tutelage (v. 102) and the prophet's vision of God placing the law within each heart and obviating the need for human teachers (Jer. 31:33-34).

Second Reading
2 Timothy 3:14—4:5 (RCL)
2 Timothy 3:14—4:2 (LFM)

These verses are a final charge to the young Timothy to carry on faithfully in ministry "whether the time is favorable or unfavorable" (4:2). Given the waning influence of the church amid the ascent of the secular, it may be tempting for contemporary ministers to suppose that our time is more unfavorable than most. This passage brings perspective. The challenges are just what they have always been: self-interested "imposters," both "deceiving and deceived," muddying the water with manipulative God-talk (3:13); failures of discernment on the part of our listeners (4:3a); and a consumer mentality that prizes comfort and convenience over truth, and threatens to go elsewhere if offended (4:3b-4). Because these verses are framed as a warning about the future ("the time is coming," 4:3), the tendency in every age is to imagine one's own time as the special fulfillment of these dire predictions. A critical perspective helps us understand that these words were likely penned by a follower of Paul after his death, evoking the authority of the apostle by describing things in the author's present as if they were yet to come.

Just as the hazards of ministry remain essentially unchanged from age to age, so also the resources for responding faithfully are a constant. First, there is the example of parents and mentors who go before us, instilling in us the convictions and training us in the practices that constitute faith (3:14, and see 1:5-6). Next, there is Scripture and its many uses (3:16), a resource that forms the young minister's faith even from the earliest years (3:15). In recent centuries, the famous phrasing about Scripture being "inspired by God" (3:16, literally "God-breathed") has supplied the warrant for elaborate and sweeping claims about the nature of the Bible—claims that have more to do with modern preoccupations with "objective" truth than with the straightforward exhortation offered in this text, namely, that Scripture is always "useful" because the God of Scripture is ever trustworthy. When read in context, one of the most striking things about the view of Scripture offered here is the way it is placed so matter-of-factly alongside the other resources that buttress faith in the face of hardship and doubt. Indeed, the most solemn and urgent charge of all is saved for last: be mindful that the work of ministry is always carried out in the presence of the living God and of God's Christ who judges "the living and the dead" (4:1).

Gospel

Luke 18:1-8 (RCL, LFM)

The lection is a parable (vv. 2-5) framed by the narrator's introduction (v. 1) and commentary placed on the lips of Jesus (vv. 6-8). Read on its own, the parable could have any number of meanings and would seem to invite interpretations related to God's concern for justice for the marginalized. In Luke's telling, however, the parable is addressed to the disciples (17:22) concerning the need for persistence in prayer (v. 1), especially in the context of waiting for the coming of the Son of Man (17:20-37; 18:8).

The parable begins by introducing "a judge who neither feared God nor had respect for people" (v. 2). This brief characterization establishes that the man is not fit to judge wisely since wisdom grows out of the fear of the Lord (Prov. 1:7). Next we are introduced to a widow and learn that she has a complaint before the judge. The details are not given, but she asks repeatedly for "justice" (v. 3). Immediately there is tension. The God of Israel has a special concern for justice for the vulnerable such as this widow (Deut. 10:17-18), but this judge has no respect for the will of God, nor do we have reason to hope for humanistic altruism. What will happen? The stage is set for tragedy, but instead there is a humorous twist. We hear no more directly from the widow; the remainder of the story is focused through the judge. What we learn from overhearing his internal dialogue serves to complicate our initial assumptions about the widow and her powerlessness. It turns out that her persistence has made a strong impression. This judge is no saint, but his commitment to injustice is simply not strong enough to weather the verbal barrage she has unleashed on him: "Though I have no fear of God and no respect for anyone, yet because this widow keeps bothering me, I will grant her justice, so that she may not wear me out by continually coming" (vv. 4-5). The NRSV's alternative and more literal translation makes the verbal beating he has been taking even more apparent: ". . . so that she may not finally come and slap me in the face."

Jesus' comment on the parable makes it clear that it is not to be understood allegorically. The justice offered reluctantly and belatedly by the "unjust judge" (v. 6) is in contrast to the justice God will "quickly grant" (v. 8). If passionate and persistent asking is effective even in the case of a godless judge, how much more in the case of God the Judge! This suggests that the most generative point of comparison is between the tenacity of the widow and the prayer life of the disciples—and by extension the reader. Note that her persistence is in pursuit of a just cause. This is an important proviso. I have heard of successful prayers for good parking spots, and once even for a convenience store with a cappuccino machine. The prayer of Jabez has been proposed as a model prayer for those who intend to do good things with the "expansion" of material blessings they request. This parable is silent on such uses of prayer, but it does invite us to make an absolute pest of ourselves asking "day and night" (v. 7) for the one thing that God wants more than anything: justice.

Somewhere between the frivolous prayer for cappuccino and the noble prayer for justice comes the vast majority of the things we talk to God about. Some of these prayers are as routine and essential as the thanks we give for our food, or the good sleep we ask for our children before turning out their lights. Others, like the ones we find ourselves mumbling in hospital waiting rooms, come from a place so deep within us that we may have forgotten it existed—a guileless place purged of pettiness, irony, and cynicism. This parable invites us to get in touch with that vulnerable place in ourselves and to spend some time there talking to God. Not that sincerity in prayer guarantees results. In a moving sermon, Flemming Rutledge tells the story of a friend who suffered for years from a host of chronic and degenerative maladies. They prayed for her constantly, but to no avail. Finally, the woman's husband spoke the unbearable truth: "Every time we pray she gets worse."1 This parable offers no theodicy in the face of such a horrible realization, but it does propose that the only thing to do in such situations is to keep praying. When prayers are answered, keep praying. When they are not, keep praying. When faith is strong, pray. And especially when in doubt, pray. Ultimately, the justification this text offers for this advice is eschatological, not practical. This is what you want to be found doing when the man comes around: "When the Son of Man comes, will he find faith on the earth?" (v. 8).

Note

1. J. Clinton McCann Jr., "Psalms," in *The New Interpreter's Bible*, ed. Leander E. Keck et al. (Nashville: Abingdon, 1996), 4:1180. Alternatively, the elevation ahead may be Zion, the journey's destination and a symbol of divine help.

October 27, 2013
Lectionary 30 / Thirtieth Sunday in Ordinary Time / Proper 25
Twenty-Third Sunday after Pentecost

Revised Common Lectionary (RCL)	**Lectionary for Mass (LFM)**
Jeremiah 14:7-10, 19-22 or Sirach 35:12-17 or Joel 2:23-32	Sirach 35:12-14, 16-18
Psalm 84:1-7 or Psalm 65	Psalm 34:2-3, 17-18, 19 + 23
2 Timothy 4:6-8, 16-18	2 Timothy 4:6-8, 16-18
Luke 18:9-14	Luke 18:9-14

First Reading
Jeremiah 14:7-10, 19-22 or Sirach 35:12-17 (RCL)
Sirach 35:12-14, 16-18 (LFM)

The lection from Jeremiah recounts the confession, lament, and petition of the people in the midst of a severe drought (14:3-4). The guilt of the people is not in question (vv. 7a, 20), but in their guilt they cry out in hope that God will act to save them. Three times (vv. 7, 9, 21) the people repeat their argument: God should save them for the sake of God's own good name, not for the sake of the people's goodness. Strikingly, this text does not speak of God's absence; rather, God is imagined as present and in their midst, yet strangely passive, like a mighty warrior "stunned" by a blow in battle (v. 9 Tanakh). In the final verses of the lection, the petition strikes upon a new and powerful argument. The gods of the nations are not real and cannot give rain; therefore, God should help them because God is the only one who *can* help them (v. 22). These themes of freely confessing sin before God and unabashedly casting oneself before the mercy of God resonate with today's Gospel lection about the tax collector who showed such humility in prayer and so, unlike the more virtuous but arrogant Pharisee, "went down to his home justified" (Luke 18:14; see below).

The lection from Sirach, a collection of teachings and proverbs dating from the early second century BCE, includes instruction on giving generously (v. 12) and with "a cheerful face" (v. 11; cf. 2 Cor. 9:7). Ben Sira's unnuanced assertion that human gifts are repaid "sevenfold" by God (v. 13) is problematic, but the next verse makes it clear that tithing should not be regarded as a technique for getting what we want from God. The end of the lection speaks about God's impartiality and emphasizes the often repeated yet always astonishing biblical claim that God's eye is especially on the financially vulnerable in our midst; in Ben Sira's context these include the widow and the orphan (vv. 17-18).

Joel 2:23-32 (RCL alt.)

Joel's word of restoration to Judah after the devastation of a plague of locusts (vv. 23-27) pivots quickly toward a more ultimate horizon of significance. Some scholars argue that talk of the sun being darkened and the moon turning to blood (vv. 30-31) refers to an ordinary desert dust storm, but it seems clear that ordinary reference has been suspended. Joel is not forecasting the weather with this talk of "the great and terrible day of the Lord." We don't expect the next sentence to explain that the following day will be partly cloudy with a chance of showers; we recognize that the genre has shifted to apocalyptic with its bid to grasp the transcendent in the midst of the mundane. In the aftermath of the plague, the prophet anticipates a time when the spirit of prophecy will fall with reckless demographic abandon on "all flesh," disregarding human status expectations (vv. 28-29, quoted in Acts 2:17). This passage recognizes that "ordinary" catastrophe—whether plague, hurricane, debt crisis, or cancer diagnosis—stirs up in us ultimate questions of finitude and dependence on God. Just then is the acceptable time to remember that "everyone who calls on the name of the Lord shall be saved" (v. 32).

Psalmody

Psalm 84:1-7 or Psalm 65 (RCL)
Psalm 34:2-3, 17-18, 19 + 23 (LFM)

In the voice of a pilgrim traveling up to Jerusalem, Psalm 84 expresses the joy of seeing the temple, perhaps for the first time (vv. 1-2). One of the most memorable images in the Psalter is the bird nesting somewhere in the temple grounds—perhaps in the rafters? The psalmist seems almost jealous of the bird's privilege of dwelling in such a "lovely" (v. 1) place, a destination the poet can only visit on special occasions (v. 3). Psalm 65 begins by celebrating God who answers prayer (v. 2) and forgives transgression (v. 3), but then moves into praise and thanks for a bountiful harvest. God is the source of life-giving water that swells the river and causes the grain fields to thrive (vv. 9-10). "You crown the year with your bounty," exults the poet, going on to personify the landscape, describing it as donning festive clothing and shouting and singing for joy at the fullness of God's blessing (vv. 11-13). Psalm 34 is an acrostic poem and, like Sirach, the text to which it responds, the genre is wisdom. A strong connection between these texts is the psalmist's reminder that "the Lord is near to the brokenhearted, and saves the crushed in spirit" (v. 19; cf. Sirach 35:17-18).

Second Reading
2 Timothy 4:6-8, 16-18 (RCL, LFM)

This reading concludes the semicontinuous series from 1 and 2 Timothy. The pathos of these final words, along with an abundance of concrete and seemingly idiosyncratic details (e.g., 4:13), has led some scholars to speculate that even if it seems likely that 2 Timothy was written by a disciple of Paul to a later generation of believers, it nonetheless includes authentic fragments. Certainly, the images of Paul as a "libation" (v. 6; cf. Phil. 2:17) and an athlete finishing a race and receiving a wreath (vv. 7-8; cf. 1 Cor. 9:24-27; Phil. 3:12-16) resonate with the apostle's self-understanding in the authentic epistles.

Unlike the other pastorals, 2 Timothy presumes that Paul is in prison (2:9). These final verses speak of abandonment both in prison (v. 9) and in his trial (v. 16). The implication is that the defense has not gone well and the end is at hand. The tone is somber, lending gravitas to the charge to Timothy in the previous verses. "As for you," says the mentor, "always be sober, endure suffering . . . carry out your ministry" (v. 5). "As for me," he continues, ". . . the time of my departure has come" (v. 6).

The image of Paul's life of service to Christ being poured out as a drink offering is homiletically rich. When you pour out a libation, you know that there is a finite amount. An end comes. Commenting on this text, Guy D. Nave Jr. observes, "While individual drink offerings were always being depleted, drink offerings were continually presented to the Lord. After one vessel was emptied of its contents, another vessel was poured."[1] Paul speaks of his own depletion in hopes of encouraging Timothy to spend himself completely for the same cause. Of course, this self-emptying has its source in a singular act of sacrifice that gathers up all such suffering into the life, death, and resurrection of Jesus. In the Disciples of Christ congregation in which I worship, the Lord's Supper is celebrated with a profound gesture. A pitcher is emptied into a cup to the last, straggling drop as the words of institution are spoken: "This cup that is poured out for you is the new covenant in my blood" (Luke 22:20). The pattern that began in the ministry of Jesus is recapitulated in the ministry of Paul, and in the ministry of Timothy, and so on, and so on. To this day, whenever a Christian pours herself out like wine upon the altar of service, she proclaims the Lord's death until he comes.

Gospel
Luke 18:9-14 (RCL, LFM)

This parable shares the theme of prayer with the previous lection (18:1-8) but leaves behind the theme of eschatology explored in previous pericopes and introduces the new topic of humility before God, which will be further explored in 18:15-17 and 18-25. As in the preceding lection, the parable is framed by an introductory comment by the narrator (v. 9) and a concluding statement by Jesus (v. 14) that provide an interpretive gloss. The parable is spoken to "some who trusted in themselves that they were righteous and regarded others with contempt" (v. 9). Based on Luke's earlier characterization of the Pharisees (16:14-15), there can be little doubt that they are the audience.

We learn what we need to know about the parable's two characters by paying close attention to their bodies as well as their words. The NRSV has the Pharisee "standing by himself" (v. 11), the physical separation reflecting his self-understanding as set apart and holy. The Greek can also be rendered "praying to himself," which could suggest that his prayer was addressed to himself rather than God, or even that he prayed "with reference to himself" but, as the final words of his prayer bear out, with a sideways glance at the taxpayer.[2] By contrast, the tax collector is oblivious to the presence of the Pharisee. He stands "far off," reflecting his self-confessed distance from God, and his posture is one of humility since he "would not even look up to heaven, but was beating his breast" (v. 13). Even without referring to all the other stories about (bad) Pharisees and (good) tax collectors in Luke, we see where this is going. In the parable's neat frame, two "go up to the temple to pray" (v. 10), and two go down, but only one "went down to his home justified" (v. 14).

Despite the many cues that encourage the reader to view the Pharisee with disdain and the tax collector with sympathy, the preacher should resist the temptation to present them as stock characters. Nowhere in this story are we told that the Pharisee is a hypocrite, nor is there reason to assume that the tax collector is a good guy once you really get to know him. In fact, the parable is quickly emptied of its power when we portray the Pharisee negatively and take the side of the tax collector. If the Pharisee is bad and the tax collector good "deep down," then this just confirms conventional wisdom about people always getting what they deserve in the end. The far better course for the preacher—both in terms of creating a compelling sermonic plot and in terms of deeply engaging the theological implications of this parable—is to explore what is good in the Pharisee and what is lacking in the tax collector. The sermon should make a genuine effort to take the Pharisee's side in the matter, at least for a while. This advice holds for many Gospel narratives. We have heard these stories many times and the tendency is to pile on immediately against the "bad guy" like enthusiastic theater-goers booing the villain of a melodrama we know too well. But these are stories of *reversal*, and reversal cannot be experienced when the beginning of our narrative sermon fully anticipates the story's "surprise" ending.

So let the sermon begin with a celebration of the Pharisee's virtues. I know which character in this story my church depends on. I know which one pays the bills, teaches the classes, stocks the food pantry, cleans up after the fellowship meals. I'd love a church full of Pharisees—people with commitment and character, people devoted enough to fast, people who actually tithe on their income. The tax collector, on the other hand, is a sellout. Rome doesn't want to know the details about where the money comes from as long as they get their share. If the tax collector and his network of toadies manage to use threats of imperial violence to collect a little (or a lot) on the side, so be it. In our own context, we are outraged by the few who financially exploit the many: pyramid-scheme deceivers like Bernie Madoff, or shady investment bankers who make nothing real but grow rich by manipulating numbers on a spreadsheet—all while protected by a government that considers their enterprises "too big to fail." On weekdays when he isn't at temple praying, the tax collector is that kind of guy. Give me the Pharisee over the tax collector any day.

And what's so bad about the Pharisee's prayer anyway? What is wrong with someone praying thanks to God that they have been spared the shame and grief of a life of adultery and theft? But there is a phrase in the Pharisee's prayer that has no business being there, a little phrase of comparison that causes a big problem. "God, I thank you that I am *not like* other people" (v. 11). This is a prayer that cannot end well because it begins by denying the fundamental kinship of all people living in the world, under God. The Pharisee has set his course, and now he must follow it to its disastrous end: "I thank you that I am not like other people . . . like this tax collector." Now he has stopped praying and started peeking. This is the story behind that posture of prayer we all learned as children: eyes closed, head bowed. There is no place for peripheral vision in prayer. One child tattles on another after the mealtime prayer: "She was peeking." "And how do you know that?" is the parent's perfect rejoinder. We peek in order to compare ourselves favorably to others. We peek in order to justify ourselves. Such a prayer can never be a plea for justification from the outside. It is always a bid for self-justification. God cannot justify this Pharisee because the position of justifier has already been filled. The Pharisee has beat God to the job and will have to settle for whatever results he can achieve on his own.

The prayer of comparison is a constant and subtle danger, even for those who know this story well. Justo González tells about a Sunday school teacher who taught this parable to his students and then led them in prayer: "Lord, we thank you that we have your word and your church, and that therefore we are not like the Pharisee . . ." We should be appalled, of course, but González points out that we should also be careful lest "chuckling at this teacher's incomprehension, we are secretly saying, 'Lord, I thank you that I am not like this teacher, who did not even understand your parable . . .'!"[3]

Notes

1. Guy D. Nave Jr., "Exegetical Perspective on 2 Timothy 4:6-8, 16-18," in *Feasting on the Word*, Year C, vol. 4 (Louisville: Westminster John Knox, 2010), 209.
2. Luke Timothy Johnson, *Luke*, Sacra Pagina (Collegeville, MN: Liturgical, 2006), 271.
3. Justo González, *Luke*, Belief: A Theological Commentary on the Bible (Louisville: Westminster John Knox, 2010), 213.

November 1, 2013 / November 3, 2013
All Saints Day / Sunday

Revised Common Lectionary (RCL)
Daniel 7:1-3, 15-18
Psalm 149
Ephesians 1:11-23
Luke 6:20-31

Lectionary for Mass (LFM)
Revelation 7:2-4, 9-14
Psalm 24:1-2, 3-4, 5-6
1 John 3:1-3
Matthew 5:1-12a

First Reading
Daniel 7:1-3, 15-18 (RCL)
Revelation 7:2-4, 9-14 (LFM)

Although set "in the first year of King Belshazzar of Babylon" (v. 1) in the sixth century BCE, this apocalyptic vision from Daniel 7 was written during, and addresses the concerns of, the time of the persecution of the Jews under Antiochus IV Epiphanes in the second century BCE. "As he lay in bed" (v. 1) Daniel sees a vision of the sea (a symbol of chaos) stirred up and spawning "four great beasts" (v. 3). Daniel is "troubled" by the vision and asks for an interpretation (vv. 15-16). The beasts symbolize four empires that dominated the region in succession: the Babylonians, Medes, Persians, and Greeks (v. 17; see vv. 4-8). The vision is presented as foretelling the rise of these powers, but the payoff is that the last of the four (under which the author and community of first reception suffered) is "predicted" to be the worst of them all (vv. 19ff.).

Tradition associates this reading with All Saints because of verse 18, which states: "But the holy ones [KJV: "saints"] of the Most High shall receive the kingdom and possess the kingdom forever—forever and ever." Critical approaches teach us that the "holy ones" are likely a reference to the heavenly host—God's angelic army that will win a cosmic victory over all earthly powers (cf. 8:10-13). Within the conventions of apocalyptic discourse, this passage names God as sovereign and exposes Antiochus as a pretender to the throne. But textual meanings are not exclusively meanings about the past. For many centuries this passage has been cherished as a word about the happy future enjoyed by God's beloved, a meaning that resonates productively with both the critical insights discussed above and other canonical passages such as the Gospel lection for the day. Even to the present day foul beasts arise from the swirling waters of chaos, threatening to crush the fragile zones of light and order we manage to carve out with our feeble efforts. Left to our own devices, we are powerless against the untamable systemic powers that threaten our small lives. But this text points beyond the horizon of things seen to a future in which God wins and those who place their trust in God are vindicated.

Moving from one of the Bible's two book-length apocalypses to the other, the reading from Revelation is a vision of the saved gathered around the heavenly throne crying out praises to God (v. 10). The structure of the lection implies that the group of 144,000 that receives the seal of God's ownership and protection (7:4) is identical to the group described in verses 9-14. The text itself seems to make a distinction, since the 144,000 are (symbolically) numbered, but the throng introduced in verse 9 is "a great multitude that no one could count" and includes not only those from the twelve tribes (vv. 5-8) but "from every nation, from all tribes and peoples and languages" (v. 9). Perhaps this second group includes the first. They are robed in white (cf. 3:4; 6:11; 7:14) and wave palm branches, a symbol of victory. One of the elders explains, "These are they who have come out of the great ordeal" (v. 14). Although it is unclear whether the first readers of Revelation endured officially sanctioned systematic persecution, these are clearly subversive words of resistance and hope for an oppressed minority suffering at the hand of imperial power. Read on All Saints, this text speaks to the conviction that those who have gone before us in faith have not died in vain, but even now gather around the throne of God. They give voice not to their own goodness or worthiness, but now as always they bear witness to the goodness of the God who saves and the Lamb who is the agent of that salvation (v. 10). The angels, too, join the throng, falling on their faces before the throne to extol God with words that tumble down upon one another in an astonishing cascade of praise: "Blessing and glory and wisdom and thanksgiving and honor and power and might be to our God forever and ever! Amen" (v. 12).

Psalmody
Psalm 149 (RCL)
Psalm 24:1-2, 3-4, 5-6 (LFM)

Psalm 149 begins with the signature phrase of the Psalter: "Praise the LORD!" Verse 4 goes on to describe the circumstances that occasion praise: a victory granted to the humble who enjoy the Lord's pleasure. This is no surprise; Scripture teaches in many places that God opposes the proud and gives grace to the humble. But what kind of victory is intended here? Verse 6 begins, "Let the high praises of God be in their throats," but then catches in our own throat as it concludes, ". . . and two-edged swords in their hands, to execute vengeance." The psalm makes a fittingly militant companion to Daniel's vision of angelic hosts winning a victory for God over all opposing powers, but as followers of the one who told his disciple to "put your sword back into its sheath" (John 18:11), we cannot embrace this poem's untroubled assertion that human violence—no matter how well intentioned—serves the purposes of God. Psalm 24 is a fitting response to the throne-room scene envisioned in Revelation 7. The theme of the sovereignty of God (v. 1) and the image of the great company (v. 6) of the purified standing in the presence of God (vv. 3-4) to receive vindication (v. 5) are especially resonant.

Second Reading
Ephesians 1:11-23 (RCL)
1 John 3:1-3 (LFM)

When Ephesians talks about the church, it can be difficult to believe that it is talking about us. In soaring prose, this epistle celebrates a mystery "hidden for ages" (3:9), namely, that God had a master plan for reconciling all people to one another and to God in Christ. The church is that reconciled people—a diverse and thriving community offered up for inspection by all powers and principalities as rock-solid proof of the wisdom of God (3:9-10). That's the Church, writ large; but then, there is church. Could it really be that our little band of diehards—aging, earnest, but sometimes ineffectual and occasionally distracted by petty bickering—is somehow a part of the grand vision offered in Ephesians? This vision of the church may be a hard sell in the wake of Christendom, but think of how absurd it must have seemed to those who first read this epistle! We are quick to fret over signs of our cultural disestablishment, but the Ephesians were a tiny and powerless minority—too insignificant in numbers and influence to warrant official notice, much less persecution. And yet they opened their mail to read that they have a great inheritance and are destined for great things (v. 11). The same God who was at work in Christ to conquer death (v. 20) and put all challenging powers under his feet (v. 22a) has chosen them and made that same Christ the head of the church (v. 22b). This kind of talk must have sounded like absolute foolishness to those little cells of believers gathering in houses throughout the empire, but they believed it. How could they have known at that time that they who "were the first to set [their] hope in Christ" (v. 12) would be the first of so many? How could they have known that when the apostle spoke of the community of saints (vv. 15, 18) it would include a throng of billions stretched across millennia?

There is a fine line between trusting God's promises and descending into a self-congratulatory triumphalism. The preacher must discern the context to know what is required, but it may be the right time for many of our churches to consider again the possibility of our own chosenness—to consider it despite all appearances to the contrary. One thing seems certain. If we are to believe that the words of Ephesians are somehow for and about us, we can only do so by understanding ourselves as caught up into the great company of saints that stretches across both time and space. To see this requires both humility and hope. Our past has not always been as glorious or commendable as we sometimes suppose, and the future—now as surely as ever—belongs entirely to God.

The opening words of 1 John remind us that our fellowship is not grounded in socioeconomic similarity, common ancestry, or compatible taste, but in something—or rather someone—that has been "seen and heard" and passed down to us in the form of testimony. The communion of the saints stretches across all time and space, but it is not "universal" in the technical sense. Rather, our common bond is sealed in an identity so scandalously particular that the earliest witnesses were able even to reach out and touch it with their own hands.

Gospel
Luke 6:20-31 (RCL)
Matthew 5:1-12a (LFM)

According to Matthew, the preaching ministry of Jesus begins on a mountain. There can be little doubt that in describing this setting for Jesus' first sermon, Matthew wants us to remember another great teacher whose career began on a mountain. Israel's greatest leader, Moses, ascended Sinai and received there the law of God, most famously expressed in the Ten Commandments chiseled in tablets of stone.

But when Jesus saw the crowds gathering and went up a mountain to teach (5:1), he did not begin with commandments—things that we should and should not do. The grammatical mood of the Beatitudes is indicative, not imperative. The Sermon on the Mount begins with a list that we have grown to cherish, but not a list of laws. Sometimes we misunderstand the Beatitudes because we try to turn them into laws. We seem to want Jesus to say, "Be this way," or "Do that." And Jesus will oblige such expectations soon enough in the chapters that follow. But that is not how his preaching ministry begins. Jesus begins instead with blessings—not instructions about how things should be, but rather a bold assertion of how things really are. He doesn't say, "Be meek," or "Be merciful"; he doesn't insist that we become poor in spirit—you either are or you aren't. He doesn't require us to mourn, or to long for justice like food in a famine (v. 6)—I suppose you either do or you don't. But what does he say? He says that such people are blessed of God. In other words, God's eye is on them; God's favor is with them; they will not be forgotten; they will be happy in the end.

The strange thing about the Beatitudes is that they seem to be a description of another world. In the world we know so well, the poor in spirit—those who are contrite of heart and know their own spiritual brokenness—don't get taken very seriously. The world we live in respects confidence and cocksure certainty and it despises poverty of spirit, which it diagnoses as neurosis and low self-esteem. Such people are dismissed, not blessed in the world we know.

The world we live in tolerates mourning for a short while and then asks it to get its act together and move on. Those who persist in mourning the brokenness of the world and their own lives are not lifted up in the world we know; they are swept aside. Mourning doesn't sell, and it doesn't buy, and it's depressing. It slows the rest of us down. Those who are deeply grieved are not blessed, not in the world we live in. In our world the meek don't inherit the earth—no, they get crushed. The meek have bad lawyers, or no lawyers at all. They are easily intimidated. They are easily manipulated. They get left holding the beads, while everyone else gets the land. In the world we know, if the meek did inherit the earth, it would be gone soon enough. They would give some of it to anyone who asked, and they would get cheated out of a great deal by con artists, and some of it they would just fail to defend properly when it was taken from them. Those who are meek don't inherit the earth we know. And so it goes. Those who starve for justice just keep getting hungrier. The merciful get taken advantage of. The pure in heart are called naïve. The peacemakers are branded cowards and have their patriotism called into question. In our world, we do not associate God's blessing with any of these things. We associate it with power. We associate it with success. We associate it with strength. To which of these Beatitudes do our politicians of both parties refer when they insist that God blesses America? Our national creed is one of confidence, abundance, and wealth, and it is in the service of such aspirations that we invoke and presume the blessing of God—and all the more stridently when the national narrative of wealth, confidence, and abundance seems most imperiled. Whatever Jesus is in fact doing when he kicks off the Sermon on the Mount with the Beatitudes, he is surely not describing the world we live in.

The lection from Luke also records these extraordinary blessings. Luke sets the sermon on a "level place" (6:17), not a mountain. Likewise, Luke's down-to-earth version of the Beatitudes leaves little room for spiritualization: the literal poor (v. 20) and hungry (v. 21) are blessed, even as the literal rich (v. 24) and filled (v. 25) are cursed with woes. In Luke's telling, Jesus addresses these words directly to the disciples (v. 20) who have given up everything to follow him. The pattern of reversing the presumed station of the poor and the wealthy is an important theme in Luke. It begins with Mary (1:53), upon whom the first beatitude of the Gospel is pronounced (1:42-45). Much of what was said above about Matthew's version of the Beatitudes applies here as well. The primary difference is that Luke's account focuses attention even more sharply on the socioeconomic implications of these strange blessings, and adds the edge of contrasting each blessing with a curse upon the privileged. For Luke, the reversal of the kingdom Jesus proclaimed is not just good news for the poor (4:18), but bad news for the rich who have had their comfort (16:25).

Framed boldly in the indicative, the Beatitudes are a daring act of protest against the current order. Jesus cannot very well insist that we be poor in spirit, but he can show us how to look upon such people with new eyes, and so gain entrance to a new world. The Beatitudes testify that it matters deeply whom we call "saint." The kingdom Jesus proclaimed is precisely a new way of seeing, a new way of naming, and so a new way of being. The current regime sweeps aside those Jesus declares blessed of God, but we are invited to look again and discern a new reality that is coming into being. When we learn to recognize such people as blessed—to call them saints—we pledge our allegiance to that new world even as we participate in its realization.

November 3, 2013
Lectionary 31 / Thirty-First Sunday in Ordinary Time / Proper 26
Twenty-Fourth Sunday after Pentecost

Revised Common Lectionary (RCL)
Isaiah 1:10-18 or Habakkuk 1:1-4; 2:1-4
Psalm 32:1-7 or 119:137-144
2 Thessalonians 1:1-4, 11-12
Luke 19:1-10

Lectionary for Mass (LFM)
Wisdom 11:22—12:2
Psalm 145:1-2, 8-9, 10-11, 13b-14
2 Thessalonians 1:11—2:2
Luke 19:1-10

First Reading
Isaiah 1:10-18 (RCL)

Isaiah of Jerusalem prophesied to Judah in the late eighth and early seventh century BCE. Chapter 6 tells the well-known story of his original call "in the year that King Uzziah died" (738 BCE), but the book of the prophet begins with the word of this lection, and it is a word of judgment. When the "word of the LORD" starts with comparisons to Sodom and Gomorrah (v. 10), one can be sure that it is not going to end well. Isaiah's oracle pulls no punches, describing worship as an infestation. "Trample my courts no more," God complains (v. 12). The gist of the critique is that cultic practice is obscene when it is divorced from justice, but the imagery of the oracle is more visceral than conceptual. This is not a catalogue of sins, but a vivid account of a broken relationship. Their worship has turned the temple into a house of horrors for God, who is portrayed as grossed out by their offerings—repulsed as if the hands lifted in prayer were filled with blood (v. 15). The concluding plea for reform makes it clear that their offenses include injustice against the financially most vulnerable in their midst (vv. 16-17).

Two things should be kept in mind when preaching this text. First, and most obviously, read in the context of Christian worship this is not a text about the sins of others. The only word of judgment we are justified in discerning in this oracle is judgment against our own cultic and ethical practices. When the worshiping community is complicit in economic exploitation, our harmonies, our litanies, and, yes, even our cute children's sermons—maybe *especially* the cute children's sermons—make God nauseous. Second, as Walter Brueggemann has argued persuasively, in our context the preacher's self-understanding should be that of the scribe, and not the prophet: "It is clear that most pastors (who have at best precarious tenure, who are administratively responsible for program and budget and institutional maintenance, and who worry about their pensions) are not free-floating voices who can simply emote."[1] Preacher as prophet is not seriously imaginable for us, and to pretend otherwise is to push the "contract" of preaching and listening to the breaking point. This insight is even more applicable in the case of a prophetic text that critiques worship, which is largely the work of the preacher. Scribe is a less glamorous but more realistic and, finally, more appropriate role. The preacher should adopt the stance of one who draws alongside the congregation under the authority of this astonishing and demanding text. As a "keeper of old scrolls," the scribe's task week after week is to keep alive the memory of the prophetic tradition through faithful acts of interpretation that invite the community to imagine its possibilities anew through the lens of the text.

Habakkuk 1:1-4; 2:1-4 (RCL alt.)

For commentary on this lection, please see the first reading for Lectionary 27 / Proper 22, above.

Wisdom 11:22—12:2 (LFM)

The Wisdom of Solomon is the work of a Hellenized Jew, writing within a century of the birth of Christ. These verses speak eloquently of the cosmos as a mere speck before the gaze of God (11:22), yet balance such apparent insignificance with the affirmation that God's love for every created thing is guaranteed by its very existence—for what can exist except that God first create and then sustain it from moment to moment (11:24-25)? This care extends also to human life, which the author construes in Platonic terms as infused with the immortal spirit of God (12:1). For this reason, God does not forsake us when we sin, but corrects "little by little" and "warns" so that, by such guidance, we will be freed from sin (12:2).

Psalmody

Psalm 32:1-7 or 119:137-144 (RCL)
Psalm 145:1-2, 8-9, 10-11, 13b-14 (LFM)

Psalm 32 provides an appropriate response to the reading from Isaiah. The selection from the prophet ends with the promise that the egregious trespasses named in the oracle will be forgiven by God. The psalm claims such mercy as an accomplishment and celebrates the renewal that comes after repentance is met by God's forgiveness. Psalm 119 is an extended reflection on and celebration of God's perfect, life-giving law in the form of an acrostic poem. The verses selected here focus on the character of God: God is righteous and God's judgments are right (v. 137). The justice of God is, of course, manifest in Torah, which is an expression of the character of God (v. 142). Psalm 145 echoes themes from the Wisdom of Solomon, including God's mercy on and compassion for all that God has made (vv. 8-9).

Second Reading
2 Thessalonians 1:1-4, 11-12 (RCL)
2 Thessalonians 1:11—2:2 (LFM)

This lection begins a semicontinuous series from 2 Thessalonians. Paul (or an associate writing in his name) addresses a church enduring persecution (1:4) with teachings about the second coming of Christ. The letter begins with a typical greeting (1:1-2) and moves into the expected thanksgiving. Paul expresses gratitude for the Thessalonian church because of their "steadfastness and faith" in the face of persecution, and because even in the face of hardship "the love of every one of you for one another is increasing" (1:3-4). The RCL conspicuously and understandably omits verses 5-10, but they are necessary to understanding the tone and situation of the letter. Whatever the first readers are enduring, their affliction is interpreted by the author as evidence that God's judgment in the form of Christ's return is certain and imminent (vv. 5-6). In apocalyptic imagery, Christ's coming is depicted as an act of fiery vengeance against those who afflict the believers (vv. 7-8)—a payback that will result in their "eternal destruction" and alienation from God (v. 9). It is understandable why both lectionaries avoid these verses, which constitute some of the most disturbing and unequivocal predictions of judgment in the Bible. The important thing to remember about this material is that it is offered as a promise of vindication to those who are pressed from all sides by forces they cannot hope to resist by their own resources. These words are best understood in terms of their pastoral function of offering comfort and hope to the desperate, not as a detailed outline of future happenings, nor as a window into the moral life of God and God's Christ. Whatever their proper use in our context, there is no excuse for financially comfortable and socially enfranchised Christians to wield these verses like a rhetorical club against those who disagree with us. In light of the horrors the first readers are going through for the sake of the gospel, Paul offers a prayer that they will receive God's power to continue against all odds in "every good resolve and work of faith" (v. 11). Finally, this word of encouragement is all the more necessary and urgent because of a potentially devastating misunderstanding on the part of the Thessalonians. Paul worries that his readers may have been "shaken in mind or alarmed" by the impression that Christ's return was already past—that somehow their present misery is as good as it gets (2:2). The doctrinal correction offered is not academic; it is a pastoral lifeline.

Gospel
Luke 19:1-10 (RCL, LFM)

As close readers of Luke's Gospel, we don't quite know what to expect from an encounter between Jesus and Zacchaeus. After all, Zacchaeus is rich (v. 2), and Luke has warned us about rich people. Jesus' mother sings of the rich being sent away empty (1:53), and in Luke's recounting of the Beatitudes Jesus pronounces not only a blessing on the poor (6:20), but a curse on the rich (6:24). Riches are like thorns that strangle the word of God before it can bear fruit (8:14), and rich characters in other parables are the foils, not the role models, for life in the kingdom (12:16; 16:19). "Indeed, it is easier for a camel to go through the eye of a needle than for someone who is rich to enter the kingdom of God" (18:25). Zacchaeus's wealth does not bode well for his encounter with Jesus. But Zacchaeus is also a tax collector, and that, strangely enough, gives some reason for hope. Jesus invites a tax collector named Levi to follow him as a disciple (5:27) and is notorious for befriending tax collectors and other known sinners (7:34). In the verses leading up to this story, a humble tax collector fares pretty well in a parable about pride, humility, and justification (18:9-14). In the topsy-turvy world of the kingdom Jesus proclaims, a rich tax collector like Zacchaeus occupies a strange and conflicted space. The reader's interest should be piqued.

Unable to catch a glimpse of Jesus because of his small stature, Zacchaeus runs ahead and climbs a tree where he expects him to pass (vv. 3-4). The image of a wealthy, full-grown man running in public signifies in the world of the story just as it would in our own context; it is an unself-conscious act of enthusiasm, reflecting a surprising disregard for the dignity appropriate to his station. "All who humble themselves," Jesus has just explained at the end of a story about a tax collector who demonstratively embodies repentance to the point of public spectacle, "will be exalted" (18:14). Compared to the sparseness of most biblical narrative, we are given a surprising number of details about these events; but such details only seem to open onto more questions. Are we supposed to imagine that Zacchaeus has come out to see Jesus because he has heard that Jesus has a reputation for befriending the despised? Is his inability to get a clear look at Jesus simple happenstance, or does it reflect the indifference or even hostility of a crowd that knows very well who he is (v. 7) and what he is trying to do? When Jesus reaches Zacchaeus's perch and looks up, he reciprocates the tax collector's bold disregard for decorum: "Zacchaeus, hurry and come down; for I must stay at your house today" (v. 5). This is not how hospitality is supposed to work, but Jesus is no ordinary guest. The request reflects both urgency ("hurry") and implied divine necessity (*dei*, "it is necessary"). Jesus' time is short as he approaches Jerusalem and the end, but he makes time for important business along the way. Zacchaeus responds quickly and willingly (v. 6).

But not so fast. Let's not forget what kind of guy Zacchaeus is.[2] As a "chief tax collector" (v. 2), he essentially purchased from Rome a license to operate a government-sponsored extortion ring. This is not something that happens by accident, or only occasionally. It is systematic robbery. As in the case of the parable of the Pharisee and the tax collector (18:9-14), the preacher should not be too quick to take the side of Zacchaeus and Jesus against the disgruntled crowd (v. 7). Jesus is only in town for the day, after all, but the townspeople have been enduring the shakedowns administered by Zacchaeus's network of lackeys for years or even decades. At this point it might be a good idea to imagine how his neighbors ate ramen noodles three meals a day, saving pennies trying to build up college savings for the kids, only to see those funds ruthlessly confiscated when Zacchaeus's research team uncovered them. And all the while, the delivery trucks keep depositing ever-larger flat-screen TVs on Zacchaeus's driveway—right next to his Lexus. There is no way to spin the business of a chief tax collector as a "job creator" that stimulates the economy. Zacchaeus got rich by making other people poor. It's as simple as that. The point of emphasizing his culpability is theological. Zacchaeus is not a good guy at heart; he is a bad guy who encounters transformative grace in the person of Jesus. The final pronouncement will be that "the Son of Man came to seek out and to save" not good people who are simply misunderstood, but rather "the lost" (v. 10).

When Zacchaeus repents, it is a matter of the heart, but it is also a matter of concrete, public practices of distributive justice. It may even be significant that in the logic of the narrative, the crowd's expressed anger at the discrepancy between what Jesus is supposed to stand for and what they have experienced of Zacchaeus (v. 7) is juxtaposed with specific and thorough promises of restitution from the tax collector (v. 8). This is a story that invites us to tell the truth about the way the wealthy exploit the poor, because such truth telling is the essential prerequisite for authentic reconciliation. Zacchaeus's promise of a fourfold repayment for fraud (v. 8) fulfills the law's strictest demands for restitution after theft (Exod. 22:1).

There are some interesting parallels between this story and the preaching of John the Baptist. Tax collectors are among those who approach John asking about the implications of his message of repentance. His response: "Collect no more than the amount prescribed for you" (3:12-13). John's challenge to the crowds that come out to meet him is also relevant: "Do not begin to say to yourselves, 'We have Abraham as our ancestor'; for I tell you, God is able from these stones to raise up children to Abraham" (3:8). In the Zacchaeus story, the stone from which God raises such surprising offspring is the rock-hard heart of a man committed to enriching himself through state-sponsored extortion. When his reconciliation to both God and the community is complete, Jesus will say of the day's unlikely events: "Today salvation has come to this house, because he too is a son of Abraham" (v. 9).

Notes

1. Walter Brueggemann, *The Word Militant: Preaching a Decentering Word* (Minneapolis: Fortress Press, 2007), 53.
2. Some scholars argue that the present tense of the verbs in v. 8 ("I give to the poor," "I pay back") suggests that Zacchaeus pleads innocence to the crowd's charges and that his restoration as a "son of Abraham" (v. 9) is a matter of Jesus confirming his innocence and declaring him reconciled. See Joseph A. Fitzmyer, *The Gospel According to Luke*, Anchor Bible (Garden City, NY: Doubleday, 1985), 1220–22. Though grammatically coherent, this reading seems to contradict both the theology of the story and the implications of v. 8b ("if I have defrauded") and v. 10.

November 10, 2013
Lectionary 32 / Thirty-Second Sunday in Ordinary Time / Proper 27
Twenty-Fifth Sunday after Pentecost

Revised Common Lectionary (RCL)	**Lectionary for Mass (LFM)**
Job 19:23-27a or Haggai 1:15b—2:9	2 Maccabees 7:1-2, 9-14
Psalm 17:1-9 or Psalm 145:1-5, 17-21 or Psalm 98	Psalm 17:1, 5-6, 8 + 15
2 Thessalonians 2:1-5, 13-17	2 Thessalonians 2:16—3:5
Luke 20:27-38	Luke 20:27-38 or 20:27, 34-38

First Reading
Job 19:23-27a (RCL)

Despite the deafening silence of God and the infuriatingly smug and safe theological platitudes offered by his friends in the face of profound and undeserved suffering, Job insists that vindication is coming: "I know that my Redeemer lives, and that at the last he will stand upon the earth" (v. 25). Placed alongside today's Gospel reading, the lectionary encourages the preacher to read these words in continuity with the church's long reception of them as an undaunted expression of hope in a future resurrection by the power of God (thus the NRSV's "Redeemer" with a capital *R*). On this reading, even though mortal flesh fails him (v. 26a), Job trusts that he will look upon the face of God and be saved (vv. 26b-27). Critical scholarship argues convincingly that the first readers of this text would have understood the invocation of the "redeemer" as a defiant insistence that, though he die without justice from God or friends, a family member with legal standing to act on his behalf will take up Job's cause and work for justice and even vengeance after his death. Read in this way, these words invite us to consider our own responsibility to advocate on behalf of those who suffer unjustly.

Haggai 1:15b—2:9 (RCL alt.)

The book of Haggai records four short oracles spoken to the governor Zerubbabel, Joshua the high priest (1:1), and all the people of Jerusalem (2:4) in 520 BCE concerning the work of rebuilding the temple after exile. The prophet gives voice to God's complaint that the returned exiles had prioritized rebuilding their own homes, leaving the house of God in ruins (1:9). The former glory of the first temple before its destruction in 587 BCE is a distant memory. Is there anyone living in the time of Haggai who can summon memories of it from their childhood, these sixty-seven years past (v. 3)? So many terrible things have happened in the meantime. "Yet now . . . says the LORD; take courage . . . for I am with you" (2:4). The promise is that the precious things that were stolen when the first temple was sacked will be returned or replaced so that the newly rebuilt temple will eclipse the former in glory (2:9). The two brief chapters of Haggai merit a close reading before preaching this text. The book is a remarkable record of what can happen when the reality of God thoroughly captures the imagination of one person. The result is daring speech that challenges the community to transform nostalgia for a glorious past into concrete action in service of God's possible future.

2 Maccabees 7:1-2, 9-14 (LFM)

The reading from 2 Maccabees is taken from a series of speeches made by seven brothers before their torture and martyrdom at the hands of Antiochus IV Epiphanes during the Maccabean revolt. These verses portray resurrection hope that sustains obedience to God's law in the face of horrific brutality. Stretching out his hands and tongue to be severed, the third brother expresses hope in the resurrection of the body: "I got these from Heaven, and because of his laws I disdain them, and from him I hope to get them back again" (v. 12). This passage resonates thematically with the Gospel lection for the day.

Psalmody

Psalm 17:1-9 (RCL)
Psalm 17:1, 5-6, 8 + 15 (LFM)
Psalm 145:1-5, 17-21 or Psalm 98 (RCL alt.)

Psalm 17, with its confident plea for God to vindicate the blameless, is an appropriate response to the readings from Job (RCL) and 2 Maccabees (LFM). Psalm 145 is attributed to Haggai in the LXX (and so the Vulgate), which may explain its choice as a response to the reading from that prophet. Psalm 98 celebrates God's steadfast love and faithfulness to Israel in the sight of the nations (v. 3), an appropriate hymn to accompany the theme of renewal in the Haggai reading.

Second Reading

2 Thessalonians 2:1-5, 13-17 (RCL)
2 Thessalonians 2:16—3:5 (LFM)

In 1 Thessalonians, Paul describes the second coming as if it could occur at any moment (5:1-11). By contrast, the author of 2 Thessalonians emphasizes that the *parousia* will not come until after a series of specific events (2:3-5). Although the nature of "the rebellion" and the identity of "the lawless one" are a mystery to contemporary interpreters, one thing does seem clear: the point of the author's instruction in these matters is pastoral. The readers can take heart in the assurance that the return of Christ is still in the future—they are not missing anything (2:1-2). The verses omitted from the middle of the lection speak cryptically of a force that "restrains" the lawless one for a time (2:6-7), but his influence is offered as an explanation for those who reject God's truth (2:9-12). The overall effect of these verses is to explain opposition to the faith community as the result of evil forces—forces that God permits to hold sway for a time, but that will ultimately be overcome at the triumphant return of Christ (v. 8). By stark contrast, the author assures the readers that God has chosen them for "salvation through sanctification by the Spirit and through belief in the truth" (v. 13), provided that they "stand firm and hold fast to the traditions" (v. 15). The lection concludes with prayers asking God's comfort and care for the readers (vv. 16-17), a request that such prayers be reciprocated on behalf of the author (3:1-2), and a confident expression of trust that with God's help they will continue steadfast in their faith (3:3-5).

This is difficult material for preaching. Few congregations are in much danger of thinking that the day of the Lord is already here, nor do we require the pastoral assurance that those who hate and oppress us are destined for destruction when Christ returns. But there may be a needful word of reminder here that the world we inhabit so nonchalantly is not as tame as it seems—that beneath the surface of things seen our very lives are the site of a contest between good and evil. In other words, the apocalyptic categories of this text invite us to recognize that the decisions we make in life are not simply the expression of our individual tastes, or the exercising of our constitutional right to do what we want as long as we don't interfere with the rights of others. Rather, whether we know it or like it or not, this text insists that our choices are secretly caught up into a larger drama. They are the expression of our loyalty either to God's will made known to us in Christ, or to the forces that oppose God's truth.

Gospel

Luke 20:27-38 (RCL)

Luke 20:27-38 or 20:27, 34-38 (LFM)

Having arrived in Jerusalem at last (19:28) and having entered the temple grounds (19:45-57), Jesus faces a series of challenges from the religious establishment there (20:1-8, 20-26). The question the Sadducees pose in this lection is the third such test. The Sadducees were the archconservatives of the religious milieu Jesus moved within—strict constitutional constructionists who adhered rigidly and exclusively to the text of Torah and resisted the hermeneutical innovations of the Pharisees who strove to adapt the law to new circumstances. For example, the Sadducees found no basis for belief in resurrection from the dead in the five books of Moses they accepted as authoritative. The Sadducees were in their element at the temple, where they had consolidated their influence through control of its grounds and rites. It's not difficult to imagine that when they learned that Jesus was in town—indeed, answering all questioners right on their own front porch—they saw it as an opportunity to put this dangerous change agent in his place.

The question they pose is intended to show the absurdity of belief in the resurrection of the dead. For the sake of argument, they concoct a hypothetical scenario about a woman whose husband dies before she could bear him a son to carry on his name. There is a law (Deut. 25:5) that says the man's brother must take her as his wife and honor the dead brother by fathering a son by her so that the man's name may live on through such progeny. The problem is that the second brother also dies without her bearing an heir. Likewise, the third brother who stepped in to fill the role dies. To make the debacle complete, seven brothers in all are imagined, and every last one of them perishes before a son is born. In our world, this situation would call for a police investigation to find out what the woman had been putting in the seven brothers' coffee. But for the Sadducees, the entire fiasco has been dreamed up for the sake of this punch line: "In the resurrection, therefore, whose wife will the woman be? For the seven had married her" (v. 33).

Before discussing Jesus' response, we should notice that this bizarre hypothetical they have constructed tells us some interesting things about the Sadducees. First of all, they are not scandalized by stories of patriarchs with more than one wife, but the idea of a woman with more than one husband strikes them as patently absurd—completely unimaginable. Second, their construal of marriage is on display: marriage has just one true purpose, just as women have but one use. They are a means by which a man's future may be secured—his life project vicariously perpetuated through male offspring.

Jesus' response addresses both their assumptions about marriage and their view on resurrection. He argues that resurrection means no more fear of death, and therefore no more concern about bearing children to fight off the specter of mortality. Indeed, unlike in this age, in the resurrection there will be no more "having" of people for purposes. No more "taking" or "giving" of women to make babies, or for any other reason (vv. 34-35). The only children will be the children of God—the children of the resurrection who enjoy God together forever (v. 36). All relationships will be equalized, transformed in that coming glory. Jesus imagines a new age in which there is no need for marriage, or at least no version of it that the Sadducees would recognize. Then Jesus goes on to make a subtle exegetical argument that turns on a grammatical point. Knowing that the Sadducees don't accept the straightforward testimony of texts like Daniel 12:2, Jesus instead cites a text from a part of Scripture they do acknowledge as authoritative. In the story of the burning bush, God says to Moses, "I am the God of your father, the God of Abraham, the God of Isaac, and the God of Jacob" (Exod. 3:6). Because the verb is in the present tense, the implication is that these patriarchs are not dead, but living—somehow alive to God in the moment God claims them (v. 38).

This text raises a number of pastoral considerations for preaching. There is something obscene about the way the Sadducees raise the question of resurrection as if it were purely academic—a brain twister for theologians. But for Jesus, now arrived in the city where he will soon die, resurrection is surely not a topic of dry intellectual speculation. Christian belief in resurrection is grounded primarily in Jesus' own resurrection as the "first fruits" of those who will follow (1 Cor. 15:20-23), not in his teachings. In other words, for Christians, resurrection is not a doctrine, but a person (John 11:25). But here we have word and deed together in the powerful testimony of Jesus articulating his own trust in God's vindication even as the end of his ministry and life draws near. This may offer a point of connection for listeners who are also wrestling intimately with the sting of death.

For those who have lost a beloved spouse, the notion of a resurrection life in which the bonds of marriage are dissolved may be disturbing. Such concerns should be addressed creatively and compassionately. After all, it is marriage as the Sadducees imagine it that has no place in the resurrection life Jesus anticipates. The Sadducees with their stunted, misogynistic vision of marriage—they who speak the word *resurrection* with a smirk and a wink—these men want to ask a question about marriage and resurrection? Very well, but the results are not likely to be pretty. So it is true that Jesus kills their question with his answer, but it is a mercy killing. "Your distorted view of marriage will be put to rest in kingdom come," Jesus seems to be saying. Still, if we use our imaginations, perhaps we can envision radically different contexts in which essentially the same question might receive a very different answer. If the asker were famished instead of self-satisfied, hoping instead of plotting, the answer might be very different indeed. What if . . . ? What if the hypothetical woman of the story were very real, and what if she took the risk one day of asking: "Lord, of the seven, it was Eli that I really loved; will we be together in the resurrection?" Do we know for sure that he would have given the exact same answer he gave the Sadducees? Or if she had asked: "Lord, they treated me like a dog, every last one of them; am I finally free of them in glory?" What answer then? Or—and now we will see if it is only Sadducees who can be scandalized by the idea—what if she had begged: "Lord, the truth is I loved all seven of them like crazy; can I have 'em all in heaven?" Who is to say by what word or gesture the Lord of life might have made her understand that in the resurrection life things will be better than we can ask or imagine?

Of course, we don't know and should not pretend to know. We may think we know what would make us happy in the resurrection. Yet all indications are that, in the end, the God of mercy will not punish us by giving us so little as that. "It does not yet appear what we shall be" (1 John 3:2 RSV); "but we will all be changed" (1 Cor. 15:51). This, after all, is the point Jesus is trying to make: whatever resurrection is, it is completely different from what we have known. And at its very center will be the One with whom we have to do, the One we have always known, however dimly, the One who has known us perfectly from our beginning. It is to God that we will live (20:38)—in God's light forever. In that light, all that is contingent, cultural, political, and, yes, even all that is religious will burn away in the great discontinuity of resurrection. But that which is real, that which endures, that which is love will abide and be revealed complete at last in that pure light. Then we will be transformed into the image of our older brother, Jesus. We will be children together under the perfect parenthood of the One who is "God not of the dead, but of the living." Then, at last, all the children of God will finally find out what it actually means to live.

November 17, 2013
Lectionary 33 / Thirty-Third Sunday in Ordinary Time / Proper 28
Twenty-Sixth Sunday after Pentecost

Revised Common Lectionary (RCL)

Malachi 4:1-2a or Isaiah 65:17-25
Psalm 98 or Isaiah 12
2 Thessalonians 3:6-13
Luke 21:5-19

Lectionary for Mass (LFM)

Malachi 3:19-20a
Psalm 98:5-6, 7-8, 9
2 Thessalonians 3:7-12
Luke 21:5-19

First Reading
Isaiah 65:17-25 (RCL alt.)

The Isaiah lection is taken from Third Isaiah (chs. 56–66). Though similar in style and theological outlook to earlier chapters, this material clearly presupposes a later historical backdrop, namely, Jerusalem after the return of the exiles (late sixth century BCE). The reference to the rebuilding of the temple in 66:1 suggests that, like the Haggai lection from Lectionary 32 / Proper 27 (above), these oracles are addressed to a people who have returned from captivity to find that the reality of rebuilding their city and their lives is far more difficult than they had hoped. Earlier chapters in Third Isaiah make it clear that the returned exiles have faced hardships and that many have responded not with covenant faithfulness, but by turning to other gods (57:1-10) and forsaking the demands of justice (58:1-12). In contrast to much of Third Isaiah, this oracle is an unconditional promise of blessing, pure and simple. The God who created all things is about to create newness for them such that former things will be forgotten (v. 17). The oracle is striking for its concreteness. The new Jerusalem of this vision is not a heavenly city, but a transformed earthly environment in which infant mortality rates plummet, even as life spans are dramatically lengthened (v. 20). The prophet guarantees that the hard work they invest in new houses and vineyards will not be in vain—no enemy will harvest what they plant or enjoy the shelter of the roofs they build (vv. 21-22). The vision ends with cherished images of a return to the harmony of creation in the beginning. God's "holy mountain" (Jerusalem) is imagined as a gathering place where prey and predator lie down together without bloodshed, and even the serpent eats only dust (v. 25).

Malachi 4:1-2a (RCL)
Malachi 3:19-20a (LFM)

The book of Malachi assumes that the Jerusalem temple has been rebuilt at last, but all is not well. The generations after the return from Babylonian exile must now contend with economic hardship and cultural decline—the harsh reality of life in the shadow of Persian hegemony. The prophet gives voice to God's charges against the compromises they have made under such pressure. Among these are the offering of blemished sacrifices in the temple ("Try presenting that to your governor," God challenges sarcastically in 1:8) and the shorting of tithes ("You are cursed with a curse, for you are robbing me—the whole nation of you!" 3:9). On the other hand, the people complain that there is no point in putting themselves out to keep the demands of covenant, because God neither rewards the faithful nor punishes the wicked: "It is vain to serve God. What do we profit by keeping his command . . . ? . . . [E]vildoers not only prosper, but when they put God to the test they escape" (3:14-15). In response to these charges we have the words of today's lection. The prophet anticipates a day when God's coming will be like heat—a consuming fire that will burn up "the arrogant and all evildoers" like a plant thrown into an oven (4:1), but also the warmth of a rising sun to bring healing on the faithful who "revere my name" (4:2). Positioned in the Protestant Bible just before the Gospels, these words have been read as an anticipation of the redemption God brings in Christ, who is identified in hymn as the "sun of righteousness."

Psalmody
Psalm 98 (RCL)
Psalm 98:5-6, 7-8, 9 (LFM)
Isaiah 12 (RCL alt.)

Isaiah 12, the psalmic conclusion to the first section of the book of Isaiah, is included in the lectionary alongside the oracle of restoration from Third Isaiah (65:17-25; see the first reading, above). Third Isaiah's promise that God will bring relief to troubled Jerusalem in the form of long life and prosperity finds an appropriate response in this psalm of thanksgiving. Isaiah 65:24 declares, "Before they call I will answer," and Isaiah 12:3 answers, "Give thanks to the Lord, call on his name; make known his deeds among the nations; proclaim that his name is exalted."

As a response to Malachi, which speaks of the coming day when God will bring judgment upon the wicked and healing for the righteous, Psalm 98 celebrates God's intervention as an accomplished fact: "The Lord has made known his victory; he has revealed his vindication in the sight of the nations" (v. 3).

Second Reading

2 Thessalonians 3:6-13 (RCL)
2 Thessalonians 3:7-12 (LFM)

This final lection from 2 Thessalonians marks a change of emphasis. Apparently leaving behind the eschatological concerns of the previous two readings, this text focuses on correcting behavior in the present. Some in the community are "living in idleness" (v. 6), disregarding both the "tradition" and the apostle's example of working in order to avoid becoming a "burden" to others (vv. 7-8). Though he had a "right" to rely on the community for financial support, Paul chose instead to work hard by way of example (v. 9). Perhaps those who are refusing to work are among those who have been deceived into believing that "the day of the Lord is already here" (2:1-3), a misunderstanding that might lead to disinterest in mundane matters like earning money. Not surprisingly, those who are not engaged in productive work have a tendency to become "busybodies," using their free time and energy to cause problems (v. 11). The correction offered in this text is straightforward: "Anyone unwilling to work should not eat" (v. 10).

In our context, words like these can do more harm than good. Several years ago, I watched a lay reader break down in angry tears as he tried to choke out the words of this lection. He works daily with people who are so disturbed and oppressed by the consequences of bad luck and/or bad decisions that they are not able to hold down a job. Christians should not let such people go hungry. It is an irresponsible distortion of the gospel we preach to allow a text like this to be read in the assembly without comment—especially in light of the self-righteous rhetoric about the evils of "entitlement" that characterizes so much of our political discourse. The key point is that this is a word against those who are able to work but, for whatever reason, refuse to do so. Like the Gospel lection from Luke (below), this text addresses the intersection between eschatological expectation and ethics; specifically, it highlights the way distorted beliefs about last things can become an impediment to right practice in the present. Even if this text is not the focus of the sermon, if this passage is read in the assembly, the wise pastor will take the time to offer some guidance about how to make sense of these words in context.

Gospel

Luke 21:5-19 (RCL, LFM)

When these verses are read in the assembly, the tendency is for hearers to immediately interpret them through the lens of the apocalyptic categories supplied by our context—everything from expectations about the triumphant rapture of the righteous to worries about eco-catastrophe. The preacher who knows her church well can anticipate these interpretive predispositions and be prepared to explain how this passage functions within Luke's narrative in order to help the congregation appropriate these words faithfully.

This lection concludes a series of readings about Jesus in the Jerusalem temple teaching the people, and in conflict with the religious authorities (19:47-48). In these verses, a lengthy speech by Jesus is precipitated by "some" (perhaps the disciples, 20:45) who point out that the temple is an impressive and beautifully adorned structure (v. 5). Thus prompted, Jesus predicts that "not one stone will be left upon another; all will be thrown down" (v. 6). His interlocutors then ask two questions: "When will this be, and what will be the sign that this is about to take place?" (v. 7).

The wide-ranging answer that Jesus gives to these questions is not straightforward and needs to be considered systematically.[1] First, in verses 8-11 Jesus describes events leading up to the destruction of the temple. This section takes the form of a warning that many things must first take place. In the days to come, the hearers should be on guard against being led astray by those who claim either to be Jesus or to speak in his name (v. 8). These false prophets will predict that the "time is near," but they should not be heeded. Jesus predicts war and political upheaval (vv. 9-10), natural disasters (v. 11a), and even portents in the heavens (v. 11b), but still the fall of Jerusalem and the destruction of the temple will not follow "immediately" (v. 9). These verses suggest that there is a lengthy script that must unfold in due course, and that the tendency of the uninformed will be to rush to judgments prematurely.

Somewhat confusingly, the next section of Jesus' response (vv. 12-19) interrupts the temporal flow by addressing matters that precede the events described in the first section above: "But before all this occurs, they will arrest you and persecute you" (v. 12). In other words, even before the extended program of events that must not be mistaken for the end, a time is coming when the followers of Jesus will be persecuted by religious authorities ("synagogues"), civil authorities ("prisons," "kings and governors"), and even their own families (vv. 12, 16). Verse 17 summarizes this prediction with a sweeping statement: "You will be hated by all because of my name." Surprisingly, Jesus encourages his followers to embrace this time of hardship as an "opportunity to testify" (v. 13). Rather than carefully preparing a defense, when the time comes to give an answer before the authorities, they can trust Jesus to supply them with irrefutable wisdom (vv. 14-15).

The final sections of Jesus' response fall outside the lection as delineated but are integral to the passage as a whole. In verses 20-24 Jesus returns to the matter of the fall of Jerusalem and the destruction of the temple that was interrupted by verses 12-19. Finally, he transitions away from talk about the fate of Jerusalem and the temple and concludes in verses 25-28 with predictions about the second coming and the end of history.

In terms of Luke's literary-theological project, we can identify two functions of this discourse. In the first place, like the rest of the Gospel, this material renders the identity of Jesus. Written after the destruction of the temple by Rome in 70 CE to readers who know how events actually unfolded, this passage depicts Jesus as a true prophet who accurately predicts the future, including the coming of false prophets who by contrast fail to interpret the signs of the times properly. Jesus' reliability as a prophet of the events leading up to the fall of Jerusalem serves to engender confidence that his predictions about the final coming of the Son of Man to redeem his followers can also be trusted (v. 28). Second, the events in verses 12-19 anticipate in detail the fate that will befall the followers of Jesus as described in Luke's second volume, Acts. To highlight just a few examples out of many, they will be persecuted, arrested, and imprisoned by kings (Acts 12:1-5), conspired against by synagogues (Acts 9:2), and have opportunity to bear witness before governors (Acts 23:24) and other leaders (Acts 4:5-12). These connections to Acts further strengthen the portrayal of Jesus as a true prophet, enhance the overall unity of Luke's narrative, and establish the deeds and sufferings of Jesus' followers as a continuation of his earthly mission in the power of his risen Spirit.

Based on this analysis, several sermonic themes suggest themselves. The first and most obvious point is that to follow Jesus means to look forward expectantly to a future in which God will get what God wants. Jesus is not impressed with Herod's beautifully adorned temple because he knows that it—along with all the human projects that occupy our attention and vie for our loyalty—is passing away. Things will not be as they are. Progressive Christians are sometimes embarrassed by, or at least uncomfortable with, the apocalyptic thinking that funds so much of the New Testament. We worry that it leads to pie-in-the-sky distraction from the pressing demands of justice and peace here and now. Such concerns are warranted. We must resist every shallow eschatology that sponsors ethical apathy, self-congratulatory triumphalism, and indifference to the plight of those who suffer now. But there is no way to make sense of the identity of Jesus as depicted for us by the only witnesses we have without taking seriously the claims of this text: the present order of things is passing away. The future belongs to God and will be uncovered on God's schedule. In light of all this, we must not become too invested in the status quo, with its measured perks and sensible prospect of short odds on salvation writ small. Instead, we must learn to travel light, ready at a moment's notice to let go of the old and embrace the new thing God has in store for us.

There is also a word of warning in this text about becoming obsessed with dates and times. For a discourse full of predictions about signs and portents, we may be surprised to realize that in the end no specific guidance about timing is given. To the contrary, the overall effect of this passage is to discourage the reader from becoming too attached to any one event or scenario as a certain harbinger of the end. The questioners ask for a road map to the future, but what Jesus supplies is a warning not to fall into the trap of prematurely supposing that our own experiences must surely be the final chapter. Letting go of our fixation on knowing every last detail about how it will all come to pass frees the mind and heart to meet the challenge to live faithfully as witnesses in the meantime.

Finally, this passage moves against the grain of contemporary strains of apocalyptic thinking that insist that to be chosen by God is somehow to be exempted from suffering—lifted above the fray and spared the hardships that characterize human life generally, and the life of the world as it slowly gives way to God's future. Whatever Jesus means when he promises, "Not a hair of your head will perish" (v. 18), the reality is that his followers must face not only the upheaval and desolation common to all, but also the special burden of enduring the attentions of enemies who make a special target of those who love what Jesus loves, say what Jesus says, and do what Jesus does. As Acts will show, for many disciples loyalty to Jesus will demand the ultimate sacrifice. The promise is not that God's certain future is an escape from the present, but that it will vindicate faithfulness in the present. In other words, according to Jesus, all that his followers endure for the sake of his name is ingredient to the future God has dreamed for the world, for "by your endurance you will gain your souls" (v. 19).

Note

1. This analysis is indebted to the literary structure outlined in Luke Timothy Johnson, *Luke*, Sacra Pagina (Collegeville, MN: Liturgical, 1991), 324–26.

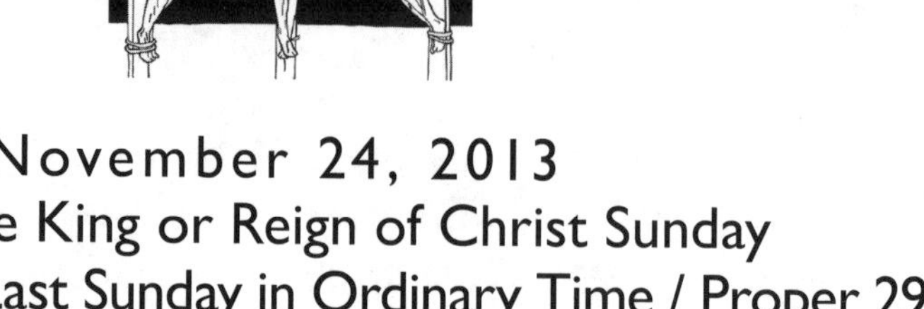

November 24, 2013
Christ the King or Reign of Christ Sunday
Lectionary 34 / Last Sunday in Ordinary Time / Proper 29
Twenty-Seventh Sunday after Pentecost

Revised Common Lectionary (RCL)

Jeremiah 23:1-6
Psalm 46 or Luke 1:68-79
Colossians 1:11-20
Luke 23:33-43

Lectionary for Mass (LFM)

2 Samuel 5:1-3
Psalm 122:1-2, 3-4a, 4b-5
Colossians 1:12-20
Luke 23:35-43

First Reading
Jeremiah 23:1-6 (RCL)
2 Samuel 5:1-3 (LFM)

The historical backdrop to the Jeremiah lection is the dispersion and exile of Judah at the hands of Babylon in the early sixth century BCE. The passage begins with a harsh indictment of the "shepherds" (i.e., leaders, probably Jehoiakim and Zedekiah, the last two kings of Judah before exile) who have overseen this fiasco. Instead of "attending" properly to God's flock, they have instead "driven," "scattered," and "destroyed" the sheep (vv. 1-2). Therefore, God promises ominously to "attend" to them for their "evil doings" (v. 2b). Because the human shepherds have failed, God will go out and perform the duty of a shepherd by gathering the remnant from the lands of the dispersion (v. 3a). God will return them to their "fold" in Jerusalem where they will thrive; and God will raise up new leaders to shepherd the people properly (vv. 3b-4). The next section, verses 5-6, elaborates on this promise by anticipating "a righteous Branch" from the line of David. With wordplay on the name and questioning the legitimacy of the failed king Zedekiah, this oracle promises that the new king will be wise, just, and righteous. The literary unit continues through verse 8 by claiming that the return from Babylon will eclipse even the exodus from Egypt as the quintessential manifestation of God's care and power. Verses 7-8 make the historical context more explicit. By ending the lection at verse 6, the historical density of these oracles is obscured, facilitating the church's appropriation of this passage as an anticipation of the wise, just, and righteous kingship of Christ (compare Luke 1:69, below).

The brief lection from 2 Samuel recounts the acceptance and anointing of David as king of the northern tribes. (For his earlier anointing over Judah, see 2:1-7.) This story about the origin of the line of David, with its emphasis on the "bone and flesh" (v. 1) ties that fund the dynastic imagination, makes a fitting accompaniment to the day's lections, which celebrate Jesus as the anointed king descended from the line of David.

Psalmody

Psalm 46 or Luke 1:68-79 (RCL)
Psalm 122:1-2, 3-4a, 4b-5 (LFM)

The beloved words of Psalm 46 eloquently claim God's power and willingness to save. God is "a very present help in trouble" (v. 1). The trouble imagined by the psalmist is nothing short of what Psalms scholar J. Clinton McCann Jr. has called "the worst-case scenario": "The 'change' in the earth described in vv. 2-3 seems like a simultaneous 10.0 earthquake and class-five hurricane, but actually it is even worse! According to the ancient Near Eastern view of the universe, the mountains were both the foundations that anchored the dry land in the midst of a watery chaos and the pillars that held up the sky."[1] In other words, the psalmist is describing a doomsday scenario in which everything that can go wrong does go wrong. The shaking mountains portend the falling of the sky and the unleashing of the chaotic waters of the sea. Nevertheless, God is sovereign even over the end of the world as we know it; therefore "we will not fear" (v. 2). No wonder, then, that lesser threats both political (v. 6) and military (v. 9) are no cause for dismay. On Christ the King Sunday, it is helpful to remind ourselves that it was the kingship of Israel's God that Jesus himself tirelessly proclaimed. In Jesus, God's invisible reign has been made so clear to us that we can even claim, in the words of this poem, that he is "God with us" (vv. 7, 11).

Zechariah's prophetic song, known traditionally as the Benedictus from its first word in Latin, beautifully expresses the Christian understanding of Jesus as the longed-for Davidic ruler. The focus on Jesus as the answer to historic Israel's expectation for salvation is striking. In depicting Jesus' messianic identity, Luke gives us a Jewish priest extolling salvation "from our enemies and from the hand of all who hate us" (v. 71). See the Gospel lection, below, for a discussion of Luke's subversive reimagining of that kingship in light of the (apparent) failure of the crucifixion.

Psalm 122 responds to the anointing of David in 2 Samuel with a hymn celebrating the city of Jerusalem as the locus of God's presence (v. 1), the secure stronghold of the Davidic dynasty (v. 3), and the site of the mediation of God's just rule through the kings of that line (v. 5).

Second Reading

Colossians 1:11-20 (RCL)
Colossians 1:12-20 (LFM)

While the day's other lections remind us that the kingship of Christ is rooted within and emerges from the struggles of a particular historical people, this reading from

Colossians highlights the universal implications of his reign. The soaring hymn to the cosmic Christ (vv. 15-20) speaks of Jesus not just as the rightful heir to the Davidic dynasty of Israel, but as the very image of the otherwise invisible God (v. 15). Not only was he present from before the creation of the world (v. 17a), he is himself the unifying principle of the cosmos (v. 17b), and so may be affirmed as somehow both the agent through which every created thing came into being and the destiny of all things (v. 16b). Using the most sweeping categories available, the Colossian hymn stakes its claim to the singular and ultimate significance of Jesus Christ.

Furthermore, this completely significant Christ—this Christ whose legitimate reign knows no temporal, spatial, or existential limits—is head of the church (v. 18). This is a claim that surely stretched the limits of the seriously imaginable for the church, which first asserted it was not an impressive institution. As readers of the New Testament, we see the early church through the lens of the literature it produced, and the historical fact of its astounding growth in the centuries that followed. But if we take a step back from that literature and suspend our awareness of how the story eventually played out, we can begin to appreciate that the cultural impact of Christianity in its first decades was negligible by any objective standard. And yet in this hymn we have the most ambitious conceivable claim about the significance of the Christ they alone proclaimed as Lord. They dared to believe the impossible. The faith of the tiny house churches of Asia Minor before Christendom should serve as a powerful witness to Christians in a context of accelerating disestablishment.

The promise and challenge of this text is that—whether we knew it or not—we were once subjects under the tyranny of the power of darkness, but now we have been "redeemed" (v. 14, i.e., "bought back at a price") and therefore "transferred into the kingdom" of God's Son (v. 13). In other words, this text is a bid to frame life and loyalty in absolute terms. Either we are subjects of darkness or we have been rescued from that fate and now live entirely within the realm of Christ's kingship. There are forces in our context that encourage us to imagine our spiritual lives as if we are sovereign consumers, standing above the fray and assembling the meaningful parts of our lives piecemeal, like diners in a cafeteria line filling their trays with a little of this and a little of that. But this text does not invite us to understand Christ as one ingredient in our well-balanced diet of commitments and affirmations. The Christ of this hymn cannot be incorporated into some larger project of meaning. He is simply too large for that. To be transferred into the kingdom of this cosmic Christ is to see everything else as subject to him. When we think along with this totalizing poem, it forces a decision either to accept Christ or to reject him on these astonishing terms. But, finally, even this implied decision gets swallowed up into a larger vision that brooks no dissent: "For in him all the fullness of God was pleased to dwell, and through him God was pleased to reconcile to himself all things, whether on earth or in heaven, by making peace through the blood of his cross" (vv. 19-20).

Gospel
Luke 23:33-43 (RCL)
Luke 23:35-43 (LFM)

According to the Christian calendar, this is the last Sunday of the year, a day to crown the year by acknowledging that Jesus Christ is king. And so from Jeremiah we read a prophecy of a future descendent of David who will be a wise and righteous leader worthy of the people's trust and respect. From Colossians we read a beautiful hymn to the majesty of the cosmic Christ, the very image of the invisible God, in whom the fullness of God was pleased to dwell, in whom the created order finds coherence, through whom God achieves reconciliation with all that God made and lost. But then, in a bizarre twist, the Gospel describes that same Jesus tortured, humiliated, and executed as a criminal. How strange that on a day when we celebrate the kingship of Christ, the Gospel lection should ask us to look full square upon the crucifixion. Why speak of crosses on a day of coronation? The answer is to be found in the inscription placed above the crucified man's head, "This is the King of the Jews" (v. 38), and in the mocking taunt of the soldiers: "If you are the King of the Jews, save yourself!" (v. 37). On the day we crown him anew in our lives, we are reminded that for those who looked upon Jesus in the flesh, his sovereignty was a morbid joke. This is strange testimony.

Luke supplies no forensic details about the crucifixion, nor does he pay any rhetorical homage to its pathos. Concerning the historical event at the heart of Christian faith, he reports simply: "When they came to the place that is called The Skull, they crucified Jesus there with the criminals, one on his right and one on his left" (v. 33). There is nothing regal about this restrained but bleak depiction. A king has power; Jesus, impaled, is powerless. A king has a domain; Jesus, suspended, cannot even touch the ground. A sovereign has subjects; Jesus has torturers and hecklers.

What Luke wants to show us about the peculiar sovereignty of Jesus, he communicates through a brief but remarkable conversation. Amid a chorus of mockers a lone voice, that of a condemned man hanging beside him, asks, "Jesus, remember me when you come into your kingdom" (v. 42). This is preposterous. At that moment you could have searched the entire human realm and it would have been impossible to find two people with less earthly hope than these conversation partners. They were Jews in a Roman world. They were condemned criminals in a world of brutal and often arbitrary law. By any reasonable human standard they were finished. They had been cast outside the city wall, stripped of all possessions right down to their bare flesh, impaled with cold iron, and hung naked to suffocate and bleed out their last hours on earth as subhuman refuse. Every possible dignity was denied them. The only remaining use the world had for them was to make an example of them—to exact the greatest possible price of pain from their bodies, the greatest possible price of shame from their personalities, before they perished. In the end, they would hang torn and lifeless, a gruesome testimony to the power and brutality of the world that rejected them—a warning to any who questioned the authority of the powers that be.

But the conversation Luke gives us is not one of despair. As they live their social death, as they stare physical death in the eye, these two speak of the future! One condemned man says to another, "Jesus, remember me when you come into your kingdom." The response evoked by this brief request is astonishing. So prompted, Jesus speaks words that belie a hidden reality rippling beneath the surface of the apparent: "Truly I tell you, today you will be with me in Paradise." He speaks like one of the kings in his own parables, serenely lavishing staggering gifts on a stunned, improbable recipient. As requests go, "Remember me when . . ." is modest; but Jesus replies with extravagant generosity. Sovereign of more than his petitioner can dream, he grants him the whole green garden of God.

This story suggests two claims about the kingship of Christ. First, for now his reign in this world is hidden, and it is hidden in suffering. Jesus did not seem a king to most on the cross, and to most eyes he does not seem one today. His cause, by all appearances, is not doing very well. Even to this day, violent power struts about on the stage of history, shouting its lines, looking very much the conqueror, the last one standing. Wherever selfishness, injustice, and violence carry the day, Christ writhes in silence beneath it all—bearing the world forward to transformations that are hidden for now. When all is finally revealed, every knee will bow and every tongue will confess who is truly Lord. But for now, Christ reigns among us in a sovereignty of suffering.

Yet, even in a world of darkness, there are moments when the majesty of the hidden King flashes briefly. This is the second claim. There are outbreaks of mercy, epiphanies of power, signs of the reign of Christ the King that can be glimpsed by those with eyes to see. The story suggests that this may happen when someone has dared in the midst of suffering and hopelessness to speak a word of faith. The criminal on the cross calls for the King. Like Israel reminding God to be God, someone calls to Jesus over the derisive laughs of his enemies and summons the kingdom with a prayer: "When you come into your kingdom." Or as we say when we pray the prayer he taught us to pray: "Your kingdom come!" At these words the face turns, the silence breaks, a King responds. Perhaps the world would get more glimpses of the Regal Face if the dying church dared to speak and to act as if a Sovereign really were among us.

Note

1. J. Clinton McCann Jr., "Psalms," in *The New Interpreter's Bible*, ed. Leander E. Keck et al. (Nashville: Abingdon, 1996), 4:865–67.

November 28, 2013 (USA) / October 14, 2013 (Canada)
Thanksgiving Day

Revised Common Lectionary (RCL)
Deuteronomy 26:1-11
Psalm 100
Philippians 4:4-9
John 6:25-35

Lectionary for Mass (LFM)
Deuteronomy 8:7-18 or Sirach 50:22-24 or 1 Kings 8:55-61
Psalm 113:1-8 or 138:1-5
1 Corinthians 1:3-9 or Colossians 3:12-17 or 1 Timothy 6:6-11, 17-19
Luke 17:11-19 or Mark 5:18-20 or Luke 12:15-21

The texts for Thanksgiving Day are too numerous to permit comprehensive individual treatments. Instead, the approach will be to integrate several of the day's lections into a discussion of preaching strategies for Thanksgiving. (For a detailed treatment of Luke 17:11-19, see the Gospel reading for Lectionary 28 / Proper 23, above.)

First Reading
Deuteronomy 26:1-11 (RCL)
Deuteronomy 8:7-18 or Sirach 50:22-24 or 1 Kings 8:55-61 (LFM)

In the fall of the year, after harvesting the good things that the land produced, the Israelite farmer did a strange thing. The very first part that was harvested went into a basket. The basket was taken to the sanctuary and placed before the altar of the Lord. And when the first fruit of the land was so presented, the Israelite would tell this story:

> "A wandering Aramean was my ancestor: he went down into Egypt and lived there as an alien, few in number, and there he became a great nation, mighty and populous. When the Egyptians treated us harshly and afflicted us, by imposing hard labor on us, we cried to the Lord, the God of our ancestors; the Lord heard our voice and saw our affliction, our toil, and our oppression. The Lord brought us out of Egypt with a

> mighty hand and an outstretched arm, with a terrifying display of power, and with signs and wonders; and he brought us into this place and gave us this land, a land flowing with milk and honey. So now I bring the first of the fruit of the ground that you, O LORD, have given me." (Deut. 26:5b-10a)

To modern ears this formal creedal language has an exotic feel. Disconnected from the lives of our ancestors as most of us are, we are intrigued by, and perhaps a bit jealous of, the Israelite's ties to the past. Storyless as we are, these words can easily be mistaken for an elegantly phrased homage to a glorious past: "My ancestor was a wandering Aramean." It sounds romantic, nostalgic, almost elegiac. But that was not the original sense of this pronouncement. The story about the wandering Aramean ancestor (probably a reference to Jacob, not Abraham) was not the ceremonial reliving of a glorious past. Rather, it was a confession of humble beginnings. It was an admission that life was not always as secure as it is now; it was a declaration of dependence on God.

For the Israelite farmer, the gift of the land meant security and life. This was no mere nomad, like Abraham, Isaac, and Jacob long before. The farmer did not travel about and hope against hope that there would be food for another day in another place. And he was not a desert wanderer like his more recent storied ancestors, waking each morning to the serendipity of manna and collecting each new day just enough for that day, one day at a time. This descendent of sojourners had come into the new technology of agriculture with a vengeance, and a (relatively) secure domestic lifestyle was the reward. No longer was he subject to the whims of happenstance. With hard work he was able to plant, to tend, to harvest, to store—able, in other words, to abide, to remain in one place with security. After so many generations of uncertainty, the Israelite farmer was in control of his destiny at last.

But when his work paid off and the security of the harvest came, the Israelite did something surprising. The farmer took the first of what the ground produced, traveled to the designated place, and spoke words that confess not autonomy and competence, but dependence and vulnerability. On the one day of the year that could so easily have come to symbolize his mastery over his environment, his triumph over contingency—on the harvest day, he took the fruit of his labor, approached the altar of God, and recited the story that said in effect: "I know that I am not in control. I farm this ground and it produces year to year, but every year at the harvest I remember that in my bones I'm just a wanderer, a nomad, an alien casting about and hoping to be fed another day. I only have what I have because when the Egyptians treated us harshly and afflicted us, we cried out to God and God brought us out of Egypt with a mighty hand, with a terrifying display of power, and brought us to this place and gave us this land, flowing with all these pleasures and comforts and securities. So now I bring the very first part of each harvest and I declare that the LORD is good, the source of all these blessings."

This story has an obvious connection to Thanksgiving, which is celebrated in the late fall and associated both historically and in the popular imagination with the bounty of harvest. But, of course, the world has moved on. What would the farmer think of us in our nice suburban houses with two (two!) cars in the garage, health-insurance cards in our wallets, and Thanksgiving Day football on the flat screen? The pumpkins on our porches and the turkeys on our tables come from the grocery store, not the field. Most of us don't even have gardens. We no longer put our hands in the black dirt or worry over cloudless skies. For most of us, planting and harvesting are dead metaphors now—a dream of a dream of a way we once were. Our illusions of self-sufficiency and self-determination run even deeper now—so deep that the Israelite could scarcely fathom our pride. We are such a long way from the wandering Aramean. We are a long way even from the farming Israelite. We are not wanderers hoping for a scrap of food and a dry plot on which to pitch a tent. Nor are most of us farmers hoping for rain or praying back the frost. We don't suffer when the rain fails or the cold comes too soon. We have come into a world of technologies that meet our physical needs almost magically, even as they threaten to separate us from the most basic truths about ourselves and God.

For the Israelite farmer, the bounties of the God-given land were both blessing and threat:

> Take care that you do not forget the LORD your God, by failing to keep his commandments, his ordinances, and his statutes, which I am commanding you today. When you have eaten your fill and have built fine houses and live in them, and when your herds and flocks have multiplied, and your silver and gold is multiplied, and all that you have is multiplied, then do not exalt yourself, forgetting the LORD your God, who brought you out of the land of Egypt, out of the house of slavery. (Deut. 8:11-14)

This warning could just as well have been penned for us. We may be in a recession, but by any realistic historical or global standard, Thanksgiving in a typical North American household is an embarrassment of riches—a shocking display of material surplus that would stagger the imagination of most of the people who have ever lived. If we can't see this, it may be because an even more shocking display immediately follows, inaugurated with an orgy of procurement beginning the very next day after Thanksgiving. Christians in the United States should spend some time pondering the implications of the annual "Black Friday" (and now "Cyber Monday") shopping frenzy in relation to the supposed gratitude of "Thanksgiving Thursday." There are strong forces at work among us—powers that seek to unsettle our grateful contentment in order to stir in us an insatiable hunger for more.

The story of the Israelite farmer is a powerful resource for safeguarding Thanksgiving from degenerating into a celebration of all the things that separate us from our need. Apart from the story of God's dealings with our ancestors and so with us, a harvest festival might serve as little more than a display of our triumph over need for another year. Especially in our North American context, displays of plenty intended to acknowledge blessings can all too easily feed an already voracious appetite for more. This is a day to remember our deep and fundamental dependence on God and to demonstrate our contentment with God's provision. Celebrated in this way, it becomes an act of resistance against a culture of unending acquisitiveness. Instead of signaling our triumph over need, Thanksgiving can serve to remind us of who we really are and how much we need God.

Gospel
John 6:25-35 (RCL)
Luke 17:11-19 or Mark 5:18-20 or Luke 12:15-21 (LFM)

Jesus warns against becoming too fixated upon the bread that fills the stomach to the neglect of the bread that endures (John 6:25-35). The crowd that "found him on the other side of the sea" (v. 25) is the same crowd that received the miraculous feeding of the loaves and the fish (vv. 1-15). They have been searching for Jesus for some time (vv. 22-24), but he calls their motives into question. They have come because they want another meal (v. 26). This passage serves as a stern warning against the so-called gospel of health and wealth, but it also asks us to think long and hard about our own motivations for following Jesus, our own expectations about what he should do for us. In response to those who interpret past blessings as a warrant for self-satisfaction—those who presume the right to ever more spectacular signs of God's care (vv. 30-31)—Jesus proffers instead the sustaining bread of his own life as sufficient (v. 35).

Thinking about Luke's depiction of Jesus in relation to the readings from Deuteronomy, we are reminded that we have for our ancestor not only a wandering Aramean who trusted God for sustenance from day to day, but also a wandering Nazarean who had no place to lay his head (Luke 9:58) but who shared table gladly with all and became for us the only meal that truly satisfies. Luke's Jesus has a great deal to teach us about the possibilities and dangers of material possessions for the life of faith. In one of the remarkable stories he told, Jesus exposes the hidden peril of focusing too much on material blessings, and the pitfall of allowing our possessions to turn us inward upon ourselves (Luke 12:15-21). This text unit actually begins at verse 13 when a man asks Jesus to make a ruling in an inheritance dispute he is having with his brother. Jesus refuses, and then introduces a parable with these words: "Take care! Be on your guard against all kinds of greed; for one's life does not consist in the abundance of possessions" (v. 15). In the story that follows, the land of a rich man produces a bumper crop. In fact, the harvest is so abundant that the man realizes he does not have enough room to store the surplus. Careful attention to the language used to describe this man's deliberations reveals a striking portrait of a personality turned back inward upon itself. Note the abundance of first-person language: "What should *I* do, for *I* have no place to store *my* crops? . . . *I* will do this: *I* will pull down *my* barns and build larger ones, and there *I* will store all *my* grain and *my* goods. And *I* will say to *my* soul . . ." (vv. 17-19, emphasis added). This man has many belongings, but he has no thought for anyone else. He cannot imagine any use for his super-abundance except to hoard it in larger storehouses. There is no mention of a family for which he might provide, nor a community of need with which he might share his good fortune. He lives entirely to himself, and as the parable reaches its conclusion, it becomes clear that he must die to himself as well, for God declares: "This very night your life is being demanded of you. And the things you have prepared, whose will they be?" (v. 20). This is the only time that God appears directly as a character in one of Jesus' parables. In addition to lending unassailable credibility to the pronouncements against the rich man's choices, this also has the effect of further highlighting his isolation. There is literally no other human in his world to share in his plenty or challenge his thinking. The only way for this man to encounter something beyond himself is to be confronted in death by the One who finally holds all people accountable. God's rhetorical question to the man (v. 20b) plays on the question about inheritance that introduces this story. A section that begins with the ambitions of a potential heir ends with a depiction of the futility of hoarding what you cannot, ultimately, keep. The alternative is to be "rich toward God" (v. 21), that is, to direct one's energies and resources outward toward the source of all blessings, and by extension toward the world and the people God loves.